T0110637

Acclaim for William Dalrymple's **In Xanadu**

"Bright, sharp, laconic and outrageous, his is an adventurous account of hippies and mad mullahs, mosques and sacred tombs, dangers and celebrations, Dionysian rituals and rich discoveries. It is full of life and very funny."
—*The Sunday Times* (London)

"Dalrymple is probably the best travel writer of his generation."
—*The Daily Mail*

"Uncommonly satisfying because of the rare skill with which Dalrymple blends his ingredients: history, danger, humour, architecture, people, hardships, politics."
—*London Literary Review*

"Dalrymple is a phenomenon and his journey a remarkable one. . . . A striking achievement."
—*Punch*

"A vivid, engaging, often hilarious account of an amazing 12,000-mile quest."
—*Sunday Express*

"Outstanding. . . . William Dalrymple is a natural writer. His models are, perhaps, Peter Fleming and Evelyn Waugh rather than more serious travellers, but he's a better scholar than either. Best of all, he has the gift of comedy. . . . *In Xanadu* marks the arrival of a new star."
—*Sydney Morning Herald*

"A fast, furious, funny read. . . . Clearly the stuff bestsellers are made of."
—*Times of India*

"A delightful book—erudite, adventurous and amusing [with] an exotic itinerary, charming companions, impossible odds, appalling discomfort and bizarre encounters along the way."
—Piers Paul Read

Also by William Dalrymple

City of Djinns

From the Holy Mountain

The Age of Kali

White Mughals

The Last Mughal

Nine Lives

William Dalrymple

IN XANADU

William Dalrymple is the author of seven acclaimed works of history and travel, including *City of Djinns*, which won the Young British Writer of the Year Prize and the Thomas Cook Travel Book award; the bestselling *From the Holy Mountain*; *White Mughals*, which won Britain's most prestigious history prize, the Wolfson; and *The Last Mughal*, which won the Duff Cooper Prize for History and Biography. He divides his time between New Delhi and London, and is a contributor to *The New York Review of Books*, *The New Yorker*, and *The Guardian*.

www.williamdalrymple.uk.com

IN
XANADU

IN
XANADU

William
Dalrymple

VINTAGE BOOKS
A Division of Random House, Inc.
New York

FIRST VINTAGE DEPARTURES EDITION, AUGUST 2012

Copyright © 1989 by William Dalrymple

All rights reserved. Published in the United States by
Vintage Books, a division of Random House, Inc., New York,
and in Canada by Random House of Canada Limited, Toronto.
Originally published in hardcover in Great Britain
by Collins, London, in 1989.

Vintage is a registered trademark and Vintage Departures
and colophon are trademarks of Random House, Inc.

The Cataloging-in-Publication data is
on file at the Library of Congress.

Maps by Ken Lewis

Vintage ISBN: 978-0-307-94888-5

www.vintagebooks.com

Illustrations

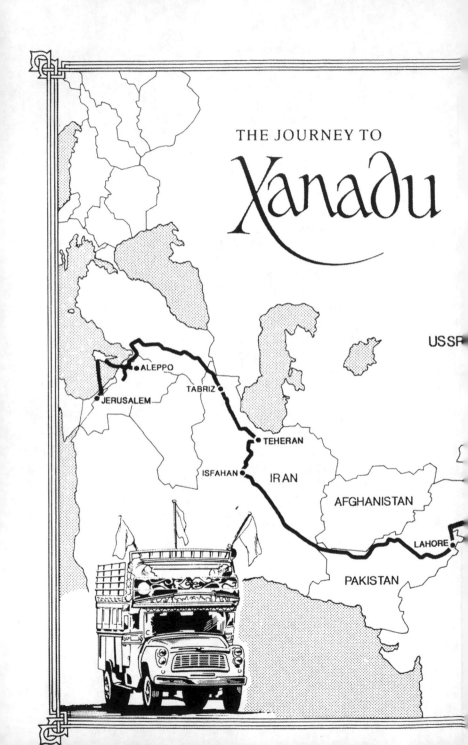

THE JOURNEY TO
Xanadu

USSR

ALEPPO
TABRIZ
JERUSALEM
TEHERAN
ISFAHAN
IRAN
AFGHANISTAN
LAHORE
PAKISTAN

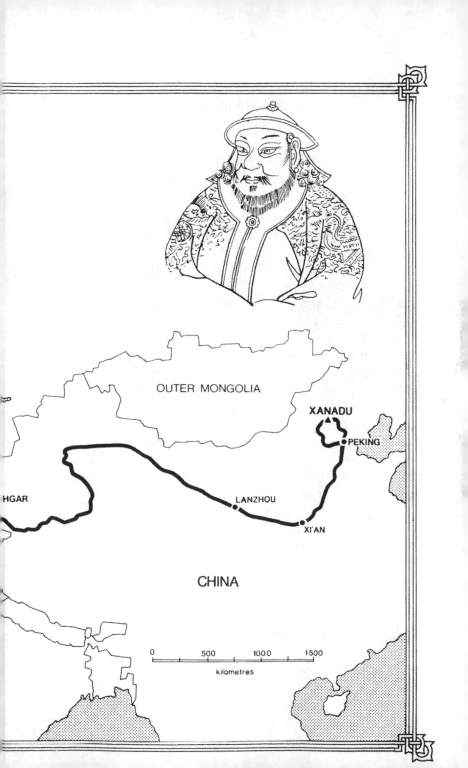

OUTER MONGOLIA

XANADU

PEKING

HGAR

LANZHOU

XI'AN

CHINA

0   500   1000   1500
kilometres

Acknowledgements

This book is already too long but it would be churlish to let it go to press without acknowledging the help and tolerance of a number of people without whom the expedition could never have taken place nor the book have been written.

Dr Simon Keynes persuaded Trinity to part with £700 to help finance the trip; in the event it proved enough to pay for everything as far as Peking. Sir Anthony Acland and Sir Robert Wade-Gery spared valuable time to help us clear diplomatic hurdles, while Anthony Fitzherbert, the Begum Quizilbash and Charlie and Cherry Parton all entertained us lavishly en route.

Back in England, Maggie Noach helped me sell the book while Mike Fishwick of Collins was kind enough to buy it; both of them provided great encouragement during the fourteen months it took to write. During that time my girlfriend Olivia Fraser and my flatmate Andrew Berton put up with me and successive drafts of my book with extraordinary tolerance and forbearance. Fania Stoney, Henrietta Miers, Patrick French, Lucy Warrack, my brothers Hewie, Jock and Rob and my long suffering mother and father were all nagged to read it. Lucian Taylor is responsible for many helpful editorial comments; on five separate occasions he spared whole days to go over the manuscript word by word. It would be a considerably longer, more pompous and boring book without his advice and cuts.

Many others have helped and I apologize if I have not mentioned everyone. Most of all, however, it must be obvious to anyone who reads this book that I owe an enormous debt to two people without whom the whole enterprise could never have got off the ground.

I dedicate this book with love and apologies to Laura and Louisa.

ONE

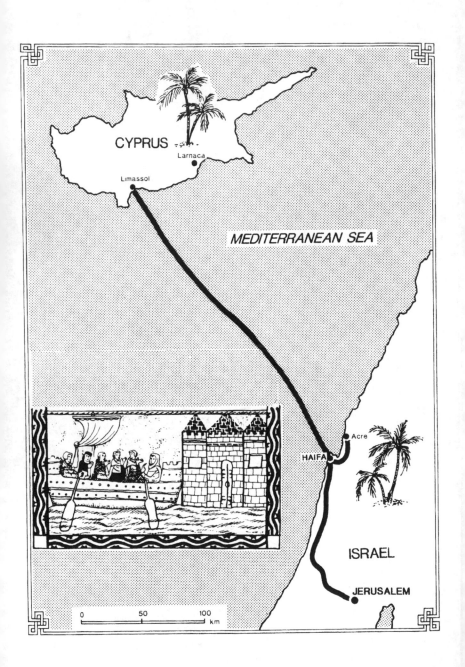

CYPRUS

Larnaca

Limassol

MEDITERRANEAN SEA

Acre

HAIFA

ISRAEL

JERUSALEM

0   50   100
                 km

It was still dark when I left Sheik Jarrah. At the Damascus Gate the first fruit sellers were gathered by a brazier, warming their fingers around glasses of sweet tea. The Irish Franciscan was waiting by the door of the Holy Sepulchre. He nodded from under the hood of his habit and without a word led me past the Armenian chapel and under the great rotunda. Around the dome you could hear the echo of plainchant as twelve separate congregations sang their different matins.

'It's not long now,' said Brother Fabian. 'The Greeks will be finished by eight-thirty.'

'That's in two hours' time.'

'Only half an hour. The Greeks don't allow us to put the clocks back. We work on Byzantine time here.'

He knelt down on a flagstone, folded his hands in his sleeves and began murmuring his devotions. We waited for twenty minutes.

'What's keeping them?'

'The rota's very strict. They're allowed four hours in the tomb, and they won't leave until their time is up,'

He hesitated then added:

'Things are a bit tense at the moment. Last month one of the Armenian monks went crazy: thought an angel was telling him to kill the Greek patriarch. So he smashed an oil lamp and chased Patriarch Diodorus through the choir with a piece of broken glass.'

'What happened?'

'The Greeks overpowered him. There's an ex-weightlifter from Thessaloniki who looks after the Greek chapel on Calvary. He pinned the Armenian down in the crypt until the police came. But since then the Greeks and the Armenians haven't been on speaking terms. Which means we had to be the go-betweens. Until we broke off relations with the Greeks as well.'

'What do you mean?'

'Last month Diodorus was crossing the bridge into Jordan when the border guards found a big bag of heroin in the air filter of his car. They released him but arrested his driver. Diodorus claimed he must have put the bag there. The driver was a Catholic.'

'So now no one is speaking to anyone?'

'I think the Copts are still speaking to the Maronites. But apart from that, no.'

Brother Fabian pulled one arm out of his habit and pointed to the dome of the rotunda.

'You see the painter's scaffolding? That's been up ten years because the three patriarchs can't agree on a colour. They'd just about settled on black when the Armenian assaulted Diodorus. Now the Greeks are demanding purple. It won't get repainted for another ten years now. By which time,' added Fabian, 'I shall be back in Donegal.'

At that moment a procession of black-clad Greek monks emerged from the Tomb, a bulbous, kettle-like structure which Robert Byron thought resembled a railway engine. As the monks stepped out some were singing anthems while others sprayed the ambulatory with holy water. They had cascading pepper-and-salt beards and wore cylindrical hats topped with black mortarboards. They scowled in the direction of the Latin chapel then marched off towards Calvary.

'Wait here,' said Brother Fabian.

He returned carrying a tin watering can and a tray of what looked like surgical instruments. He handed me the tray then walked up to the tomb, bowed, bent double and squeezed under the low, cusped arch. I followed. We passed through the dim first chamber, then stooped into the inner sanctum. The holiest shrine in Christendom was the size of a small broom cupboard. Raised on a ledge was the Stone of Resurrection and on top of it rested two icons, a tatty Mannerist painting and a vase containing seven wilted roses. Twelve lamps were suspended from the ceiling by steel chains. Fabian knelt down, kissed the Stone and murmured a prayer. Then he rose.

'We've got until twelve-thirty,' he said.

From a recess in the first chamber he produced a small stepladder. He climbed up onto it, unclipped a hook from the wall-ring then let go of the pulley. The four Catholic lamps descended. They were made of beaten bronze and were very tarnished and very old. Finely incised on the outside were the figures of cherubim and a six-winged seraph. Motioning that I should pass the watering can up to him, the friar arched over the lamps and very carefully poured oil from the can into three of them. As he did so each one guttered.

'I thought these lamps were miraculous. They're supposed to be eternal flames.'

'That's what they say,' said Brother Fabian, now struggling with the wick of one of the lamps. 'But you try and change the oil without them going out. Take it from me. It's absolutely impossible. Damn it! This wick's finished. Pass me up the string.'

He pointed to the tray of surgical instruments. I found a ball of string and passed it to him.

'So there is nothing miraculous about these lamps?'

'Nothing at all. Pass the scissors.'

'What about the oil itself? Is it chrism? Olive oil from the Mount of Olives?'

'No it's ordinary sunflower oil. Comes from a box in the sacristy. Damn this lamp! We'll have to have a new float. Pass one up will you?'

'Float?'

'One of those cork things.'

I passed him a spare from the tray.

'Where's the girl?' asked Fabian from the ladder.

'I don't know. Probably asleep.'

'Is she your . . . friend?'

'What do you mean?'

5

Fabian winked at me.

'You know. . . .'

'She's not my girlfriend, if that's what you mean.'

'And who's this Italian you were looking for?'

'Polo?'

'That's the one.'

'He's . . . different.'

'And he told you this oil was miraculous?'

'I suppose he did, indirectly.'

'Well you can tell him from me it's quite ordinary.'

'That would be a little difficult.'

Fabian let this pass.

'You say he took this oil east with him?' he continued.

'Yes.'

'What did he carry it in?'

'I don't know. A goatskin flask, perhaps.'

'He'd be a bit old fashioned then.'

'A bit.'

Fabian put the finishing touches to his new wick, put it back in the oil then lit it from the one remaining unguttered lamp.

'You still want some of this oil?'

'Please.'

I handed him a small plastic phial.

'Not goatskin.'

'No. It comes from the Body Shop in Covent Garden.'

Fabian took the bottle, removed the top, and carefully dipped it in the sump of the fourth lamp. It filled, slowly. Then he handed it back to me.

'Good luck finding your friend.'

Marco Polo came to the Holy Sepulchre in the autumn of 1271. Jerusalem had finally been lost to Islam thirty years previously, and the Sepulchre would have been semi-derelict when Polo saw it. The Turks who captured Jerusalem in 1244 had butchered the priests inside, desecrated the tombs of the Kings of Jerusalem, and burned the church to the ground.

Since then, the city had passed into the hands of the Mameluke Sultan, Baibars I, an upwardly mobile ex-slave who had once been returned to the market place by a dissatisfied buyer on account of his excessive ugliness. By the time Polo came to the Levant ten years later he had made himself the most feared and most powerful figure in the Middle East, defeating the Mongols and driving them back east of the Euphrates.

At the same time Baibars was slowly and methodically evicting the crusaders from their last toe-hold on the coast of Palestine. As I passed through the St Stephen's Gate on my way back to Sheik Jarrah I saw an emblem of Baibars' placed high above the portal. It must have been newly carved when Polo arrived in Jerusalem. The symbol was a pair of lions rampant about to attack a small rat. The lions, which were shown with powerful haunches, long claws and magnificent heraldic tails, represented Mameluke Egypt; the cornered rat, the crusaders. It was a sadly accurate picture: in 1263 Baibars had sacked Nazareth and burned the outskirts of Acre. The following year the crusader fortresses of Caesarea, Arsuf and Athlit all fell before his siege engines. In 1268 Antioch was captured by Baibars after a siege of only four days. But it was in the spring of 1271 that the crusaders received their greatest shock. Krak des Chevaliers, the headquarters of the Knights Hospitallers, was considered by all sides to be impregnable; in 1188 it had defied even Saladin. But on March the third Mameluke troops appeared unexpectedly below the castle, and soon the fortress was invested. Despite heavy spring rains arbalesters were brought up the hill from the valley bottom and after a short bombardment the Egyptians broke into the lower ward. The depleted garrison of three hundred fought on for another month until, on April the eighth, they surrendered, having received a forged order to do so, purporting to come from the Grand Master of the Hospitallers in Tripoli.

The loss of Krak was as great a boon to the prestige of Baibars as it was a blow to that of the Franks. Yet Acre, the capital of the Crusader Kingdom since the fall of Jerusalem, was at this critical point in a state of vigorous civil war. None of the crusaders was taking an even remotely responsible attitude to the survival of the Kingdom: this was left to the Papal Legate, Theobald of Piacenza. Theobald was a man of great severity and dignity, a friend of St Thomas Aquinas and a confidant of the kings of England and France. Appointed Archdeacon of Liège, he left his position and retired to the Holy Land after disagreements with his bishop who was attempting to turn the Liège episcopal palace into a bordello. In Acre Theobald succeeded in negotiating a temporary truce between the Genoese and Venetians, and persuading the local nobility to cooperate with Prince Edward of England who had just arrived at the head of an English crusade. But he lacked the authority or the power to do anything more radical to save the Kingdom. Then, in the late August of that year, Theobald was elected to the papacy. He heard of his appointment in early September and took the name Gregory X.

Gregory realized that the only possible hope for the crusaders was to make some sort of pact with the Mongols with whom they shared a common Egyptian enemy. Not only did this make good strategic sense, there were growing indications that Kubla Khan was considering embracing Christianity. This was not as unlikely a proposition as it sounded. There were many Eastern Christians among the Mongol ranks and already there had been military cooperation between Bohemond, the crusader Prince of Antioch, and Hulagu, the Mongol Prince of Persia. But Gregory had conceived a more daring and ambitious plan than simple cooperation. He wished to convert the Mongols to Christianity and to turn the Great Khan Kubla into the spiritual son of the Roman Pontiff. The Mongol Empire ranged from the Euphrates to the Pacific; it was the largest empire the world had ever seen. Gregory understood that if it could be turned into a Christian empire, the days of Islam would be numbered and the Crusader Kingdom saved.

Gregory's first action as Pope was thus to recall to Acre a

Venetian galley that had just arrived at Ayas in Asia Minor. On board were two Venetian brothers, Niccolo and Maffeo Polo along with Niccolo's seventeen-year-old son, Marco. Two years previously, in the spring of 1269, the two elder Polos had suddenly appeared in Acre. They said they had just returned from Xanadu, the summer palace of Kubla Khan on the Mongolian steppe. They were the first Europeans ever to claim to have travelled so far east, and their tale appeared to be true. When they were brought before Gregory (then still Papal Legate) they told him their remarkable story and showed him the Tablets of Gold given to them by Kubla Khan. On these were inscribed orders that the Polos should be 'supplied with everything needful in all the countries through which they should pass – with horses, with escorts, and, in short, with whatever they should require'. According to the brothers, Kubla Khan was a man of rather different temperament to his grandfather Ghengis. He had shown great interest in Christianity and had given them a letter in which he asked the Pope to send him 'a hundred persons of the Christian faith; intelligent men, acquainted with the Seven Arts, and able clearly to prove to idolaters and other kinds of folk, that the Law of Christ was best, and that all other religions were false and nought'. The brothers said that if they could prove this, Kubla Khan and all his subjects would become Christians. The Khan had also asked the brothers to bring back to him what he had heard was the most sacred of Christian relics, a sample of oil from the famous lamps which burned in the Holy Sepulchre.

The Legate realized that this was a crucial chance for Christendom. But in 1269 there was no Pope, as Clement IV had just died and the cardinals had yet to summon the energy to meet and choose his successor. The Polos had no choice but to go to Venice and wait until a Pope was elected. By the spring of 1271, despite mounting public indignation, the cardinals appeared to be no nearer reaching a decision. Seeing this, the Polos decided to return to Acre, this time with Marco. There they announced to the Legate that Pope or no Pope they were going to return to the Khan 'for we have already tarried long, and there has been more than enough delay'. They set off east in the last days of August.

Meanwhile in Viterbo the papal election had turned into an international scandal. In order to speed a decision, the civic authorities had locked the cardinals in the Papal Palace, threatened a starvation diet and removed the roof 'to allow the divine influences to descend more freely on their counsels'. This unusual approach to the workings of the Holy Spirit proved a surprising success. The cardinals delegated the decision to a committee of six who, anxious to get away, elected Theobald that same day. A week later news of the decision reached Acre and the Polos were recalled. The new Pope immediately gave them permission to go to Jerusalem to fetch the Holy Oil. He also provided the expedition with, if not one hundred, then at least with two intelligent men of the Christian faith, Friar Nicolas of Vicenza and Friar William of Tripoli, the two most senior friars in the Holy Land. Pope Gregory gave to the friars extraordinary powers of ordination and absolution, and to the Polos letters and presents for the Great Khan. The party, now five strong – the two elder Polos, Marco, and the two friars – finally departed in early November.

At my primary school we knew all about Marco Polo. He wore a turban, a stripy robe a bit like a dressing gown and he rode a camel with only one hump. The Ladybird book which had this picture on the cover was the most heavily thumbed book on the school bookshelf. One day, my friends and I put some biscuits in a handkerchief, tied the handkerchief to a stick and set off to China. It was an exhausting walk as there were no camels in Scotland, and by tea time we had eaten all our biscuits. There was also the problem that we were not absolutely sure where China was. It was beyond England, of that we were certain, but then we were not absolutely sure where England was either. Nonetheless we strode off manfully towards Haddington where there was a shop. We could ask there, we said. But when it began to get dark we turned around and went home for supper. After consultation we decided to put the plan on the shelf for a while. China could wait.

In fact, no one had ever been much more successful than us in following Marco Polo. Many had, like us, set off in his tracks but no one had ever managed to complete the journey. In the nineteenth century Afghanistan was too dangerous; in the twentieth, first Sinkiang, then the whole of China was closed to foreigners. By the time China began opening up in the early eighties, Afghanistan was closed again, this time because of the Soviet invasion. Now, while the Soviets are withdrawing, Iran and Syria have both closed their borders. But in the spring of 1986 the opening of the Karakoram Highway, the mountain road which links Pakistan with China, made it possible for the first time, perhaps since the thirteenth century, to plan an overland route between Jerusalem and Xanadu and to attempt to carry a phial of Holy Oil from one to the other. The war in Afghanistan prevented the whole of Polo's journey being followed but in principle it was now possible to follow almost all of it, and to complete the journey. It was my then girlfriend Louisa who spotted the small article in the *New York Herald Tribune* which announced the opening of the highway and together we decided to mount an expedition to follow in the Venetian's footsteps. The previous summer I had walked from Edinburgh to Jerusalem following the route of the First Crusade. That journey had ended at the Holy Sepulchre; Marco Polo's journey began where the other finished. It was the obvious sequel.

For a month Louisa and I planned the expedition. We argued over maps and atlases, sat in the Cambridge University Library reading up the history, toured the different embassies; I even managed to persuade my college to part with £700 to help finance it. With exams looming, I then disappeared into my books for two months, forgot about the trip and saw very little of Louisa. A fortnight before we were due to depart I met Lou for a drink outside a pub in Hammersmith. There, between delicate sips of sweet white wine, I was presented with a *fait accompli*. There was (sip) a new man (sip) and a new destination (sip); 'Edward' and 'Orkney' respectively. Reeling from the blow, I went off to a dinner party where I poured out my heart to the stranger who was sitting on my left. The recipient was called Laura. Although I had never met her before her reputation had gone before her. She was renowned as a formidable lady, frighteningly intelligent, physically tough, and if not conventionally beautiful, then at least sturdily handsome. I had heard that she was an Oxford ice-hockey blue and a scholar; I also knew that she was a fearless traveller. During her father's latest posting in Delhi, Laura had taken the opportunity to explore the entire subcontinent. Stories of her feats of endurance were common currency; if one half of them were true, she had by the age of twenty-one made Freya Starke look like a dilettante. It was said that travelling on her own she had penetrated the most inaccessible corners of the Deccan, cut a swathe through the jungles of Bengal, scaled some of the highest peaks in the Himalayas. Her finest moment had come in the communal riots that engulfed Delhi on the death of Mrs Gandhi. Trying to rescue a Sikh friend from street gangs, Laura had been cornered in a cul-de-sac by a party of rapists intent on violation. She had beaten them off single-handed, and, so the story went, left one of them permanently incapacitated.

I had not been told that Laura was as impulsive as she was formidable. At the end of supper she announced that she would take Louisa's place, at least as far as Lahore, whence she could make her way home to Delhi. She had been planning to explore the Andes, but the Ayatollah's Iran sounded just her cup of tea. She would ring me in three days' time to confirm.

Three days later, at the ominously early time of seven-thirty a.m., the telephone went. Of course she was coming, she told me. If I would meet her at the Syrian embassy in one hour we could begin collecting the necessary visas. Over the next two weeks Laura swept me around London as she slashed at red tape, assaulted passport officials, and humbled the bureaucracy of the Asian embassies. Under her supervision I was inspected, injected and protected against diseases I had never dreamt existed. My maps were thrown away and replaced with a set that looked as if they had been prepared by the CIA: they were covered in unexplained figures and inscribed the chilling warning AIRCRAFT INFRINGING UPON THE NON-FREE FLYING TERRITORY MAY BE FIRED UPON WITHOUT WARNING.

Meanwhile, the full weight of Laura's connections was put into the planning of the expedition. Through devious means, visas were obtained for us for Iran. A way was found to get us from Israel to Syria: telex messages to Odessa led to us obtaining tickets for a ship which ran between Haifa in Israel and Limassol in Cyprus; berths were then booked in another ship which ran from Larnaca, at the other end of the island, to Latakia in Syria. There were still some problems. We had to make sure that the Israelis did not stamp our passports, nor let the Cypriot authorities indicate in any way how we had come to their island. If we failed in this we would be unable to enter either Syria or Iran. There were also worries as to our reception in Iran. The previous year a British student of our own age had been arrested while travelling through the country and was still languishing in an Iranian jail on espionage charges. Most serious of all was the shadow of gloom cast by a travel article which appeared in *The Times* only two days before our departure. It claimed that while the Karakoram Highway was indeed open to foreign travellers, only those foreigners who were part of a tour group would be allowed into China. The only exceptions were those who had booked accommodation at Tashkurgan, the first town in China. This, claimed the article, could only be done via Peking, and took six months to arrange.

The next morning I got a phone call from Louisa. She had heard that I was still planning to go on the trip. She would be back from Orkney by mid-August. Would I like her to come on the second half of the journey, from Lahore to Peking? I said yes. I did not tell her about the article. That hurdle would have to be jumped when we came to it.

Thus I committed myself to travelling across twelve

thousand miles of extremely dangerous, inhospitable territory, much of which seemed still to be closed to foreigners, with two companions, one a complete stranger, the other completely estranged. Perhaps I should have consulted a doctor; instead I went to a travel agent and bought a ticket to Jerusalem.

I got back from the Holy Sepulchre in time for breakfast. Laura and I were staying, on slightly dubious credentials, at the British School of Archaeology, the creation of the great Dame Kathleen Kenyon and still surviving as a piece of turn-of-the-century Oxbridge-in-the-Orient. Sheer obscurity seemed to have saved it from the late twentieth century in general and government cuts in particular. It was the home of a collection of shy, bookish scholars who pottered away digging up remote crusader castles in the Judean Hills and editing multi-volume works on the Roman sewer systems of Jerusalem. The week we were there the diggers had just found a small, rather plain waterleaf capital which was the cause of great excitement.

The tone of the school was formal. This was particularly so of the meals, and of these, none more so than breakfast. The school serves certainly the best (and possibly the only) bacon and eggs east of Rome. However, not wishing to embarrass any local Palestinian archaeologists who might be staying, the school also serves a supplementary course of feta cheese, olives, tomatoes and pitta bread – and throws in watermelons, yoghurt, toast and marmalade for good measure. This agreeable feast is served in two shifts. The first is at five a.m. and is meant for the diggers. The second and slightly larger sitting is at eight a.m. and is intended for researchers, post-excavation experts and anyone else who has managed not to be woken up by the diggers three hours earlier. On the morning in question this included Laura, who was deep in her bacon and eggs when I returned from my rendezvous with Brother Fabian. I was looking forward to spending a leisurely few days at the school, seeing Jerusalem and generally acclimatizing before setting off to the unknown horrors of Syria. But it was not to be.

At breakfast Laura produced for the first time a document that was to terrorize the rest of the trip: Laura's Schedule. This harmless-looking piece of paper was filled with a series of impossible deadlines culminating in the laughable goal of reaching Lahore by the end of August. Its immediate import, however, was that we were to leave Jerusalem at lunchtime. My protests were quickly quashed. If I wanted to see the city a last time I was free to do so, Laura announced, but I had to report back by twelve-thirty. One of the researchers, a young hen-pecked academic doing a PhD on Mameluke pottery took pity on me and gave me a lift to Jaffa Gate in his van; I had three hours to explore.

The town had woken since my dawn visit. Occidentals now outnumbered orientals by about two to one. The streets were filled with elderly Saga pensioners on pilgrimage from Preston; in the Via Dolorosa weeping Evangelicals sung 'Kum-ba-ya' against the background of wailing *muezzin*. There were a few miserable-looking Presbyterians, some rotund Eastern European widows and an Ethiopian cleric in his flowing cassock of grey serge. Pallid, short-sighted Orthodox Jews shuffled past clutching Uzi sub-machine guns. The Arabs – wearing pin-stripe for practicality, and *keffiyeh* to attract tourists – had taken up station outside their shops: *Rainbow Bazaar, The Omar Khayyam Souvenir Museum, Magic Coffee House, The al-Haj Carpentry Store*. To get to the Dome of the Rock there was no option but to run the gauntlet:

'Yes please, you like?'

'Wallah! I give you souvenir, no price. Come with me.'

'Upstairs sir, I show you *everything*.'

'Sir, sir, you want guide? I show you church six thousand years old. No problem!'

'Friend! My carpet awaits you.'

This pantomime of subservience has gone on day after day for centuries. Jerusalem has always been a tourist town. The pilgrims have changed, religions have come and gone and empires with them; only the knickknack sellers remain. The objects in their shops are a fascinating compendium of the junk on sale all over the Islamic world. There are the same hookahs that are on sale in Istanbul outside Hagia Sophia; there are the soap-stone boxes from the bazaar in Agra; painted wooden camels familiar from Cairo. Christian religious souvenirs are generally imported from Europe: Palestine does not claim the azure madonnas or the plastic Stations of the Cross but the crucifixes are stamped 'wood from the Garden of Gethsemane' and marked up 200 per cent. Nothing appears to be of native manufacture.

The Dome of the Rock is a world apart from this chaos. The great marble platform of the Haram al-Sharif may be one of the Holy Sites of Islam but apart from Friday prayers it is nearly always deserted. It is only when you get here and have a moment to sit, and think, and look back, that you come to realize how little the tawdriness matters and how beautiful Jerusalem still is: the bleached stone, the hills, the miles and miles of untouched crusader bazaar, the white walls of Suleiman the Magnificent.

The charm of the Dome of the Rock takes a little longer to appreciate. The gaudy Ottoman tile work and the flashing dome have both been recently renovated by the Jordanians and in no way prepare one for the breathtaking beauty of what lies inside. The golden mosaic work bears the hand of the Byzantines: the amphorae and the cornucopiae, the acanthus leaves and the geometric designs, are all in the old Hellenistic tradition. So is the building itself. It is the climax of a tradition of centrally planned churches that embraces St George in Thessaloniki, San Vitale in Ravenna and, long before either of these, Santa Constanza in Rome. The Dome is the smallest, yet despite its size it is still the most impressive. Its marble work is more refined, its mosaics more harmonious, the whole more satisfying. But the Dome is not, of course, a church (although the crusaders turned it into one during their occupation of Jerusalem). It was built as a mosque, and was probably the first such; certainly it was the first major artistic endeavour of Islam. It was built by Caliph Abd al-Malik in 687 and so is the rough contemporary of the Synod of Whitby and the very earliest Saxon churches in England: the crypts at Hexham and Ripon, and the choir of Bede's church at Jarrow. It was as old by the time of Marco Polo as most of the mediaeval abbeys in England are today. The specifically Islamic character of the building becomes apparent on a second glance. Already the arches have the beginning of a point, and in the mosaics there are no saints, no angels. The Koranic ban on the portrayal of living creatures had already taken effect.

But only when you study the Dome for a considerable time does the full programme of its builders become clear. Suspended in the vinescrolls, low down on the inner arcades, are the insignia of the defeated Byzantine and Sassanian empires: crows, double- winged diadems, jewels and breastplates. They have been hung on the walls of the mosque like hunting trophies on the walls of an English country house. Far from being a purely religious or aesthetic monument, this first mosque is a celebration of victory. The Koranic scrolls are chosen to show Islam as the successor to Christianity; the same spirit located the building directly on top of the Jewish temple and used captive Greeks to build it. The Dome dominates Jerusalem and deliberately eclipses the buildings of Judaism and Christianity. It is an indication of both the self-confidence and the intolerance of the new Islamic conquerors of Jerusalem. Ravishing to look at, it is, in a way, a deeply disturbing building.

If history repeats itself anywhere, it does so in Jerusalem. When the crusaders captured the city they slaughtered the Muslims (many of whom took refuge on the roof of the Dome) as well as the Jews and the native Christians whom they had purportedly set out to help. The bazaars which today give the Old City its character were punched through the homes of its previous occupants. Now the Jews, more subtly but equally firmly, are evicting the Palestinians. Israeli soldiers terrorize the Old City; the Orthodox are slowly colonizing the Muslim, Christian and Armenian quarters of East Jerusalem. Since 1948 the Christian population has dropped from thirty-five thousand to eleven thousand; there are no opportunities for the young people beyond selling knickknacks or washing dishes. Only the lazy stay; the ambitious and the better educated emigrate.

In the queue for the bus to Acre I talked to a young Jewish soldier and his girlfriend. They were both tall, brown, well-built and good-looking; the boy ate a packet of crisps, the girl wrapped herself around the boy. Had it not been for the machine guns that both were holding it might have been a homely scene. They were friendly; both were highly educated and at first seemed liberal and thoroughly reasonable. But when the conversation turned to Israeli affairs their replies were chilling. When I asked the boy whether he minded policing the West Bank and enforcing the illegal occupation of Jordanian territory he said that it was not a duty so much as a right, a privilege. The girl agreed. She complained that in the Israeli army women were trained to use rifles and even shown how to drive tanks, but then only given clerical jobs. She said: 'What's the use of being taught to use a gun if you're then not allowed to shoot with it?'

For two thousand years Jerusalem has brought out the least attractive qualities in every race that has lived there. The Holy City has had more atrocities committed in it, more consistently, than any other town in the world. Sacred to three religions, the city has witnessed the worst intolerance and self-righteousness of all of them.

Israeli buses are the fastest, most comfortable and efficient in Asia. They are the only ones in which you can write a diary and read the results afterwards. But the view from their windows is invariably depressing: you read much about how the Israelis have made the desert flower, but little about the cost. The dual carriageway from Jerusalem winds past not a land of milk and honey, but a scape of scarred hillsides, rubbish dumps, telegraph wires, pylons, concrete, dirt and dust. The towns are charmless and ugly; there is barbed wire everywhere. Perhaps inspired by the view, an American *kibbutznik* began a long lamentation behind me. She talked without pausing for an hour and a half:

'. . . my cousin speaks better Hebrew than I do it's kinda intimidating he went on a kibbutz and worked with chickens . . . there are six major cities I gotta see my interests are very diverse . . . look Burger Ranch well fancy that burgers in Israel . . . home is a big air force base East Coast absolutely gorgeous my boyfriend Rob he's graduating in statistics wants me to get a lot out of this . . . I guess I could do it but I'd prefer not to enough problems I have allergies neuroses I'm a vegetarian I could really use a sterile environment my analyst childhood problems some long name for it cruise long holiday . . . Rob and I difficult time this girl in the statistics department we will work it out . . . I'm very curious links Zen Buddhism Jewish mysticism *kibbutznik* philosophy. . . .'

It grew worse as we left the hills. Outside all was shoddy and new: a sprawl of supermarkets, warehouses, drive-in cinemas, factories and military installations – all imposed over the old Palestinian villages, bulldozed after their inhabitants were evicted in 1948. On the coast between Haifa and Acre we passed a line of luxury concrete hotels hung with fairy lights and giving onto private beaches occupied by fun fairs and night-clubs. The Israeli woman next to me pointed it out proudly. 'Look,' she said. 'We have everything!' Not wishing to give offence I nodded. But I thought: No. You've taken the oldest country in the world, one of the great centres of civilization, a kind of paradise – and you've turned it into suburbia.

New Acre confirmed my prejudices. It has the decaying, unloved look of a provincial Californian town of the late fifties – all parking lots and spurious palm trees. But its building has at least spared Old Acre from the horrors of Israelification. Old Acre has survived as an Arab ghetto. It is run-down and the old weathered stone is crumbling, yet to come to it from New Acre is like chancing upon an unexpected oasis in the desert. It is still essentially a mediaeval town and there are few buildings which post-date the Ottoman period. Marco Polo could probably still find his way around without too much trouble. The *funduq* of the Italian communes have been rebuilt as Mameluke *han*, the churches turned into mosques and the mole in the harbour topped with new stone to shelter the fishing boats – but all these occupy the same sites and preserve the same dimensions as the crusader originals.

Mediaeval opinion was divided about Acre. Many thought the safety of its harbour, the cosmopolitan population and the fortunes that could be made there all compensated for its failings, namely 'diseases, evil smells and corruption of the air'. Others were less sure. The priggish Muslim traveller Ibn Jubayr was a particularly fierce critic. 'Its roads are choked by the press of men, so it is hard to put foot to ground,' he wrote. 'Unbelief and unpiousness there burn fiercely, and Pigs [Christians] and crosses abound. It stinks and is filthy, being full of refuse and excrement.'

Nor was it just Muslims who were aware of Acre's failings. As the thirteenth century progressed, the place became increasingly unruly so that by the middle of the century it was suffering from a chronic crime problem. By the time Polo came here, it resembled, in the words of James de Vitry, one its bishops '. . . a monster of nine heads, each of which is fighting the other. Nightly men are murdered within the city, men are strangled, women poison their husbands, whores and drug vendors are prepared to pay high rents for rooms, so that even priests lease houses to them. . . .'

Surprisingly little has changed. We were still sitting at our café in the Old Town when we were approached by a tall sun-tanned Arab boy. He wore Bermuda shorts and a T-shirt which read TURBOSURF SENIOR WINDSURFER. There was an air of corruption and decadence about him, but he offered us a room for a pittance and we accepted: I had only £600 to see me through to Peking, twelve thousand miles away. This was not going to be a deluxe holiday, whatever else it might promise. As he led us to his house through a maze of back alleys, Hamoudi told us of all the different narcotics he would be prepared to part with, for only a small consideration, should we so wish. After he had finished I congratulated him on his English.

'Where did you learn it?' I asked.

'In jail,' he replied.

He led us up a flight of stairs, under a line of drying nappies, into one of the filthiest houses I have ever seen. From down the end of the corridor came the wail of a screaming baby. In another room, whose door was open, we saw what I took to be his father, an enormously fat Arab gentleman who was sprawled toad-like on a bed. He had button-black eyes, wore a dirty shift and in his mouth was lodged the brass filter of an out-sized hubble-bubble. In the following twelve hours we passed the door of that room several times, yet Hamoudi's father never seemed to move. He never blinked, never scratched himself, never left his station to eat or to wash. He certainly never spoke. The only indication that the man was alive were the aquarium-like sucking noises that emerged from his *nargile*.

Hamoudi led us into an empty room at the end of the corridor. The paint was peeling, a naked light bulb dangled from the ceiling and the whole place smelt strongly of livestock. Hamoudi went out into the corridor and pulled two stained mattresses into the room. While Laura washed, Hamoudi fetched two cups of Turkish coffee and, as a present for me, a pile of Arab soft porn. 'Gearls,' he explained, displaying a set of black jagged teeth. He sat on the bed, flicked through his magazines and treated me to an anecdotal history of his sex life. Hamoudi's existence seemed a fairly comprehensive passage through the different vices. There was little he had not bought, sold, smoked, sniffed or made love to. In particular he had had many gearls, he told me: Swedish, French, Italian, Israeli – but, he confided, the Bulgarians were undoubtedly the best. I should try one sometime. Hamoudi rambled on until Laura returned from her shower and evicted him.

When we emerged it was late evening, and the light was beginning to fade. We wandered through the bazaars as the fishmongers were beginning to shut up shop, and the old Arabs who had been sitting outside, leaning on their sticks began to hobble off home. We visited the Palace of the Hospitallers, buried since the fall of Acre in 1291 and recently excavated by Israeli archaeologists. The refectory is one of the finest crusader buildings to survive anywhere. It has magnificent vaulting held up with three monolithic round pillars, as huge and heavy as those in Durham Cathedral, only simpler, with no chevron work or decorated capitals. The Hospitallers' refectory at Krak, built in happier times, is as elaborate and refined as anything to survive from the Middle Ages in Europe. This was very different: dating from the very end of the crusader period, it is sombre, defensive architecture, utilitarian and practical with no unnecessary details or distractions. It is the architecture of a people with their back against a wall.

From the Hospitallers' Palace we passed through the old Genoese quarter and arrived in what had once been the quarter of the Venetians. The Italian communes had claimed these areas in the early twelfth century as a condition for helping with their original conquest and had since zealously guarded their privileges and rights within the walls. Here they mixed with their own people, spoke their own language, and were disciplined by their own laws. There was a commune bath and a commune bakery to cater for particular tastes and habits, a commune church to bless and bury in a familiar tongue, among compatriots. To these quarters the Italians carried the feuds and rivalries that proliferated in mediaeval Italy. The vendettas of the family, the factions of Guelph and Ghibelline, the rivalries of Genoa and Venice, all these were brought to the Holy Land to add to the divisions that already complicated expatriate life there. Yet while the Italians dominated the commerce of the Crusader Kingdom they tried wherever possible to keep to themselves, preferring to live with a little Italy of their own creation, disdaining the ways and habits of the other Franks. It may just have been my imagination, but I thought that Acre still had a slightly Italian feel to it. Its coarse mediaeval stonework, the peeling stucco, the play of light and shade in the piazzas, the smell of baking bread, the horseshoe arc of the sea walls – all this brought back memories of Italian sea ports.

One hundred yards in from the sea front was the Khan al-Alfranj. The *han* was a fourteenth-century Mameluke structure, but stands on the site (and incorporates much of the masonry) of the Venetian *funduq*, the caravanserai where the Polos would almost certainly have lodged during their visits to Acre. During the months of the *passagium*, between Easter and late autumn, the *han* would have been full of sea captains, merchants and sailors. Here they would wake and sleep, eat and drink, buy and sell, free from the laws and customs of the Kingdom of Jerusalem. It is a quiet place now. You enter the compound under a narrow arch of red and white polychrome keystones, past a pair of old metal-reinforced gates still hanging from their original rusty hinges. The windows are covered with white-painted shutters, there is washing hung up from the balconies. There is a faint sound of hammering from a coppersmith's shop. Along three sides of the *han* are lines of blocked-up, eliptical arches, left open on the fourth side to provide shelter for upturned dinghies, tangles of netting, lobster pots, and a single ancient car, now pillaged of its seats, headlights, windshield, and driving wheel.

When the Polos came here for the last time in November 1271, the months of the *passagium* were past and the *han* must have been almost deserted, just as it was now. Sitting down in a last pool of evening light to write up the logbook I wondered what Marco must have felt the night before he was due to set off from the relatively familiar world of the westernized Crusader Kingdom, into the unknown Orient. He was about the same age as I and presumably of similar inclination. Nor was the world we lived in so very different. There was a remarkable similarity, for example, between the Crusader Kingdom and the State of Israel. They had similar boundaries, both were ruled from Jerusalem, and both were effectively supported by the West. Taking advantage of Arab disunity, they were both established by force and maintained by violence. They faced the same problems: Arab aggression outside, insufficient numbers within. In both, Arab and newcomer tended not to mix or intermarry: religion and culture divide the two now as it did then.

As we left the Khan al-Afranj we were invited into the shop of an Arab *terzi* (tailor). There we drank *cay* and talked about the problems of the Arabs in Acre, then as now, better integrated than most places: Ibn Jubayr remarked on this in the twelfth century while Hamoudi, who exhibited all the vices of the West in one body, is evidence of it today. The *terzi* was a tall man, unshaven, shambolic and friendly. But when I asked him about his relations with the Jews he was surprisingly eloquent.

'We live in peace in Acre,' he said. 'Here the Jew and the Arab are friends. On Saturday nights the Jews come here, play cards, smoke and drink coffee. The people want peace. Only the government does not.'

'What do you mean?'

'We live here under an undeclared apartheid. It is just like South Africa. For the Jews there is democracy. They have freedom of speech, they can vote for whichever government they like, can go where they like and talk to whom they like. For us it is different. We are here on sufferance. We are called into police stations if we are heard talking about politics. We are never sure we will get justice in court: if we have a plea against a Jew, then probably we will not. We are not allowed to join the army in case we turn sides. Because of this we cannot get any good jobs; for these you need security clearance. Most of us end up washing dishes or working as manual labourers; if you are lucky you can become a garbage collector.'

He laughed and sent a boy off to go and get some more tea.

'You see this shop? It belonged to my father before 1948, yet now I have to pay rent to the town council for it. If I was a Jew I would be given it, free. The taxes for us are very high. Many of the young – they are very angry. If this was their government they would not mind. But they do not want to pay the tax which will buy the tank which will kill their brother Arabs. It also means we cannot compete with the Jewish shopkeepers. They do not pay rents for their property so they can sell everything cheaper than us. The Israeli government does nothing for our people.'

'What do you think will happen?' asked Laura.

'How do I know? Some Arabs say: this is Palestine we must kick the Jews out. Also there are many Jews who call us dogs, animals. They say: we must clear the land of the Arabs. Both are wrong. We are both human. We both need to live. We must live together.'

The boy returned and handed round the cups. It was mint tea. When he was ready the *terzi* continued:

'Every morning I think that there could be peace. When I open the shop up in the morning Jews will drink coffee with me. Sometimes if I have problem with my telephone, my Jewish friend will say: use mine. Many of them are such lovely people. If only we could live in peace with them and there were no fighting, no killing. . . .'

Laura and I sat on a tower on the Cape of Storms in the old Pisan Quarter. It was a beautiful night and we sat in silence looking out over the sea, mulling over what the *terzi* had said. Then the peace was broken by two visitors.

Arab 1:	Where are you from?
WD:	Shshsh.
Arabs 1 and 2:	Shshshshshshshsh.
(*Silence, then:*)	
Arab 1 (*to Laura*):	You wanna buy carpet? I give you good price.
Laura (*dignified*):	Please. Not today. We're watching the sea.
(*Another pause, then:*)	
Arab 2 (*in whisper*):	That is nice watch. You sell?
WD (*abrupt*):	Shut up! Or go away.
Arab 2 (*annoyed*):	How long you stay in Acre?

25

WD (*repentant*):	We're off tomorrow.
Arab 2:	Where to?
WD:	Peking.
Arab 2:	Where?
WD:	Peking. In China.
Arab 2 (*furious*):	You think me fool? You think me animal? I tell you. Arab man very clever. We invent astronomy! We invent mathematics! Arab man finest artists in world. (*Pause. Then:*) Where are you really going?
WD:	Peking.
Arab 2:	You are crazy man.

(*Exit Arabs 1 and 2.*)

After supper we returned to our room. Hamoudi was out on the prowl but his father was still sprawled on the bed with his hookah bubbling away. The soft porn which had been thrown out of the room by Laura had reappeared; otherwise, to our surprise, our room did not look as if it had been tampered with nor our luggage ransacked. The only sign of life was one of Hamoudi's cats noisily crunching a mouse on my mattress. Laura went to bed, while I sat in the corridor scribbling in the logbook. A few mosquitos wheeled around a light bulb; many more wheeled around me, nibbling on my ankles and forearms. After an hour, I gave up. I felt very tired.

I got out the maps and drew a black line between Jerusalem and Acre. It was about a quarter of an inch long. Lahore was three feet away at the edge of the map. Peking lay halfway across the room on an entirely different sheet. It seemed a very long way indeed.

TWO

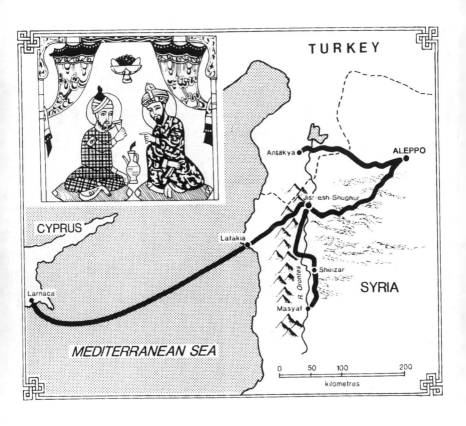

TURKEY

Antakya

ALEPPO

Jisr-esh-Shughur

CYPRUS

Latakia

Sheizar

R. Orontes

SYRIA

Masyaf

Larnaca

MEDITERRANEAN SEA

0   50   100   200

kilometres

Latakia is a filthy hole; I had forgotten how bad it was.

The town smells of dead fish: you can smell it three miles into the Mediterranean. At the first whiff, the passengers finished their drinks at the bar, and closed their *tawla* (backgammon) boards. They gathered their luggage into piles, collected their wives, and wiped their children's faces. By the time the lights of the town became visible on the horizon, the gangplanks were already clogged with excited Arabs jostling to be the first ashore. There were westernized Lebanese in polyester suits and flares; they held black attaché cases in their right hands. Beside them stood Druze straight out of a David Roberts' picture, squat and snub-nosed in khaki jackets, cavernous *charwal* trousers and red and white *keffiyeh*. Their *charwal* dangled heavily between their legs and their *keffiyeh* were thrown over their shoulders and held in place by a thick headband of black cord. They were silent and sullen and small. The Jordanians were more cheery. They waddled around in dirty white shifts, and nursed large distended bellies and crowds of spoilt children. The Syrian peasants were the worst. They pulled and shoved at their trunks and sacks, knocking into the Druze and arguing with their neighbours. Then they would recognize a friend and fight their way through the crowd to embrace him and kiss him on both cheeks. They chewed pistachio nuts, scattered the shells and chattered incessantly.

Laura and I were at the back of the queue, and stood next to a group of four huge men who looked even more out of place than we did. They had pale white skin and large white biceps, grey ankle-socks, shorts, and close-fitting T-shirts. They talked

Russian among themselves and explained to us in French that they were teachers. Later one of them said they were engineers. Presumably they must have been KGB.

Our liner docked soon after 10 p.m. The port was hung with multi-coloured lights and a scattering of charcoal braziers gave off a warm red glow. They lit a scene of bustling anarchy. Thousands of Arabs were massed baying on the quay and within seconds of us touching the pier head, hordes of them had swarmed up the walkways and along the guy ropes. It took well over two hours to fight our way ashore. The girder-faced receptionist broke down in tears as a party of Palestinians took a short cut over her desk, scattering her papers, and an epileptic had a fit on the lower deck amid a car-pet of pistachio shells. One old woman fainted. As we tried to edge our way towards the gangplank, a Lebanese merchant began quizzing us on our journey:

'Good sir, why are you coming to Syria?'

'We are following Marco Polo.'

He considered this as he fought his way forward.

'This Marco Poodle – he is Englishman?'

'No,' said Laura, stepping over the epileptic. 'Italian.'

'Oh.' Then: 'When was Mr Poodle coming to Syria?'

'Many years ago.'

'He is still alive?'

'No.'

'Then why do you follow him?'

In European ports immigration officials are hard to avoid. In Syria you need the instincts of a homing pigeon to find them. They lurked in a large and dimly lit hangar, through a laby-rinth of alleyways full of growling mongrels, past loading cranes, skips, piles of rusting wire and tangles of disused net-ting. In one corner an official was standing on a platform with a pile of passports, auctioning them off to anyone who raised their hand. At the opposite end two harassed clerks in military uniform were slaving over a pair of enormous ledgers. Shriek-

30

ing Arabs were waving their passports at them, and shouting their date of birth and the details of their grandparents' religious beliefs. In between sat miserable groups of women, children and packing cases, and near them, on one side, sprawled a group of immigrants sucking feverishly at hookahs. It reminded me of a Hieronymous Bosch hell-scene. A hand clutched my arm; it was the merchant again.

'Good sir,' he said. 'This country has no order. You should come and stay with me in Lebanon.'

'That's very kind.'

'I live in Ba'albek. It is a very beautiful town.'

'So I have heard,' said Laura, 'but isn't it now the head-quarters of the Hezbollah?'

'Yes it is. They are good men, Hezbollah. Very religious peoples. Always they are giving prayers.'

'Really?' said Laura. 'Well you know that's awfully kind of you, but I'm afraid we are in rather a rush. We've got to be in Pakistan in one month.'

Later, when the merchant had gone, I asked Laura why she had been so quick to refuse the invitation.

'Do you know who the Hezbollah are?' she replied.

'Never heard of them. But they sound rather charming, don't they?'

'They're the most extreme terrorists in the entire Middle East, responsible for most of the recent kidnappings in Beirut. They keep their prisoners in the Sheik Lutfullah barracks in Ba'albek. We wouldn't have lasted two hours had we gone to stay with that man.'

She gave me one of her withering looks.

'You know, William, you really should read the papers.'

I left Laura with the luggage while I went to retrieve our passports, and register with the clerks. Having queued and fought and sworn my way to the front I was then redirected to a different hut which dealt with Europeans. Here I was per-suaded to part with an 'entry tax' and face a lurid inquisition.

'Why you come Syria? You like Arab peoples? Good. You like Arab boys, eh? No? Arab womens then? No? Who then?

31

(*Opens Laura's passport.*) This picture your wife? She pretty womans. How much she cost? No – not your wife. Girlfriend then? If you drink *raki* then you make your girlfriend many times in one night. Once I make my girlfriend THIRTEEN times. You not believe? Thirteen times I tell you. My friend Abdul – he knows. Hey Abdul, I make my friend thirteen times, eh? You see. I very virile man. *Big* minaret! Abdul knows, eh Abdul?'

(Continues describing minarets, drinking feats, girlfriends etc. etc. until I manage to move the conversation back onto passports. Then:)

'This is you? Hey Abdul, look at the picture of the Ingliz! He wears necktie and jacket! You look very high man, very rich man. No? Neither? Why then necktie? You poor man? How come to Syria then? I don't believe. I poor man. You want *raki*? We ALL want *raki*! Abdul, fill my glass. Yes! Yes! You no like Arab boys? I know nice place. You don't want? Nor want womens? I tell you Arab womens the best in world. No? What can I say? More *raki*. You want stamp? Abdul, he wants passport stamp! Here. You my friend. I give you special stamp. No extra cost. Allah be with you. Goodbye, my friend. Yes, next time we go with little boys. ABDUL, THE *RAKI*.'

I fled. I found Laura and got a taxi to a hotel. It was a horrible place, with a pigeon in the shower, but at least the door locked. We shut out Arabia and went to sleep.

The following morning started badly. After a hazardous shower, we went down for breakfast. The proprietor narrowed his eyes at us:

'Que cherchez-vous?'
'Vous avez des oeufs?'
'Oeufs mauvais.'
'Du fromage?'
'Fromage mauvais.'
'Une tasse de thé?'
'Thé mauvais.'
'Pouvez-vous nous appeller un taxi?'

'Taxi m . . . O.K. Je vais vous appeller un taxi. Mais ça va couter cher.'

He rang for a taxi, and added it to the bill.

A twenty-minute ride took us to the bus station, through the ruinous streets of Latakia. It is a hideous place, but strangely fascinating. The streets seem almost wilfully neglected; Roman columns, Byzantine capitals, Arabesque lintels and Ottoman vaulting lie together on roundabouts and street corners, great dusty piles of masonry mixed up with plastic bottles, abandoned shoes and broken water pipes. The food – if you can find it – is the worst in the Middle East, the people the least friendly. They mix Arab deviousness with colonial French arrogance, and add to this a surliness which is uniquely their own. Yet beneath the ugliness, grime and smut, there is a sense of the corrupt which is curiously compelling. There is something conspiratorial about the beckoning pimps and the cockroach cafés, something which always makes one want to pry behind the closed doors and shuttered windows.

If this is true of Latakia as a whole, it is particularly so of the bus station. It is a large, flat wasteland on the outskirts of the town, the sort of place which the traveller occasionally comes across, into which all transportation leads and from which none ever seems to emerge. The previous year I had got stuck here for what seemed like weeks, under constant assault from nut vendors and noxious-smelling kebab salesmen, terrified by the mobs of unruly Arabs who would converge on incoming buses, howling horribly as if bent on their destruction.

But this year, with Laura in the lead, it all seemed much easier. We got aboard on our third attempt. Ten school years of cold scrum practice in wet, February North Yorkshire were finally put to good use; we charged forward like a pair of prop forwards, swinging our rucksacks, mercilessly knocking everyone flying; only the Bedouin got in before us. We seized a patch of floor beside the running board which we shared with a weak-bladdered billy goat and defended it against all comers.

Inside, the bus was lovingly dressed up, rather as the English decorate their Christmas trees. Plastic birds balanced on plastic leaves; garlands of azaleas and silver tinsel hung around a framed picture of the Syrian president, Haffez Assad. The roof was coated in gaudy polychrome lino, and along the length of the bus, shiny baubles, plastic Korans and large bunches of plastic grapes swung from the luggage rack. The passengers were less lovingly cared for, squashed into an impossible space with their baggage, their children and their livestock. A few were in a bad way: some of the old men had that glazed, shell-shocked look that comes over you after a few hours at the Latakia bus station.

But before long things began to improve. In low gear the old bus chugged off, up into the Syrian Jebel, the lovely hill country which divides the coastal plain from the valley of the al-Garb, and beyond that the Badiet esh-Sham, the Great Syrian Desert. As we went we shed some of our excess passengers and climbed on up through sweet-smelling slopes of mimosa, and past thickly wooded banks of cypress, spruce and cedar of Lebanon.

Our destination was the village of Masyaf. Although Polo never came to Syria and instead went straight to the Kingdom of Lesser Armenia, he does discuss a sect who in 1271 had their headquarters at Masyaf, the order known to history as the Assassins. For centuries the Assassins embodied everything that Europeans distrusted in Asia. They were fanatical Muslims said to indulge in strange sexual perversities and unusual narcotics. The tales smack more of *One Thousand and One Nights* than real history. Yet where it is rare among millions of similar myths from the East is that when stripped bare by modern historians the reality is quite as interesting as the myth.

The Assassins were a militant wing of a heterodox Sh'ia sect, the Isma'ilis. For a short time in the eleventh century the Isma'ilis had gained political power in Egypt under the Fatamid caliphs, but in Persia and elsewhere in Islam they remained an unpopular minority who were intermittently persecuted. 'To kill them,' wrote one Persian mullah, 'is more lawful than rainwater. It is the duty of sultans and kings to conquer and kill them, and cleanse the surface of the earth from their pollution. It is not right to associate with them, nor eat meat butchered by them, nor enter into marriage with them. To shed their blood is more meritorious than to kill seventy infidel. . . .'

It was in response to this persecution that the Assassins were founded, and under their first Grand Master, Hasan-i-Sabbah, they became the original terrorist group. Their first victim was the Seljuk vizier of Persia, Nizam al-Mulk. He, Omar Khayyam and Hasan were said to have been school friends, but Nizam tried to control the growing powers of the Isma'ili and in 1092 he was stabbed to death in his litter by an Assassin disguised as a Sufi holy man. He was on his way from the audience hall to the tent of his harem.

Hasan built up his followers into an order, united in strict obedience to himself. During the twelfth century large numbers of princes hostile to the Isma'ili met their death by the Assassins' daggers: the Prince of Homs was followed by the Prince of Mosul, the Wazir of Egypt and even the heavily guarded crusader king, Conrad of Jerusalem. Their enemies were forced to take elaborate precautions to protect themselves. When Polo's predecessor in the East, Friar William of Rubruck, arrived at the Mongol capital of Karakoram in 1254, he was amazed at the security arrangements. 'We were separately brought in and they asked us where we came from, and why, and what we wanted. And they proceeded to question us minutely,' he wrote. It was only later that he discovered that the interrogation was a response to the intelligence that no less than forty Assassins were abroad in the town, and that in various disguises they had all been sent to murder the Khan.

Such behaviour left the Assassins with few friends. Little was known about them and wild rumours abounded. Muslims said they ate pig meat and prayed with their backs to Mecca. There were rumours of sorcery. Stories even reached Christian Europe. 'They are accursed,' wrote the priest Brocardus. 'They sell themselves, are thirsty for human blood, kill the innocent for a price and care nothing for life or salvation. Like the devil they can transfigure themselves into angels of light.' Others echoed his words. 'They make use of all women without distinction,' wrote one anxious cleric, 'including their mothers and sisters.'

Against this sort of sensationalism, Polo's description of the sect is sobriety itself. Yet it is one of the most beautiful passages in *The Travels*:

> Now the Old Man of The Mountain caused a certain valley between two mountains to be enclosed, and had it turned into a garden, the largest and most beautiful that ever was seen, filled with every variety of fruit. In it were erected pavilions and palaces, the most elegant that can be imagined, all covered with gilding and exquisite painting. And there were runnels too, flowing freely with wine and milk and honey; and numbers of ladies and all the most beautiful damsels in the world, who would play on all manner of instruments, and sung most sweetly, and danced in a manner that was charming to behold. For the Old Man desired his people to think that this was actually paradise. . . .
>
> Now no man was allowed to enter the garden save those who were intended to be his Assassins. And there was a fortress at the entrance to the garden, strong enough to resist all the world. The Old Man kept at his court a number of youths of the country and to these he used to tell tales about paradise. Then he would introduce them into his garden, some four or six or ten at a time, having first made them drink a certain potion which cast them into a deep sleep, and then causing them to be lifted and carried in. So they awoke and found themselves in the garden, and deemed it was paradise in very truth; and the ladies and damsels dallied with them to their hearts' content, so that they had what young men will have; and with their own good will they would never have quitted this place.

Now when he wanted one of his Assassins to send on any mission, he would cause that potion whereof I spoke to be given to one of the youths in the garden, and then had him carried into his palace. So that when the young man awoke he found himself in the castle and no longer in paradise; whereat he was not over well pleased. And the Old Man would say to such a youth: 'Go and slay So and So; and when thou returnest my angels shall bear thee to paradise.'

So he caused them to believe; and thus there was no order of his that they would not affront any peril to execute, for the great desire that they had to get back to that paradise of his. And in this manner the Old One got his people to murder anyone whom he desired to be rid of. . . .'

Polo's story of the Garden of the Old One is based on the Assassins' Persian stronghold, Mulehet, the Eagle's Nest. But in 1271 this no longer existed, having been overrun and destroyed by the Mongols a few years before, leaving Masyaf as the headquarters of the order. To a certain extent the early ideals had degenerated by the end of the thirteenth century, and the *fida'i* were frequently hired out as mercenary assassins. Yet they were still capable of heroics. When the crusader prince, Henry of Champagne, visited Masyaf he was taken around the battlements of the castle by the Grand Master. The Grand Master asked the prince if he had any subject as obedient as his own, and without waiting for a reply made a sign to two of his *fida'i*. They immediately jumped off the tower on which they were standing, and plunged straight to their deaths on the rocks below.

But even complete obedience could not save the Assassins. As befits fairy-tale villains they came to a sticky end. They had fallen foul not only of the Mongols, but of the other great power of the day, the revolting Mameluke sultan, Baibars. In 1273, he marched into the al-Garb and laid seige to the castle. It was taken by storm less than a week later and every Isma'ili was put to the sword. Before he left, Baibars built a victory tower. It was twenty feet high, and made out of the skulls of the defenders.

We arrived at Masyaf in the late afternoon. It had turned unusually chilly for high summer and clouds were billowing over the battlements. In the fields along the al-Garb, the cotton was just beginning to ripen and a line of mules was bringing the first sackoads of white buds up to the town for weighing.

We were tired and dusty after five hours of travelling, and stumbled out of the bus into two wicker chairs placed against the stone wall of a tea house. A boy dressed in a long gown of blue and white striped cotton brought a pot of cinnamon tea, and grapes on a silver tray; we sat munching them in silence, eavesdropping on the conversations around us. At the next table two middle-aged men in shirtsleeves were playing *tawla*; they had suntanned faces, uncovered balding heads, and plump midriffs. Beside them sat a third man, who watched the play and occasionally leant over to offer advice. He was dressed in full *jellaba* and *keffiyeh*, and through the V-neck of his gown you could see a string vest. Nearby, at different tables, sat two old men with wrinkled foreheads and heavy glass hookahs. They would gaze thoughtfully at us, then at the backgammon players, then at each other, and when they drew on their hookahs the water in the glass bulbs would make a muffled bubbling noise.

An Arab boy walked over to our table and asked if he could sit down.

'My name is Nizar al-Omar, the Merchant's son,' he said. 'I like for you. You like for me?'

I looked at Laura.

'Yes,' I said. 'We like for you.'

We did like for him. He was a tall, fragile boy with a light moustache on his upper lip, and the narrow, stooping manner of someone who is aware of his size. He looked delicate, sensitive and slightly effeminate.

'I think you are English,' he said.

'We are.'

'Good,' he said. 'I am student of English. I like English people because they speak very good English.'

'It's as good a reason as any.'

'Come,' he said. 'We are friends. Tonight you stay with my house.'

We got up and followed him through the steep, winding lanes. Masyaf reminded me of an Italian hill village. It was clean, and high and narrow, built of old, undressed stone. The houses were entered through first floor doors, up wooden banisters, and the windows had rough-hewn wooden frames which were covered with latticed grilles. We turned left down an alleyway, climbed some stairs and left our shoes outside the front door. Nizar's elder brother was playing cards on the floor. He got up when we entered and shook our hands.

'Do you know Werner?' he asked.

'Werner who?'

'Werner the German. He is my friend.'

'I'm afraid we're English.'

'But England is near Germany, isn't it?'

'Quite near.'

'I am sorry,' he said politely, and resumed his game. The family was as welcoming and hospitable as only Arabs can be. Laura and I sat on a sofa and made friendly gestures while the household was paraded before us. We smiled at four younger brothers, and two little sisters in frilly dresses, before being introduced to the mother who was known as Um-Aziz, mother of Aziz. She was a great beaming woman, still beautiful, with clear china-blue eyes shining out from an elaborate wimple. She said: 'saalam alekum', smiled again and slipped off into the kitchen.

'My house is yours,' said Nizar.

More to the point, his supper was ours. His mother returned with a tray full of Arab delicacies. As we sat on great camel-hair cushions the size of a large mattress, an undreamt-of spread of food was laid before us: white goats' cheese softened in boiling water, stuffed aubergines, curd, peppers, dates, tomatoes, green olives, houmos in sunflower oil, kidney beans, bowls of saffron and turmeric-coloured sauces, great sheets of flat, chapatti-like bread. We hadn't eaten for twenty-four hours and were ravenous. Nizar and his brothers joined us on the floor sitting cross-legged around the tray and scooping up the sauces with little corners of chapatti bread. It was a completely different concept to the Western idea of a meal, where everyone has their own separate portion. This was a communal meal – for the menfolk, at least. Laura was the only girl eating, and as we gorged the women waited on us, filling our glasses with more tea, and replenishing the bowls over and over again. When a boy wanted something he would clap his hands and a sister, or even his mother, would come scurrying from the kitchen.

When the meal was over we lay back on the cushions and digested our meal with the help of yet more pots of scented tea. Were we full? Were we comfortable? Was our journey tiring? Could we bring ourselves to forgive this humble fare? Would we accept their apologies? No wonder the Arabs have endeared themselves to generations of European travellers. The conversation was slow, formal and courteous, so much so that it seemed somehow archaic, fabulous, as if we were eighteenth-century gentlemen on a grand tour, rather than grimy undergraduates on a long-vac jaunt.

We reclined, and followed the example of the brothers. Some snoozed. Some played backgammon. Everyone belched. But before long Nizar went and fetched a new radio cassette recorder from his bedroom and my eighteenth-century fantasy evaporated. The first channel he picked up was a muezzin wailing despairingly to himself. Nizar looked embarrassed and turned the dial. We got a Turkish football report then some Changing-The-Guard-At-Buckingham-Palace music. Nizar blushed and turned the knob a little further.

'. . . a very taut, sensitive study. . . .' said a voice on the radio. Nizar smiled.

'London,' he said, pouting slightly. ' "Kaleidoscope".'

He sat down and looked intently at the radio.

'. . . wry . . . sensitive . . . deeply poignant,' said the radio '. . . lesbianism . . . warmly compassionate. . . .'

'The learned ones of England discuss great literature,' said Nizar. 'Much is their wisdom.'

The following day we visited some castles.

The fortress at Masyaf is a wonderful ruin, straight out of one of the gloomier corners of a Burne-Jones canvas. It is grim, dark and brooding, with an air of Jack and the Beanstalk: 'Long ago there was a wicked ogre who lived in a big castle on a steep mountain. . . .' It squats heavily on a pinnacle of rock above the town, framed on one side by the peaks of the Alawi mountains, on the other by a windbreak of cypress and the flapping felt tents of a Bedouin encampment. Its weak curtain and irregularly placed, irregularly shaped towers of rough-cut granite can never have been a very serious deterrent to an attacker, yet it is just the sort of castle you would expect an Assassin to live in.

We skirted the walls, but the main gate was locked and the custodian would not let us in. He was an old man with skin like walnut bark and the left side of his face was drawn into a paralysed grin. Drawing on his hookah he coughed deep, choking coughs and spat the catarrh on the ground beside him. He sat in a little tin shack propped up against the foot of the castle rock. We left him there, firing his catapult at the children who were taunting him. Then, despite Nizar's protests about the dirt on his new trousers, we wriggled into the castle through a gap under the postern salient.

Inside it was dark and smelt of dust and bats' droppings. When our eyes adjusted, we could see stretching out ahead of us long, vaulted corridors buried halfway to the capitals. On either side lay the plain rectangular cells of the *fida'i*. We picked our way over fallen masonry, and wandered through the castle, silent and respectful, as if in a cathedral. It was a gloomy, eerie place full of sad, empty halls and echoing, rubble-filled cisterns. Preserved by centuries of warm Mediterranean weather it seemed only newly deserted and so doubly melancholy.

After passing through the length of its buried catacomb-passages, we climbed the winding stairs of a tower and stood on the battlements, looking down over the al-Garb. I tried to link the ruins with the legends I had pored over in libraries in Cambridge. Where was Henry of Champagne standing when the *fida'i* leapt over the walls? Where was the library which so impressed Yves the Breton? During a truce he had been sent as an envoy from the French crusader, St Louis, and had been allowed to delve among the scrolls of the Assassins. Among a myriad of spells, cures and incantations he had found the text of an apocryphal sermon addressed by Christ to St Peter, who, the sectaries told him, was an incantation of Abraham, Noah and Abel. When he returned to the crusader camp at Acre, he took with him presents from the Old Man of the Mountain which included a 'crystal elephant very well carved, and an animal they call a giraffe, also in crystal, balls of divers sorts also in crystal, and backgammon and chess boards, and all these were ornamented with amber, and the amber was attached to the crystal by fair filigree of pure gold. When the coffers in which these things were packed were opened it seemed as if the whole chamber were filled with spices so fragrantly did these things smell.'

After Masyaf, the second castle we visited was a disappointment. We took a bus some fifteen miles down the al-Garb and arrived at the Sheizar soon after midday. The castle was badly ruined and the village at its base was an unappealing expanse of mud brick and dung.

But, with a little imagination, you could just see why the crusaders tried so hard to capture the fort they called 'La Grande Cesare'. In its day it must have been an impressive sight. It stands on a great hogsback ridge above a bend in the Orontes, with sheer cliffs on two sides, and a steep slope on the third. The slope was glazed with a smooth glacis of neatly fitted stone, the cliffs topped with a curtain wall and on the fourth side, where nature provided no defence, a great fosse had been sunk into the rock, one hundred feet deep by thirty feet wide. This was crowned with a keep of carefully dressed yellow-ochre stone, its smooth face broken by courses of reused classical columns laid horizontally into the wall.

We entered the castle through its great Saracenic gateway, and climbed up along the length of the hogsback to the keep, where in the cool of the shade we sat and chatted until the sun had sunk lower. As with Masyaf, Sheizar is more remarkable for its romantic associations than its architecture. Anyone who knows the Marcher castles of Edward the First or the keeps of the Scots Borders can easily be disappointed by the much-vaunted crusader castles, which, with the exception of Krak, Sahyoune and Safita are often quite modest buildings. Where they are exceptional is in the depth of their recorded history, and this is especially so of Sheizar, where the memoirs survive of one of its castellans, the urbane and civilized Usamah ibn-Munquid. Usamah lived a century or so before Polo, but his writings give a unique picture of everyday life in the mediaeval Middle East and, perhaps more than any other manuscript of the period, put flesh and blood on the dry bones of the world of Polo's *The Travels*.

Usamah was a gentleman and a scholar. He was observant, literate and intelligent yet obsessed with the twin loves of the mediaeval nobility – war and hunting – so that in his memoirs some very touching, homely scenes sit alongside gruesome descriptions of battles, wounds and natural disasters. At their best the memoirs read rather like an eleventh-century version of Turgenev's *Sketches From A Huntsman's Album*.

In Sheizar we had two hunting fields, one in the mountains to the south of the town for partridges and hares; and another on the bank of the river in the cane fields to the west, for waterfowl, francolins, hares and gazelles . . . Those were carefree days. . . .

We would start for the hunt from the gate of the lower town, then walk to the marshy cranebrakes. The

cheetahs and sakes [large hawks] would be kept outside the field, while we would go into the brakes with
the falcons. If a francolin rose, the falcon would strike
it. If a hare jumped we would throw a falcon upon it. If
the falcon seized it, well and good; otherwise as soon as
a hare got beyond the canebrakes, the cheetahs would
be loosed upon it. . . .

My father had a way of organizing the hunting party
as though it were a battle or a very serious affair. No
one was supposed to engage in conversation with his
companion, and everybody was expected to have one
concern only, scanning the ground to spy out a hare or
a bird in its nest. . . .

Through a long series of anecdotes, Usamah, like Turgenev,
gradually builds up a wonderful picture of the country life of
his time. We meet the two Majaju brothers who rent Usamah's
mill at Sheizar. The mill is profitable, but is next to a slaughter
yard which is full of hornets, and one of the brothers is stung
twice and dies. We meet al-Zamarrakal, the old brigand, who
Usamah encounters dressed in women's clothing about to
steal horses from the crusaders. A day later he sees him again,
wounded, but a horse, a shield and a lance the richer. We meet
Muzaffar, the merchant, who suffers from a scrotal hernia and
is cured by eating stewed ravens.

Usamah had a magpie mind and nothing was too silly or
inconsequential for inclusion. Thus soon after a serious passage about a siege of Sheizar by the Byzantines and their terrifying mangonels, Usamah recounts a number of ridiculous
stories about a cat who committed suicide on seeing a lion
skin, his fearsome warrior uncle who was terrified of mice,
and a tame lion in Damascus which was chased around a
courtyard by an angry sheep.

Usamah was a maverick, eccentric enough to record these
stories (and in his old age to compile the *Kitb al-'Asa*, the 'Book
of the Stick', an extremely odd anthology of anecdotes, prov-
erbs and sayings all on the subject of sticks), but he was also a

war hero who repeatedly repulsed the massed attacks of the crusaders, and a serious poet whose town house in Damascus became a literary salon for the intelligentsia of the most cultured of Arab capitals.

But perhaps the most interesting aspect of Usamah's books are his reflections on his European neighbours, the crusaders. He admired their military skill, their courage and their horsemanship. But the aesthete in him was disgusted by their habits and bored by their conversation: 'They are animals,' he wrote, 'possessing the virtues of courage and fighting, just as animals have only the virtues of strength and carrying loads – but nothing else.' A story from the memoirs illustrates the point:

Usamah was in his family's bath house at Ma'aret when a Frankish knight wandered in stark naked. The Franks refused to conform to the Arab practice of wearing a cloth round their waist when bathing, and the knight went up to the bath attendant, Salim, an old retainer of Usamah's, and snatched away his loincloth. When he saw that Salim had, in the Arab manner, shaved his pubic hair, the knight got in a great state of excitement and bawled at the top of his voice across the bath house, 'Salim! It's magnificent! You shall certainly do the same to me.' To Usamah's horror the knight lay on his back. 'His hair,' he comments 'was as long as his beard.' But there was worse to follow. When the bath attendant had shaved him, the knight felt the place with his hand and, says Usamah, 'found it agreeably smooth. "Salim," cried the knight, "you will do the same for my dama." ' The knight sent a valet to fetch his wife, and when they returned and the valet had brought her in, she too lay down on her back and was shaved while the local Arab gentry looked on. Usamah was disgusted: 'The knight thanked Salim,' he adds, 'and paid him for his services.'

By five the sun had sunk low, casting long shadows over the broken walls and fallen pillars of the castle. The mid-afternoon haze had disappeared and you could see clearly down the valley, over the fields to the tell of Apamea, and the barley-sugar pillars of the old Roman Imperial Stud; beyond rose the mountains, butter-coloured in the evening light. Nearby, a cloud of dust indicated that shepherd boys were already leading their flocks back home for the night, and we slid down the glacis and walked over to the old arched bridge which spanned the Orontes. In the evening cool the women of the town were doing their washing in the river and the handles of their basins flashed in the sun. A little boy in shorts led a milk cow through the sedge and bulrushes, and over the piles of clothes drying on the riverbank.

We sat on the bank and dangled our feet in the water. Nizar said that sometimes when he was a boy he used to come to Sheizar to fish. He would sit in the dust in the shade of a tree reading a novel, with his line tied to a branch and a maggot wriggling in the current. If he caught something he might roast it on a charcoal fire; or else he would sell it to the villagers and when he had saved enough money he could take a bus into Homs and buy another novel. Perhaps he would get a Joseph Conrad or another Thomas Hardy. He liked Thomas Hardy. I talked to Nizar of Usamah and told him the story of the Majaju brothers whose mill must have stood nearby. He shrugged his shoulders.

'Your English books are full of good things. I am not understanding why you like so much our Arab writing.'

'Usamah is also full of good things.'

'Not so full as your Henry Fielding.'

'I've never read any Fielding.'

'Oh, Mr William, you are big fool. Missy Laura has read much Henry Fielding, I think.'

Laura nodded.

'Henry Fielding,' said Nizar smacking his lips, 'is the father of your English fiction.'

'What about Chaucer?'

'I do not know this Chaucer. He is older than Henry Fielding?'

'Certainly.'

'And he is good writer?'

'Very good.'

'I think you wrong. If Chaucer was good writer I would hear his name on "Kaleidoscope". All the good writers they are on "Kaleidoscope". But never your Mr Chaucer.'

'Is Shakespeare on "Kaleidoscope"?' asked Laura.

'No, but sometimes I have heard him and his renowned company mentioned. You know of Shakespeare, Mr William?'

'A little.'

'He was great English playwright and patriot, and he was a friend of the Arabs.'

'Are you sure?'

'Oh yes, he was great English playwright.'

'No, I mean about the Arabs.'

'Mr William, at my university I am studying a drama called *The Merchant of Venice*. It is about a good merchant called Mr Anthony, and a wicked Israeli called Mr Shylock. Always Mr Shylock he wants the body of Mr Anthony, but in the end because he is wicked, greedy and a Jew, the judge throws him in prison and he is killed. It is a great symbol of the struggle of the Arabs and the Israelis.'

'That can't have been the original meaning.'

'Oh, you are wrong. Mr Shakespeare loved very much the Arab people. So did your Lord Byron.'

'He didn't like Jews either?'

'No, Mr William. Always you make mistake. Mr Byron didn't like the Turks. Always he is fighting with the Arabs against the Turks who many years ago were enslaving the Arab peoples.'

'I didn't realize. I thought he fought with the Greeks.'

'Mr William, I tell you only the truth. Obviously you are not knowing much about your English literature.'

That evening I almost crawled my way back into favour by reading some Hardy poems into Nizar's precious tape recorder, but I don't think he ever took me seriously again. After supper he and Laura discussed the great literature of the English peoples while I sat next door and wrote up my logbook.

Attempts to leave Masyaf early the following morning met with only limited success. Arabs delight in long and emotional farewells, and as a result by one o'clock we had only got as far as Jisr esh-Shughur a couple of miles away at the top of the al-Garb. With our phrasebook Arabic we were unable to establish whether we had missed the bus to Aleppo, or whether it was about to come. After a two-hour wait it became clear that we had just missed it, and we decided to hitch. Our first lift – in the back of trailer with two fat Arabs and a pile of watermelons – took us only three miles, at a speed which never exceeded walking pace. We then waited beside the road for a further hour before a yellow taxi drew up. The passenger leant out and offered to take us to Aleppo.

'You're English, aren't you? I can tell you're English.'

'How do you know?'

He looked at Laura's feet.

'Only the English wear socks under their sandals. Come on, get in.'

He had a flattish forehead, thick, curly, black hair and a magnificent loo-brush moustache which threatened to engulf the whole bottom half of his face. Krikor Bekarion looked pleased to see us. He was a Christian Armenian, he told us, whose family had fled from Erzurum in 1917 during the massacres, and had managed to get to Beirut where they had set up a shoe-making firm. Then in 1976 they had been driven out of Beirut and had moved to Aleppo where they started all over again. But Krikor did not like Syria ('too much politics, not enough profit'), and so had moved to Germany where he ran a shady-sounding 'import/export' business. Finally he had ended up in Athens where he now possessed a restaurant, a nightclub, two girlfriends (one Greek, one English – it was she who wore socks under her sandals) and a Mercedes. He was coming to Aleppo only briefly, he said, to visit his brother, and was pleased to have us for company. He liked the English, and thought the people of Aleppo both dull and difficult – 'always they make problems'.

'It is too late to cross the border,' he said. 'Tonight you will stay in Aleppo and we will go dancing.'

'There are nightclubs in Aleppo?'

'My cousin has nightclub. Nice place. Much drink, many girls.'

'I didn't realize there was a nightlife in Syria. I thought Muslims disapproved of that sort of thing.'

'They do. This nightclub is a Christian nightclub. No Muslims. Lots of fun.'

Krikor took out a cassette from his bag, and told the driver to put it on.

'Michael Jackson,' he said. 'Music for Christians.'

He showed us the cross hanging around his neck and winked conspiratorially.

The country around Jisr had been particularly lovely, rolling hills like the Cotswolds, clothed in fields of cotton, maize and tobacco, and broken by clusters of olive trees in the manner of a Tuscan painting. The villages were raised up on tells, small groups of beehive huts surrounded by belts of orchards, and as we sat by the roadside peasant farmers had ridden past on donkeys, saddlebags bulging with peaches and apples and cherries. But as we drove, the landscape flattened out and the cotton fields gave way, first to withered sunflowers then to tufts of coarse, black scrub-grass. Aleppo lies on the edge of the Badiet esh-Sham between the desert and the arable land of the littoral; it is a trading post linking farmland and sea trade with desert caravan.

The town is small and compact. There are no suburbs, just a series of police checkpoints, then the town and, looming above it, the great earthen dome of its citadel. We dropped off our rucksacks at Krikor's brother's house (in the curiously named Sulemaniye Hawaii Telephone Street) then headed for the Bekarion shoe factory in the Aleppo souk.

The souk was straight out of *Sheherazade*. We followed Krikor into the vaulted half-light squeezing past donkeys, beggars and wooden-wheeled barrows. The only illumination came from portholes cut into the roof, and from these shafts of light streamed down, illuminating some stall holders like prima donnas, and leaving their neighbours in near darkness. On either side, sitting cross-legged in arcaded booths, vendors shrieked at us to stop and look and buy. As in a mediaeval European market, each trade was organized into a distinct area, and we would pass lines of Arabs slowly stirring sinister-looking vats of liquid soap then turn a corner and find ourselves amid the spice vendors, and the air heavy with cumin and tumeric, cardamoms and peppers, saffron and aniseed. I paused by one shop and sniffed in the sacks. Krikor stopped and hissed at me:

'These men are Muslims.'

'I know, but what's this?' I said, pointing to a sack of white powder.

Krikor frowned and asked the spice seller.

'It is camomile.'

'And this?'

Krikor again asked the merchant, then translated:

'Rosehip.'

'And this?'

I pointed at a jar of grey-brown crystals, with the same consistency as Floris bath salts.

'It is the ground testicle of Jacob's sheep. The Muslims think it helps them please their women.'

Passing through the silk and linen merchants, the carpet sellers and butchers we arrived at the Armenian area of the souk – the Streets of the Jewellers, the Ironmongers, and the Cobblers. Suddenly everyone knew Krikor. Men rushed out from stalls gabbling in Armenian – a language that makes German sound soft and cadent – and, hugging him to their breasts, gave him the Armenian kiss, a peck on each cheek followed by three more on the lips.

'These people love me,' said Krikor modestly. 'All are glad to see me.'

It did appear to be true. A large, loud, jostling, gossiping crowd gathered around us trying alternately to fete us down the cobbles, load us with presents (I was given a fez of bright pillar-box red), and drag us into booths to ply us with thick, sweet cups of Turkish coffee.

But we were soon brought back to earth. Never have I seen a place like the Bekarion shoe factory outside textbook pictures of sweat-shops in the Industrial Revolution. It lay at the bottom of a flight of stairs in the Street of the Cobblers; we left our escort at ground level and descended into the hot, hammering depths. Krikor's brother – older, fatter and more corrupt-looking than Krikor – sat like a Mogul on a raised dais at one end of the room, while all around him machines whirled and lasts clattered. The floor was littered with old pieces of cut leather, and half-made or discarded shoes cluttered the bench tops. Around the debris buzzed a workforce of ragged children. Apart from Krikor's brother and a pockmarked foreman with a cadaverous grin, none of the factory's staff had yet reached puberty. I asked Krikor who the children were.

'They are the children of Muslims.'

'Why aren't they at school?'

'Because my brother has bought them.'

'Bought them?'

'Yes. Their parents are poor and they want money for *raki*. So they lease their children to my brother for one year.'

'And does your brother pay them?'

'Don't be stupid. If he paid them there would be no profit.'

'But that's slavery.'

Krikor shrugged his shoulders.

'They like it here. My brother feeds them, and they enjoy themselves. Look they are all happy.'

A little boy came up with two cups of Turkish coffee and a saucer full of salted melon seeds. He looked absolutely miserable.

'It's disgraceful,' said Laura.

'It's profit,' said Krikor.

*   *   *

We left Krikor and agreed to meet in Sulemaniye Hawaii Telephone Street later that evening. Wandering back through the souk it seemed as if Krikor's remarks were a key to understanding Aleppo. Profit; the previous year in Damascus I had heard the Aleppans described as bourgeois merchantmen; a Damascus funeral was said to be more fun than an Aleppo wedding. Now, compared with the busy, teeming streets of Damascus, the rows of smart merchants' houses did seem somehow stuffy and respectable.

The monumental architecture of the town seemed to reflect this. The Ummayad mosque and the citadel were two of the finest buildings that we saw in the East, but there was a utilitarian spirit about them that distinguished them from the run of Islamic buildings. There was none of the luxuriant frivolity of Damascus, none of the foppish gaiety and colour of Isfahan.

Superficially the Ummayad mosque does resemble that in Damascus. Both were built in the eighth century, and they share the same open-court plan, like a Cambridge college; the same prayer-hall with a nave and two transepts and a square minaret that is really a church tower. All this is an inheritance from the pre-Islamic tradition of Byzantine ecclesiastical architecture, except that the mihrab is in the south wall, so that prayers face the long side of the rectangle, not the narrow. Yet the Aleppo mosque is a much more stern building than that in Damascus. There are no mosaics, no arabesque fantasies, no kufic inscriptions. The only decoration is a simple inlay pattern in black marble in the courtyard floor – something St Bernard allowed even in his Cistercian monasteries. But where Cistercian simplicity was born of austerity, one suspects that in Aleppo it was born of economy. 'Why should we have mosaics?' one can hear the merchants ask. 'How much do they cost?' 'I don't think we can afford Corinthian capitals.' So it is. There are no mosaics; the capitals are plain. Even the carpets look cheap.

The citadel is also puritanical in spirit, but here the restraint is informed not so much by meanness as by a strict functionalism. It is a vast, totalitarian mass of mustard-coloured masonry, with totalitarian qualities – simplicity, scale and symmetry – like the Fascist architecture of Italy, or the Stalinist architecture of Soviet Russia. It is the building of a megalomaniac, awesome and unassailable, all towers and walls, with a mountain for its glacis and a pair of fortresses as its gates.

Less threatening but equally disturbing is a tomb in the gatehouse. Passing through a maze of dog-leg turns, gates and portcullises you come to a gloomy hall with a large wasps' nest in the vaulting. There, raised on a dais, covered with flowers and offerings and swamped by layer upon layer of rustling, kufic-encrusted silk, lies one of the two reputed bodies of the patron saint of England (the other is at Ramleh near Jerusalem). Quite what St George is doing in either place I have been unable to discover.

The history of Aleppo is terrible stuff: a long succession of massacres and sieges disappearing into the mists of Syrian prehistory. First held by the Hittites, it was captured in turn by the Philistines, Assyrians, Babylonians, Persians, Greeks, Romans, Persians (again), Byzantines, Arabs, Mongols and Ottomans, each of whom vied to outdo the carnage of their predecessors. The Assyrians were the most imaginatively sadistic: they impaled the town's menfolk on their spears and feasted for two days while their victims groaned to a slow death.

In between invasions Aleppo was ruled by a succession of aristocratic thugs who exacted outrageous taxes and perfected ingenious ways of bankrupting their burghers.

In all the town's history there are only two cheering anecdotes. The first tells of the Arabs who captured Aleppo by dressing up as goats and nibbling their way into the city; the second concerns Abraham, who is supposed to have milked his cow on the citadel's summit. It is not much in ten thousand years of history, especially when the one story ends in a massacre (after the Arabs killed the guards and opened the city gates to their friends) and the other is a legend, and untrue. It is the result of a misunderstood derivation of the town's (Arabic) name Haleb, which comes not from the Arabic for milk (*halib*) but a much older word, possibly Assyrian, connected with the mechanics of child abuse.

As promised, Krikor took us to his cousin's nightclub. I don't know what we expected, perhaps some dark cavern filled with belly dancers and Moroccans in white tuxedos, but it surprised us both. It lay a fifteen-minute taxi drive outside Aleppo, a vast open-air amphitheatre cut out of the hillside. On terraces along the raised back ridge were placed table and chairs for a thousand people separated by climbing vines weaving through trellising, orange trees, and pots of holly-hocks and azaleas. At the bottom, in the old orchestra well, was a sunken dance floor. On the stage, an Armenian band was backing a wailing chanteuse. Her song, plainly a tragedy, combined all the drama of a Verdi aria with the earsplitting torture of loud feedback. She moaned and groaned, writhed, sobbed and screeched her way towards some searing, long-awaited climax. It was a horrible sound. We took our seats and watched.

'Lovely, lovely,' said Krikor. 'This is famous Armenian song about the massacre in Van. Ees very, *very* beautiful.'

'Weeeeeeaaaggh' sang the singer. 'Crooooooosk unkph weeeeagh.'

I had never heard a language less suited to singing than Armenian.

'Skrooooo Vonskum Vvvvaaaaaaaaaaaan.'

'It's nice here,' said Laura.

Krikor shook his head lyrically.

'Lovely,' he said. 'I tell you this place makes good business. Big profit.'

As we chatted, moustached waiters in fancy dress ('traditional national costume') came up with a bucket of hot coals and a clutch of hookahs. They put one beside Krikor and me, stuffed the end with tobacco and hot coals, then took our orders. They returned a few minutes later with a selection of kebabs, a substantial glass of *raki* for Krikor, some weak Syrian beer for me and a glass of whisky for Laura.

'My cousin has another restaurant like this outside Beirut. Makes big profit too. Ees a lovely place. At night you can watch the rockets going over.'

'Fireworks?' asked Laura.

'No,' said Krikor. 'Killing rockets. Lovely, lovely sight. When they explode there are sparks everywhere. Ees very good view from my cousin's restaurant.'

'Isn't it awfully dangerous?' asked Laura.

'No, the restaurant is very safe. Beirut is a good town. Many nightclubs, many girls, much dancing. There are some problems – bombs, kidnapping, gun fights, but nothing serious.'

'You are brave.'

'No brave. Always I carry two guns and a grenade. But I don't often use them.'

'Often?'

'Not often.'

'Only sometimes?'

'Occasionally. Last time I went to Lebanon some Arabs made problem for my friend. They wanted to kill him. So I shot them both.'

'You killed them?'

'Sure. It's no big deal. But it's important to be armed. Even here I carry this.'

Out of his pocket he produced a pistol. It was small and black with a short, snub nose.

'How long have you been carrying that?'

'Always I carry.'

'That is very foolish,' said Laura. 'It might go off in your pocket one of these days.'

Krikor smiled. 'Come on,' he said. 'Have some *raki*.'

We got quite drunk. Krikor told us about the roses he used to cultivate in his garden in Beirut. He loved roses, he said, and he started on a long joke about roses, two homosexual Turkish gardeners and a spade, but it didn't translate well (the punchline hinged on the similarity of the Armenian words for digging and buggery) and instead we talked about Krikor's restaurant in Athens. I said I didn't like Athens; you couldn't get a proper breakfast, only soft biscuits and weak coffee. Krikor said he never got up before lunch so he didn't find that a problem.

'Have another drink,' he said, rearranging the coals on top of his hookah with a pair of copper tongs. Soon we were dancing to Django Reinhardt songs played by the Armenian band. The chanteuse had disappeared, and the centre stage was now held by two elderly Armenians, one playing some sort of accordian, the other propping up an enormous *saz*, a plucking instrument which looks like a cross between a double bass and a banjo. The dance floor was dominated by a wedding party and as we shuffled we were followed around by someone making a video of the wedding. He had a large camera, an assistant with a bright light and a long electric cable over which everybody fell. One of the wedding party asked Laura to dance and, scared to risk Armenian wrath by dancing with somebody's wife or girlfriend, I continued waltzing with Krikor. He seemed to feel less self-conscious about it than I did.

We drank more Syrian beer and talked to an Armenian friend of Krikor's who said that he had been involved in the shooting of a Turkish diplomat in Paris. Krikor then danced with Laura and I talked to the friend.

'I hear you're from Edinburgh,' he said.

'Yes.'

'Do you like Aleppo?'

'It's very pretty.'

'I hate it,' he replied. 'It's dirty, boring and full of Arabs.'

He took a gulp of his *raki*.

'I should never have left Paris,' he said somewhat theatrically.

He had been happy in Paris. He had learned karate and jujitsu and had a French girlfriend. They had gone to Bruce Lee films together on the Champs-Elysées. He told me all the problems involved in killing diplomats in foreign countries. Like Krikor he was a keen gardener and I told him the joke about the spade, the Turkish homosexuals and the roses, but he didn't think it very funny either, and went on to tell me about new kinds of plastic explosive. He plied me with *raki*, and gradually he began to blur so that all that remained in focus were his huge, hairless hands which would fly into the air as he told of the bombs he had let off outside Turkish embassies around the world.

When daylight came we decided to return home. Before I was shoved into a taxi I remember the amphitheatre describing wonderful circles around the heavens and the floor pitching to and fro beneath me. I broke into a rendering of 'The Bonny Earl of Moray'. Krikor said it sounded like an Armenian song. The Scots and the Armenians were brothers, he said. What about the English? said Laura. The English were our brothers too. We were all brothers. Of course we were. Ye highlands and ye lowlands oh whaur ha' ye been. Ees a good voice. Thanks. They've killed the Earl o' Moray and they've laid him on the green. Lang may his lady look frae the castle doon, till she . . . You're dribbling, William. Sorry. You never could take your drink. Till she sees the Earl o' Moray coom sound'ring through the toon. Lovely, lovely; ees really beautiful. Where are we, anyway? Nearly there.

The taxi dropped us off and we stumbled around the streets of Aleppo searching dazedly for Sulemaniye Hawaii Telephone Street. I sang 'The Skye Boat Song' and Krikor clapped.

After two hours' sleep we woke feeling like death. Krikor came to see us off. He gave us both an Armenian kiss and said goodbye.

'What will you do today?' asked Laura.

'My brother will tell me about his shoes and I will be bored. Then I will sit alone in the flat and drink.'

'I'm sure it's not as bad as all that.'

'Do you think they have sick bags on these buses?'

'Shut up, William.'

'Be careful with the Turks. They are bastards. Evil men. *Bang!* They kill. Rob money. Rape womens. Big problem.'

We crossed the border without incident but just before Antioch I was sick, and sick again at Mersin. We reached Ayas soon after sunset, and went to sleep on the beach.

THREE

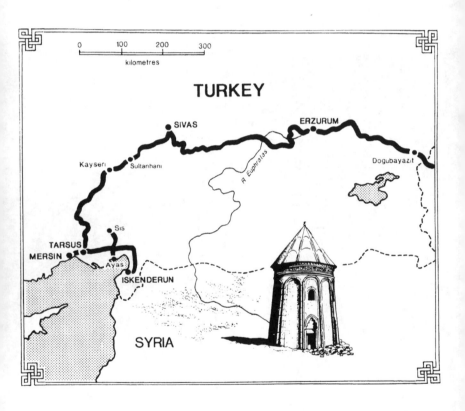

0   100   200   300

kilometres

TURKEY

SIVAS

ERZURUM

Kayseri   Sultanhani

R Euphrates

Dogubayazit

Sis

TARSUS

MERSIN

Ayas

ISKENDERUN

SYRIA

Modern Turks are a far cry from the turbaned, sabre-wielding dervish – the Terrible Turk – who haunted Europe for so long. Today Turks tend to be curious, kind and slightly earnest; certainly that was the case with the Turkish student whom I found standing over us, clipboard in hand, when I awoke the following morning.

'Good sir,' he said. 'Tourists are my friends. Permit me to welcome you to Turkey.'

'Thank you.'

'Sir, you like Turkey?'

'It's wonderful. Jesus Christ, what time is it?'

'This time is seven clocks and fifteen minutes. Good sir, my friend, what is your business?'

'I'm an aspiring writer.'

'Good sir! Are you famous?'

'No. What do you want?'

'Sir, I am a student of tourism at Mersin University. Permit me to ask you a few questions in connection with studies I am engaging.'

He was off. For thirty-five minutes I lay on the beach, trussed up in my sleeping bag while the Turk fired an endless series of questions, noting down my replies on his form. Had I beer   rkey before? For how long? Where did I go? Where was   g this time? Sir, please forgive the question, why was I going to Iran? Didn't I know about the modern tourist facilities available in western Turkey? Didn't I know about the beach resorts at Bodrum, Canakkale and Antalya? Every modern convenience a tourist could dream of was available. Sunbathing, windsurfing, sailing, modern hotels with luxury fittings, casinos. Didn't I know about the new facility in Ayas? A motel with a flushing toilet in every chalet. . . .

He came to the end of his questionnaire, wished me 'happy tourism', and strutted off towards the town with the boy-scout air of a job well done. I had forgotten how boring Turks could be. I got up and went for a swim.

It was early morning and the water was completely still and clear. The sun had just risen over the Syrian Jebel and the mountains stretched out at a right angle to the Turkish shore, a solid ridge leading down towards Beirut, Tyre and Sidon. There was a slight haze over the water. I swam out to sea.

Turning and looking behind me, I saw the old harbour. For the century following the Mongol invasions, Ayas had been the busiest port in the entire Mediterranean. The long overland trade routes which stretched through Turkey and Iran to China, India and Samarkand terminated here, and it was to Ayas that merchants from Italy, Egypt and all over the Mediterranean came to buy the merchandise of the East. Polo describes it as 'a city upon the sea . . . at which there is great trade. For you must know that all the spicery, and the cloths of silk and gold, and the other valuable wares which come from the interior, are brought to that city. And the merchants of Venice and Genoa, come hither to sell their goods, and to buy what they lack.'

There was now little left to indicate its former prosperity. It was a small, ramshackle place, not the 'wretched village of fifteen huts' described by Yule at the end of the last century, but not much grander either. The harbour was formed of two moles, one ancient and half-sunk, the other modern and topped by a sea wall. Around the shoreline stood the ruins of the sea gate and sea walls, crumbling masonry towers now used by the fishermen for storing their creels, nets and harpoons. Further back, but still within the mediaeval walls, stood a few later buildings: wooden merchants' houses with latticed windows and carved balconies, a domed Ottoman mosque, some fishermen's cottages, flat-roofed and dung-walled. Debris and flotsam lay scattered around, piles of discarded tackle, troughs for sheep and fodder for cows, an upturned dinghy, a billy goat picking among old fish boxes. On a nearby tower, a pair of storks with scarlet walking-stick legs had made a nest of driftwood, and beneath it fishermen were mending their nets and untangling their lines.

The younger men were thuggish-looking, muscular creatures, their faces tanned and tough, sitting about half-naked on fallen pilars, smoking. Their fathers kept to the sea wall, two hundred yards away. From the waist up they looked like Geordies. They wore tweed jackets, shirts with large collars, fine clipped moustaches and on their heads dirty tweed flat caps. Given a pint of brown ale their top halves could have comfortably fitted into any Jarrow pub; only their flapping *charwal* trousers betrayed their true provenance. They looked amiable and slightly senile, very far from the brutal despots or the blushing homosexuals described by nineteenth-century travellers in Asia Minor, who inspired Byron's remark:

> I see not much difference between ourselves and the Turks, save that we have foreskins and they have none, that they have long dresses and we short, and that we talk much and they little. In England the vices in fashion are whoring and drinking, in Turkey sodomy and smoking, we prefer a girl and a bottle, they a pipe and a pathic. They are sensible people.

But in Polo's day, Ayas was not under Turkish control. In the eleventh century Armenian refugees from the Caucasus had fled to the southern shore and captured Ayas and a string of hilltop fortresses. Here they settled down to a curiously pointless existence. Summers were reserved for futile campaigns against their Turkish neighbours, or spent indulging in long, torturous vendettas, raiding each other's castles, carrying off cattle, sheep and women. The winters were given over to devising sadistic means of killing off their prisoners (a Byzantine bishop was put into a sack with his dog, rashly named Armenian, and left until the beast devoured his master), while the women were left to dream up even uglier names for their children (Ablgharib, Kogh, Dgha and Mleh were all popular favourites for the boys). There was no more unpleasant race in Asia, and the Armenians were renowned as such throughout the civilized world. In the *Directorium ad passagium faciendum* a Dominican who had travelled in Cilicia wrote to warn the Pope of the horrors he came across on the southern shore.

> The leopard cannot change his spots, nor the Ethiopian his skin[wrote the Friar]. The Armenians simply partake of every error known in the east.... Their king had nine children, and all, sons and daughters alike, have come to a violent end, except one daughter and no one knows what her end will be. One brother killed another with a sword; another poisoned his brother; another strangled his brother in prison, so that they all murdered one another till only the last was left and he was poisoned and died miserably.

Doubtless, Cilician Armenia would have continued in such a manner, had not a new and powerful force pulled it firmly onto the world stage.

In 1241 the Mongols appeared at the borders of Persia and defeated the Seljuk Turks, the Armenians' greatest enemies. The Mongols were uneducated tribesmen who believed in enjoying life's simpler pleasures. Ghengis Khan expressed their philosophy most succinctly. 'Happiness,' he is recorded to have said, 'lies in conquering one's enemies, driving them in front of oneself, in taking their property, in savouring their despair, in outraging their wives and daughters.'

These were unmistakeably men with whom the Armenians could do business.

In 1253 the Armenian king, Hethoum, set off on the long journey to the Mongol capital of Karakoram. His embassy was a complete success. He got on excellently with the new Great Khan, Mongka, and returned laden with presents and promises of a Mongol–Christian alliance to win back lost Armenian territory and liberate the Holy Land from the Muslims. During the next decade Armenian troops fought beside the Mongols when they swept into Palestine, and in March 1260 Hethoum rode down the streets of the Arab capital of Damascus with the Mongol general, Kitbogha.

The Mongol alliance did not just bring stability to the Armenian Kingdom; it also brought enormous wealth (something always close to Armenian hearts). The Mongols encouraged merchants to venture the long overland route from China, through Turkestan to Ayas, and the *Pax Mongolica* established in the vast empire led to a boom in the spice and silk trade, with Ayas as the main port of exchange. The Armenians were quick to exploit the new opportunities. Their merchants made easy fortunes acting as middlemen between Chinese, Persian and Italian merchants, and the royal coffers bulged as the Kingdom taxed every transaction that took place in its bazaars. The presence of so many merchants also brought new markets for the local produce of the fertile coastal plain and the timber of the Taurus forests. It was this that caused the general prosperity that Polo witnessed. 'The country has numerous towns and villages,' he wrote, 'and has everything in plenty.' He was less impressed with the Armenians themselves. 'In days of old the nobles there were valiant men, and did doughty deeds of arms; but nowadays they are poor creatures, and good at nought, unless it be at boozing; they are great at that.'

But the position of Cilician Armenia at the edge of the Mongol world also brought its dangers. When the Muslims counter-attacked under Sultan Baibars, defeating a Mongol army at Ain Jalud and advancing into Palestine, it left the Armenians in an uncomfortable frontline position. In 1266 Baibars took advantage of King Hethoum's absence to rout a small Armenian force near the Syrian Gates. He burned Ayas and the capital of Sis, and retired to Aleppo with great caravans of booty. The Kingdom recovered, but was badly shaken.

Polo arrived at Ayas only five years later in late November 1271. Sometime soon after his arrival a rumour spread that Baibars had set off northwards from Damascus with a large force, and panic swept the port. The two friars who had been sent with the Polos to help convert Kubla Khan fled back to

Acre with the Master of the Templars; the Polos alone remained. . . .

As I swam back to land (watching, as I did so, a cluster of little boys hiding behind a rock on the seashore, tittering as Laura rose from her sleeping bag and began to change), I wondered what were the Polos' motives for continuing on their expedition when Kubla Khan's instructions to bring 'one hundred men well versed in religion' had become impossible to fulfil and the risks to the expedition were increasing. Looking at Ayas from the sea, it was easy to appreciate the panic. The town lies on the shore under a slight dip of land. Its land walls still stand in some places to their original height, and were clearly never very substantial. Had Baibars decided to attack the port again, there would have been no hope of resisting him. Why then did the Polos decide not to join the friars in making their escape to the relative safety of Acre?

Polo has been extravagantly praised over the years. Tim Severin has called him 'a genius', Eileen Power thought it was 'impossible to exaggerate the extent of his accomplishments' and that his 'curiosity was insatiable'; Elizabeth Longford believed he possessed 'enthusiasm and a photographic memory'. Hotels have been named after him, designer jeans shops, Chinese restaurants, and Eastern-style Soho strip joints. His book ('the greatest travel book ever written', according to John Masefield) has been turned into a strip cartoon, a one-man show at the Edinburgh Festival, even a million-dollar television drama, broadcast across Europe and Asia, starring Burt Lancaster as the Pope, and Leonard Nimmoy (Mr Spock) as Kubla Khan.

Yet the book is surprisingly dull. Polo did not set out to write an account of his travels, despite the name by which it has always been known, nor did he write a description of a diplomatic expedition originally launched to try to save the Crusader Kingdom. It is not even a general account of the lands he passed through. He says nothing about the sights he saw (he does not even mention the Great Wall of China), and includes very little about Asian social mores (which might have made really interesting reading). Instead he wrote a dry, factual guide to commerce in the East, a book by a merchant for other merchants, containing mainly lists of the merchandise available for sale on the caravan routes, as well as advice on how to overcome the difficulties that might be met along the way: where to stock up with provisions, where to keep an eye out for robbers, and how to cross a desert. It is not a romance, nor a book of wonders, nor a history of the world in the manner of Herodotus. For all Rustichello's elaborations, Polo's book was written as an ordinary merchant's manual, and was essentially very similar to other manuals of the time, such as the *Pratica della Mercatura* of the Florentine, Francesco Pegolotti. Indeed, of its type it is a very fine example. For all its overlay of romance, Polo's *The Travels* contained more accurate and detailed information about the place of origin of the luxury Eastern goods and the Silk Road than was available at the time from any other source, in either the Islamic or the Christian world.

Polo was not the romantic gallant that legend has made him out to be; he was a hard-headed merchant's son taking a calculated risk on a potentially lucrative expedition. The Venetians were always lukewarm about the concept of crusading and the Polos seem to have soon forgotten the original purpose of their journey. One can only judge Polo from the evidence of *The Travels* and in the light of this his motive for continuing east from Ayas was simple: profit. Nor was he heading into the unknown. The elder Polos, like, no doubt, many before them, had already made the journey to China, and knew that the risks were not too great; indeed once out of Cilician Armenia and the reach of the armies of Sultan Baibars, the journey would probably be relatively easy. The Mongols had built caravanserai along the length of the trading routes and had made safe the roads. *Pax Mongolica* ruled. They also had the additional boon of the Gold Tablet from Kubla Khan, a safe conduct from the Supreme Khan himself. There were some dangers certainly – a party of Frankish merchants had been pillaged near Amassya only a few years before. But the mediaeval merchant had always to take risks, and travel within the Mongol empire was probably considerably safer than in Europe. Fifteen years later when they returned to Venice they were rich men (so much so that in 1362, nearly one hundred years later, Polo's descendants were still arguing over the ownership of the palace which had been acquired with the profits of their forefather's China expedition). The Polos certainly took a gamble when they watched their friars flee back to Acre, and loaded up their caravan for the long land journey to Xanadu, but it was a calculated gamble – and it paid off.

The morning was given over to indolence. I picked half-heartedly through the ruins, but apart from one magnificently vaulted room with bevelled stone voussoirs – perhaps the old Venetian or Genoese consulate – there was little of interest left standing. Successive sacks by Mameluke raiding parties had taken their toll.

I made for a café beside the harbour where I found Laura deep in a romantic novel. Laura's penchant for Mills and Boon was a new and unexpected side to her character. The same girl who had swept all before her in the ice-hockey pitches of the Home Counties, who had beaten off a party of rapists during communal riots in Delhi, who had subdued the dons of Magdalen and amazed the boardrooms of the City of London, this same Laura turned out to be nourished by a literary diet of *Prince of Darkness, The Rose of Biarritz, Silent Stranger* and *His Name was Passion*. Clearly, beneath the ferocious, ice-hockey-stick-wielding exterior there lay deeper currents. I ordered a glass of beer (Turkey brews a strong German-tasting lager named Efes Pilsen) and opened Runciman's *Fall of Constantinople*.

Three Turks sat at the next table. One, potbellied and clean-shaven, appeared to be the proprietor. He was lecturing his two friends and gesticulating vehemently. I longed to know what subject could merit such gestures: capital punishment? Deep sea fishing? Castration? His two friends watched him throughout their meal. The elder of the two was having trouble with his stuffed aubergine. He bent down so low to the table that the bristles of his beard almost touched the dish. The sleeves of his jacket had got involved too, and as he wiped them clean, he coughed, spat into the napkin and dropped it onto the floor. The other man wore a stained white vest and had dark brown skin and a labourer's biceps. He had a piece of bread on the end of his fork and was mopping it round and around the tin plate.

When the fat proprietor had finished his lecture, he looked across at our table.

'Deutsch?'

'English,' said Laura.

'Ingliz,' the fat proprietor explained to his friends.

'Turkey good?' he shouted, asking the same question that was to be put to us by every Turk we met over the next fortnight.

'Turkey good,' we replied as we did to every subsequent inquiry. The Turks are very sensitive about their country.

The fat proprietor raised his glass.

'Sherife,' he said. 'Ingliz – chin-chin.'

The waiter brought over a grubby document, creased at the corners and covered with tea stains.

'Ingliz menu,' he said, beaming at Laura.

We opened the menu and studied it closely.

KUJUK AYAS FAMILY RESTRANT

INGLIZ MENUYU

SOAP

Ayas soap
Turkish tripte soap
Sheeps foot
Macaront
Water pies

EATS FROM MEAT

Deuner kepab with pi
Kebap with green pe
Kebap in paper
Meat pide
Kebap with mas patato
Samall bits of meat grilled
Almb chops

VEGETABLES

Meat in earthenware stev pot
Stfue goreen pepper
Stuffed squash
Stuffed tomatoes z
Stuffed cabbages lea
Leek with finced meat
Clery

SALAD

Brain salad
Cacik – a drink made ay ay
And cucumber

FRYING PANS

Fried aggs
Scram fried aggs
Scrum fried omlat
Omlat with brain

SWEETS AND RFUITS

Stewed atrawberry
Nightingales nests
Virgin lips
A sweet dish of thinsh of batter with butter
Banane
Meon
Leeches

It was a difficult choice. Laura chose some soap, an almb chop and a bowl of leeches. I opted for a meat pide. Then, for pudding, I ravished some virgin lips.

After lunch, revived by a draught of Turkish tea – hot, sweet and very strong – we shouldered our backpacks and tramped off on the dirt track which led towards the old Armenian capital of Sis. It was still very hot and the countryside was flat and dustily fertile. Small cottage gardens full of vegetables (soon perhaps to be mutilated at the Kujuk Ayas Family Restrant) gave way to larger fields of cotton and tobacco, lined with windbreaks of cypress. In one field the harvest had already taken place and the meadows were filled with gleaners, faces lowered towards the stubble, amid a scattering of beehive hayricks. Ahead of them a last solitary reaper was bent over his scythe; it was like a marginal illustration from a Gothic psalter, or a 'Season of the Month' on the misericord of an abbey quire. We tramped on until exhausted, then sat and waited for a lift. A tractor stopped, and we clambered up into the trailer.

Inside was a vast earth-mother swathed in voluminous wraps of calico and taffeta. Beside her was a small boy, presumably her son. She clucked around him like an old broody hen, wiping his nose and removing hay from his hair. She said nothing, but belched occasionally and fed herself noisily from a nose-bag. Good looks have been shared out unevenly among the Turks. Their men are almost all handsome with dark, supple skin and strong features: good bones, sharp eyes and tall, masculine bodies. But the women share their menfolk's pronounced features in a most unflattering way. Very few are beautiful. Their noses are too large, their chins too prominent. Baggy wraps conceal pneumatic bodies. Here must lie the reason for the Turks' easy drift out of heterosexuality.

The citadel of Sis rises out of the coastal plain, a solitary conical hill in a flat landscape. At the base of the near side of the hill lay an encampment of Yuruks, one of the last surviving tribes of Turcomen nomads. There were four or five purple felt tents and some wagons, around which sat some wild, dark-skinned women dressed in bright Rajasthani prints, some huge wolf-like dogs, and a few filthy children. I later learned that the encampment was semi-permanent; the Yuruks had settled there a decade before and worked as day labourers in summer, and lived by basket-making and horse-trading in winter. There had recently been an initiative by the government to try and settle the Turcomen, and several hundred had accepted houses in Mersin, where they sat in the bars drinking Efes Pilsen and doubled the crime rate over-night. Others had taken the houses but returned to nomadism in summer; land reclamation had stolen from them many of their traditional pastures, and it was difficult to remain peripatetic for twelve months a year. True nomads are now very few in number.

The tractor driver dropped us off in the market place in the centre of Sis, and leaving our rucksacks at a café we set off up the steep cobbled streets towards the citadel. After a while the houses and farmyards gave way to orchards and olive groves and we climbed on up, past the first line of walls, through the outer wards. Above, the great citadel perched on the cliff edge, its horseshoe towers jutting out on overhangs of rock. We passed through the ruins of the old lower town, where the traders and artisans once lived. Little remained of it for, like Ayas, it had been burned by the Mamelukes: in 1266, King Hethoum returned from an expedition to find 'Sis and its chief church given to the flames, the tombs of the kings and princes violated, and their bones torn from this last resting place, burned and scattered as ashes to the wind.' There was nothing left of the Armenian cathedral and the patriarch's palace, both of which were still in use when Sir Henry Yule was writing, late in the last century.

As the incline increased, the soil got thinner and the orchards were replaced by gorse, thistles and yellow cow pars-ley. We made slow progress or, rather, I made slow progress while Laura shot ahead and I limped up after her. Although it was mid-afternoon, it was still hot, and my shirt was saturated.

Occasionally I would collapse on a ledge, my head resounding to the military band thumping away in my temples, and douse myself with the tepid chlorinated water from the water bottle. Laura seemed impervious to the heat, the exertion, or the imminent danger of dehydration or heart failure. At first she was impatient with me ('Oh get on with it!' 'You should lose weight.' 'When was the last time you took any exercise?') but by about halfway up she seemed to come to terms with the fact that she was not travelling with an athlete and began to tempt me up with gentle, clucking pensioner-talk ('Come on now, only a little bit further.' 'Just think, nearly there!' and, 'Oh well done; one last effort now.')

We made it up in three-quarters of an hour, a remarkable feat I thought, though Laura seemed less impressed by the achievement. I sat on the crenellation of a tower and caught my breath. Then, slowly, I got up and looked around.

It was a fine castle, magnificently positioned, and intriguingly similar to some of the crusader castles I had seen in Syria the previous year. Not only was the general plan the same – a series of horseshoe towers hugging the contours of the cliff, with the keep built into the curtain wall, not separate from it as in Europe – but the masonry was dressed in an identical manner: each block carefully chiselled into an elaborate, embossed shape. Exactly the same features can be found at many of the earlier crusader castles, for example the great fort of Sahyoune, in the Syrian Jebel above Latakia. When the crusaders first set off from Europe to the Holy Land, the art of fortification was still undeveloped and historians have been baffled as to how the crusaders were able to build such remarkable and ingenious castles within a few years of arriving in Palestine. If the early castles are similar to those of the Armenians, then it may be possible that the crusaders learnt the art from them. The unstudied ruins on the hilltop of Sis may contain the clue as to the origin of the crusaders' innovations in castle building – innovations that were in turn transmitted back to Europe to revolutionize castle building there.

Whether or not this was so, it was wonderful to have the freedom to speculate. In Europe detailed research has dropped a weighty academic veil between the amateur antiquarian and his ruins. He must tread carefully for he treads on someone's PhD. In contrast, the state of Cilician archaeology is only as advanced as its English equivalent was at the time of John Aubrey and William Stukeley, and the traveller can still write books of dilettante observations like Stukeley's *Itinerarium Curiosum*, without fear of being contradicted. He is on virgin territory.

I thought of the bloody Armenian chronicles that I had read in translation in the libraries of Cambridge. Very few of the castles mentioned have ever been identified with the small crumbling ruins which dot the plains and hilltops of Cilicia. Where is Binag, the castle of Sempad the Marshal? Where is Tchelganotz or the great monastery of Trazarg? After being caught and manacled in *flagrante delicto* on a clandestine visit to the brothels of Antioch, King Rupen was forced to retire here and spend his declining years in book illumination and penance. What has happened to Molevon, Neghir or Skevra? What of Maidzar? In 1245 the Armenians swept out of here and won a great victory against Kai Khusrau the Turk, but the Armenians have gone and its site lies forgotten.

From the top of the keep we looked out over the fertile Cilician plain, in Polo's day still a malarial swamp, 'by no means a healthy region, but grievously the reverse', and through the haze to the nearby Armenian citadels of Toprakkale and Yilan Kale, the Castle of the Snake. Below, a Yuruk was cantering towards the nomad camp, throwing up a slipstream of dust, and between the purple tent tops small plumes of smoke were rising from the evening fires. The flat roofs of Sis lay to the left, partially obscured by the hillside, and behind us, the peaks of the Anti-Taurus rolled off towards the Cilician gates. On a distant slope you could just see a horse trap moving slowly uphill, pulling a tethered milk cow behind it.

After a while I broke the silence.

The Khan al-Afranj, Acre.

The Gok *medresse*, Sivas.

The Citadel, Aleppo,
seen from the gatehouse.

The *ivan* gateway of
the Shifaiye *medresse*,
Sivas.

Fisherman, Ayas.

Laura in battle dress about to
enter Iran.

'We could be the first people to have seen this view for hundreds of years,' I said, moved to unusual lyricism.

'Balls,' said Laura. 'People come up here all the time.'

As she spoke, a pair of goatherds appeared with their flock from behind the citadel walls. We had not seen them climbing up behind us, nor, until that moment, had they seen us. They looked at each other and, intrigued, walked towards us to investigate further. The elder came very close, pointed, then burst into fits of hysterics. His brother joined in and the pair rolled about on the keep's flagstone floor.

'It's those shorts of yours,' said Laura disdainfully (referring to my precious pair of long, baggy empire-builders). I had the impression that the goatherds had found us both equally amusing, but kept a tactful silence and we set off downhill to collect our rucksacks.

Here we were given a more respectful reception. The café was now crowded with the (male) *jeunesse dorée* of Sis, and we were sat down beneath a freize of posters of Sylvester Stallone and Madonna, and were plied with bottles of Coca-Cola. Twenty new pairs of stone-washed jeans clustered around.

'Oh sir, may I ask question?'

'Certainly.'

'The English people. Do they need PT teachers?'

'Oh, there's an enormous demand. Every day you read about the lack of PT teachers in the papers.'

'Oh, sir.'

Another boy pushed forward.

'Sir, sir. Do the English women want to marry Turkish men?'

'Ask Laura.'

'Madam. Do the English women want to marry Turkish men?'

'A few might,' said Laura, noncommittally.

'Sir –' it was the PT teacher again '– do you know aerobics?'

'No.'

'No?'

'No.'

'No.'

'But all England knows aerobics. It is the modern method of keep fit.'

He looked genuinely shocked.

'Well you must know breakdance.'

'I know a little rock and roll,' replied Laura.

'Rock and roll,' said the boy, 'is very old fashioned. Do you know any other dance?'

I thought foolishly of the postcards of the Ka'ba at Mecca that I had, at enormous expense, brought from a Pakistani grocery in Cambridge in order to try and woo my way into Muslim hearts. With a sheaf of Samantha Fox pin-ups Turkey could have been mine.

'Do you think they would like the Gay Gordons?' I asked Laura.

'Who is gay Gordon?' asked the PT teacher.

'He is a dance.'

'A new one?'

'Brand new.'

'You will teach us?'

The tables and chairs were cleared into a pile at the far end of the room. Laura and I took our position in front of twenty Turks, all chattering excitedly. Laura raised her hand and everyone shut up. I got into position, one hand holding her right hand above her right shoulder, the other grasping her left hand at waist height. We stood still for a dramatic, silent moment while I cocked my head in a show of mock confidence and tried desperately to remember what I had been taught by the Huskey-clad Scots woman in the cold village hall near Portree.

Then we were off, Laura in the lead. We hopped up the length of the room, pirouetted and headed back the way we had come. We turned, and did the same in reverse. We twinkled back and forward, clockwise and anti-clockwise, hopping and swaying our way around the length of the café until we drew to a halt near the great samovar at the end of the room.

We bowed, and the Turks bowed back. Most of them looked utterly bewildered by our demonstration. But Gay Gordon was modern, and they were determined to master him.

We lined them up in pairs according to height; two fragile-looking farmers' sons at one end, a couple of yelling savages, fat as bouncers, at the other. Laura stood on a bench and shouted 'one, two, *three*!' As if kicked from behind, the line moved off towards the samovar. Our Gay Gordon was not an enormous success. We failed to demonstrate properly how to manoeuvre at the end of the room and the dance soon ended in a calamitous pile-up.

But we were not to be allowed off without teaching them something. Despite our choreographic failure they cried for another dance and Laura suggested we try to teach them an eightsome. Someone was sent off to find the village musicians. A few minutes later two men appeared bearing a long balalaika and a pair of small calfskin drums. We got them to play something that sounded roughly like the correct rhythm, dismissed the savages and some other less enthusiastic dancers, then organized the remainder in two circles. The fragile boys were in my circle; Laura got the PT teacher.

Surprisingly, this time our teaching was successful, perhaps because the eightsome was not unlike some Turkish dances. We showed them how to *pas de bas* and set, and how to turn each other. Then we demonstrated how to spin the centre of the circle and cross in a figure of eight. The musicians struck up the beat: twang-twang-twang Padum! Padum! Padum! The *pas de bas* remained a stumbling block, but they all seemed to enjoy themselves and all in all took to reeling with remarkable ease.

After our exertions we felt we had earned the offers of supper which were thrust upon us; the night bus did not leave until eight o'clock and we had worked up a healthy appetite. We were billeted with a boy called Rajep who had been Laura's partner in the eightsome. He was, so he told us, not only from the richest family in the village, but also the cleverest. He studied law at the Bosphorus University in

Istanbul – and had a T-shirt to prove it. He was appalled to learn that we both studied history. 'In Turkey history has no value,' he said as he walked us to his home. 'The only serious subjects are engineering, medicine, law and economics.'

He was, however, reasonably impressed that we were from Oxford and Cambridge: 'I have heard people say that they are quite good universities.'

We were taken to his house, and sat outside beneath the fig trees. It was evening and outside the compound you could hear the dogs of the town barking. They always began howling at this time of day, during the evening call of the muezzin, and generally took at least half an hour to calm down afterwards.

'My father did not want me to go to university,' said Rajep. 'He thought it would be anti-Islamic, and only let me go after I begged him on my knees. The people here are very conservative, and they are frightened of progress. There are many – how do you say? – fanatics. They do not like what Attaturk did for this country: creating democracy, making industry, freeing the women. Many of the old men want their mullahs to rule them, like in Iran.'

'Do you still go the mosque?' asked Laura.

'Sometimes. I believe in Allah and read the Koran, but do not like the mosque. The mullahs do not talk to me or my friends because we go to university, and they will not discuss our ideas with us. This country has two problems. One is the mullahs, the other is the army – both want to rule the country, and to stop democracy.'

'I thought the military had stepped down,' I said.

'No. It is better now, but still we do not have full freedom. Many of my cousins are socialists, and there are many problems for them. My cousin – my uncle's son – was arrested for his socialism and given electric shocks by the police. They wanted him to tell them the names of all his friends, but he refused and denied everything, and eventually they let him out of prison. Still he talks about the prisons. The robbers, they beat up the political prisoners and the guards they beat up everybody. There are gangs, and many killings. Another problem for our country is that the military censor the Press: we still do not have a serious newspaper. When the military came they closed down all the good ones and left only the bad. Like *Tan* – have you seen *Tan?*'

We certainly had. *Tan* was a wonderful paper, a strange cross between the *Guards' Magazine*, the *Church Times* and the *Sun*. Most of its news items concerned the highly respectable doings of the President, General Kenan Evren, or those of the senior mullahs, but on the outside were splashed huge colour pictures of topless Western tourists photographed on the beaches of the Aegean coast. If none were being worn, bikini bottoms were always drawn in, and any visible nipples were covered with a tiny black mark. Underneath were captions reading something along the lines of, 'Lovely Helga comes from Copenhagen where she studies geography. This is her second visit to Turkey. "I love Turkey," says Helga. "Kebabs are my favourite food." '

I asked Rajep if he found it difficult being educated when the rest of his family were not.

'Sometimes there are problems. But I respect my father. He and my grandfather have worked hard and expanded our farm. When my grandfather came here much of this was waste, and we were given only very little land. Now we have nearly one thousand hectares.'

'You are not natives of Sis?' I asked.

'No, no one here is. We all came from Salonica after the Great War.'

'What happened to the original inhabitants?'

'I do not know. I know no history. Ask my grandfather.'

Rajep took us inside, where we found his grandfather sitting at the table in the stone-flagged living room. He was a typical Geordie-Turk, all flat cap and wrinkles, but you could see that he had once been a handsome man, and he still had an air of authority about him. He spoke no English so we had to go through the tedious procedure of channelling our conversation through Rajep, who acted as interpreter.

'My grandfather wants to know whether you are Muslims.'

'I'm afraid not.'

'He asks whether you are Christians.'

'We are.'

'My grandfather wants me to tell you that it does not matter. . . .'

'Oh, good.'

'. . . and that he had many Christian friends when he was a boy in Salonica. He says he had a pretty Christian girlfriend.'

'A Greek girlfriend? Wouldn't that have been regarded as rather wicked? I thought the Greeks and the Turks were traditional enemies.'

'No, my grandfather says that you are wrong. In Salonica the Greeks and the Turks were friends. He says the Greeks were kind people and were often helping the Turks. Only the governments did not like each other. He says he was very sad to leave Salonica. The houses were wooden and it was very crowded, but they had everything they wanted. He says that his father had a shop and also a farm outside the city where they grew cotton.'

The old man paused, trying to picture in his mind the images of seventy years before. From the kitchen came the sound of clattering as Rajep's sisters prepared our supper. After a second he continued; his grandson translated:

'In 1919 they were given the order to leave. Everyone was very sad. They said goodbye to all their friends and took what they could in a cart to Thrace. They stayed in Edirne for one year, but cholera broke out and he and two brothers and one hundred others decided to leave and look for land elsewhere.'

'And who was living here? What happened to the Armenians?'

'My grandfather says that when he arrived here the Armenians had already fled. He says that they got an idea to make their own country from the French. Turkey was very weak after the First World War, so it was a good opportunity for them and they started to attack villages and kill people. Many men were still away in the army, so they slaughtered the women and children. But Attaturk defeated them and they

80

lost everything. Many Armenians died, but the reason for the most deaths was hunger and cholera.'

'So the Armenians fled from Sis, and he did not have to fight for this land?'

'That's right. He says there had been a big battle a year before at the village of Gazi Kuju, and when he came here the land was empty. His eldest brother went on to Maras and there he had to fight with Armenians and the Greeks. But here they just moved into the old houses, and the one hundred settlers were each given twenty hectares. He says his land had never been used and he had to clear it of trees.'

From the kitchen there was a shout as the sisters brought in piles of food on a tray. There was a *chorba* soup, some pilau rice with pieces of chicken, couscous and stuffed aubergines. The old man smiled and his face wrinkled up like wood bark. It was only then that I noticed quite how old he was.

Over his soup he continued talking.

'My grandfather says that later some Armenians returned. They had become Muslims, and tried to hide that they were not Turkish. He says that every one knew that they were Armenians, but they allowed them to settle and have some land. He says that everyone was very sad.'

'Why?' asked Laura.

'Because there had been too many killings and too many deaths.'

After supper we refused an offer of a bed for the night, and jumped on a tractor going to Mersin. In retrospect this was a big mistake. It was a night of unmitigated horror probably best conveyed through the entries I made at the time in the logbook:

8.00 p.m.   No sign of bus.
            We drink *cay*, and I teach Laura *tawla*.
            Mersin bus station is nearly as filthy as that at
            Latakia.

8.30 p.m.   Laura goes off to look for a loo.
On the way someone throws a shoe at her.
When she returns I read her an entry from the
guidebook: 'Turkish buses are fast, comfort-
able and always run on time. They are fun and
so are the bus stations.'
Neither of us laugh.
No sign of the bus.

9.00 p.m.   More backgammon.
Still no sign of our bus.

9.30 p.m.   As before.

10.00 p.m. The bus has turned up!
It's a luxury bus and our fellow passengers
are a dowdy bunch of pseudo-European
Turks. Laura is sitting on one side with a
moustachioed businessman wearing flares. I
am next to a woman with a screaming baby.
Both of us are over the wheel. The bumpiest
place.

10.30 p.m. Set off two hours late, only to stop at the
bus station in Tarsus, the home of St Paul.
Enough to give anyone wanderlust: loud
Turkish music and some sort of mewing Turkish transvestite. He/she/it tells me Tarsus is
'very romantic place'. It wore thick mascara,
pink lipstick and held a small yellow hand-
bag.

12.00 p.m. Woken by conductor who suggests we eat sup-
per.
Driver gets out and washes his bus.
Laura and I drink *cay*.
Return to find the baby has been sick.

3.00 a.m.   Woken by conductor who offers us a biscuit.
The driver is outside washing his bus.

Laura and I get out and drink *cay*.
The baby has vomited again.

4.00 a.m. Bus stops again.
Conductor shakes us awake and offers us another biscuit.
We swear at him.
Driver gets out and washes his bus for a third time.
Woman gets out and hoses down her baby.

5.30 a.m. Sivas bus station.
Cold.
Exhausted.
Penniless.

6.00 a.m. We change ten dollars with two stranded Americans.
The taxi drivers are all still asleep.
Drink more *cay*.
Discover that my plastic shampoo bottle has broken.
There is Head and Shoulders all over my wash bag, my clothes and, horror of horrors, my books.

9.30 a.m. Taxi into Sivas.
Book into Hotel Seljuk: The familiar sewer-stench of Turkish plumbing – *and* Germans doing press-ups outside my room. They tell me they have bicycled here from Tiero del Fuego: 'Ze Andes ver ze best bit.'
Pass out to the sound of grunts outside.

I was woken by a gentle knocking on the door. Opening one eye I saw that Laura wasn't in the room, so heaved myself out of bed, expecting to find the Germans on the other side inviting us to come and look at their bicycles or perhaps go on a jog with them. My fears were needless; it was something wholly preferable. In the doorway stood the hotelier. He was holding a breakfast tray. A few minutes later he returned with a bucket of piping-hot water. He bowed as magnificently as an Abyssinian slave from *The Arabian Nights* and withdrew. This was more like it. I washed, got back into bed, rolled into the comfortable mid-mattress trough, and demolished the contents of the tray: sliced tomatoes, olives, crusty bread and white feta cheese. Sipping a tulip glass of tea, I looked out of the window at the bustling bazaar.

Sivas was transformed since our arrival at dawn. The Geordies were out in force, with their velvet mosque caps and heavy tweed jackets, although sadly their trousers lacked the capacious crotch-line favoured in Cilicia. However, this was more than compensated for by the women's outfits. A respectful six paces behind their menfolk, trailing children and shopping bags, walked a series of shapeless conical sacks. There was no sign of the enticing headdresses we had so admired in Syria; the women of Sivas literally wore garden sacks over their heads.

Everyone in Sivas seemed to be on the move. Boys dodged the carthorses to carry trays of tea to the shopkeepers. Horse traps streamed into the town, carrying farm workers and great yellow pumpkins for the market. Gangster cars – Sivas's ageing taxi fleet of 1930s Chevrolets – crawled down the streets behind flocks of fat-tailed sheep. It was tempting to go out and explore further but, on balance, I decided it was just too comfortable in bed. So I stayed put, sipping tea and reading the expedition bible, Sir Henry Yule's 1929 edition of *The Travels*, which had somehow managed to escape the morning's eruption of shampoo.

My copy of Yule is in two volumes, and weighs over a stone. Both volumes are bound in buckram and have bottle-green leather spines. They are full of beautifully printed woodcuts in the style of David Roberts, and contain a large full-face portrait of Polo and an even larger one of Sir Henry. (He has a long beard and is shown at his desk, pen in hand, writing his manuscript on vast quarto leaves: the very picture of a Victorian explorer.) Both volumes are full of inserted plates – a facsimile of Polo's will, a large copperplate dedication to 'Her Royal Highness MARGHERITA [very big letters], Princess of Piedmont', and a three-foot-long 'reduced facsimile of the celebrated Chinese Inscription of Singanfu, in Chinese and Syriac characters' – but it is the maps which always please me most. I have wasted hours poring over them, following across Asia the dots, dashes and crosses representing the different journeys of the Polos. During the expedition, on arrival at a new town the first thing I would do would be to consult the Grand Master Map to see how far along the dashes we had got.

Sivas was not marked on the GMM, but did appear on the first of the smaller maps, a little circle with 'Savast' written beside it. According to the map, after leaving Ayas, Polo had crossed into the territory of the Seljuk Turks. I knew a little about the Seljuks, having met them the previous year when following the First Crusade. They were the greatest of all the waves of nomadic peoples that swept down out of the steppes and headed for the warm south. They conquered Persia in the early eleventh century, and had appeared on the Byzantine border by the late 1050s. Their leader was Alp Arslan ('The Conquering Lion'), a giant of a man, whose stature was increased by his habitual top hat, and whose moustaches were so long that they had to be knotted behind his head before he went into battle. Against such opposition Byzantium crumbled. At the battle of Manzikert in 1071 the Seljuks shattered the Greek army, captured the Emperor, Romanus IV Diogenese, and swept into Asia Minor. Neither the Byzantines nor the crusaders ever managed to win back the lands for Christendom. Over the following century the Seljuks gradually settled in the old towns and villages, creating a powerful state, a flourishing economy and an impressive and original culture.

Reading Yule in my hotel bedroom, it was clear that Polo had failed to distinguish between the Seljuks and their great enemies, the still-nomadic Turcomen, ancestors of the Yuruks we saw at Sis. He lumps them together as inhabitants of a province he calls Turcomania and claims, rather snootily: 'These are rude people with an uncouth language of their own. They dwell among mountains and downs where they find good pasture, for their occupation is cattle keeping.' The only civilized inhabitants of 'Turcomania' were the surviving Christians, the Armenians and the Greeks who:

> . . . live mixt the former in the towns and villages, occupying themselves with trade and handicrafts. They weave the finest and handsomest carpets in the world, and also a great quantity of fine and rich silks of cramoisy and other colours, and plenty of other stuffs. Their chief cities are Conia, Savast (where the glorious Messer Saint Blaise suffered martyrdom) and Casaria. . . .

Considering that Turkey was a country Italian merchants knew well, and in which they had much trade, Polo's account is surprisingly inaccurate and I thought it odd that Yule did not comment on this in his voluminous footnotes. Although in the late thirteenth century the Seljuk state had been disrupted by the Mongol invasions, their civilization was still at its zenith. Caravanserais were being built along the trade routes, hospitals and mosques were springing up everywhere, and sophisticated Turkish merchants dominated the trade of their country. Particularly surprising are Polo's remarks about silk and carpet production. Both these trades were Turkish introductions into Asia Minor, both were produced by Turks, and in Turkish styles. The Greeks and the Armenians did contribute to the trade, but they never controlled it.

Nowhere would this have been more true than in Sivas, which in 1271 was in its golden age. Before the Mongol invasions Sivas, though important enough to have been the burial site of one of the greatest of the Seljuk sultans, Keykavus I, was always secondary to the capital at Konya. With the political decline of the latter which followed the Mongol victory over the Seljuks at Kuzadag in 1241, the position was reversed.

Perhaps inspired by a desire to preserve their culture, now threatened by the latest eruption from Central Asia, the Seljuk warrior aristocracy responded to the Mongol invasions with a wave of patronage. The year Polo came to Sivas, 1271, no fewer than three new colleges had been commissioned for its university, and the town shot to fame as one of the great centres of learning in Islam, rivalling even the great school at Amassya. Sivas was renowned especially for the Shifaiye *medresse*, the great medical school and mental hospital.

The money which financed these foundations came not from war or farming, but from trade. The opening of the trans-Arabian trade routes which followed the establishment of the Mongol empire made Sivas an important junction of roads leading east from Ayas and the Black Sea ports. Surviving trade registers both from Europe and Asia emphasize the importance of Sivas as the commercial centre of the Seljuk Empire. In 1280, Genoese notaries were drawing up accounts in the *funduq* of a Sivas merchant called Kamal al-Din. Pegolotti in his *Pratica della Mercatura* says that by 1300 the Genoese had established a permanent consulate in the town and that police guarded the road: merchants bound for Sivas had been pillaged both at sea, by pirates, and by robbers in the hills between Sivas and the coast. Big bazaars, robbers, groupings of merchants – these are just the sort of thing that Polo normally comments on. Yet for once he is silent on commercial matters, and singles out Sivas not as a trading centre, but as the site of the martyrdom of the 'glorious Messer Saint Blaise'.

According to Yule almost nothing is known about the historical St Blaise, except that he was bishop of Sebaste (Roman Sivas) and was martyred during the persecutions of Diocletian. However, lack of facts never stopped mediaeval hagiographers from assembling impressively detailed saints' lives. According to the late, apocryphal, and apparently completely fictional *Acts of Saint Blaise*, the bishop 'dwelt in a cave where he was fed by birds and wild animals who came to visit him in crowds and would not depart until he extended his hand in blessing

and healed any that were ailing'. This curious ministry continued until the saint was discovered by a party of hunters
searching for animals to be killed in the Sebaste amphitheatre
(Christians had run out). Blaise was promptly arrested and
taken back to Sivas with them. It was an eventful journey.
Blaise not only persuaded a wolf to return a pig he had stolen
from a penniless widow, but also saved a boy fatally choking
from a fishbone in his throat. Sentenced to death, his 'flesh was
torn by iron combs such as are used to card wool' and as a result
Blaise became the patron saint not only of wild animals, pigs
and sore throats, but also of wool merchants.

When Yule was writing, the tomb of St Blaise was still ven-
erated in Sivas and, inspired by my reading, I finally dragged
myself out of bed to go and search for it. It was surprisingly
chilly outside. It had been a high, clear cloudless day and
now the sun was sinking low the temperature was dropping
rapidly. Sivas is one of the coldest towns in Turkey and in
winter its streets are permanently covered in thick snow.
Occasionally, as a framed photograph in the hotel showed, the
snow could rise to cover the gables of the houses. Even now, in
high summer, those women who were not in sacking were
wrapped up in warm cotton doublets, swathing kerchiefs and
thick pleated Kashmiri-style trousers.

I wandered around the slopes of the citadel in the centre of
the town where Yule says the tomb used to be, but there did not
seem to be any sign of it. Even the old men in the *cay* shops
could not help. In a way this was hardly surprising. Blaise was
never an important saint in his own town; his fame was
greater further away. In the early Middle Ages his cult had
spread fast, collecting further legends as it went. By the eighth
century churches were dedicated to him in both Milan and
Genoa. By the ninth, 'Blas' had become a popular saint in
Germany, and the abbey of Metz claimed to possess a bit of his
skull ('remarkably thick, brown in colour and about eleven
centimetres in size'). He remained popular among Germans
ever after, except with the sailors. Blas in German means
wind. Even in the nineteenth century 'mariners avoided pro-

nouncing the name of this [saint's] feast . . . and looked upon winds blowing on that day as prognostic of tempests blowing throughout the year'.

The British knew better. Blaise did not mean wind. It meant fire. According to a seventeenth-century dictionary, St Blaise's day was when '. . . country women goe about and make goode cheere and if they find any of their neighbor women a spinning, they burne and make a blaze of fire of the distaffs, and thereof called St Blaise his day'. To this day, most Catholic churches in Britain mark the third of February with the ceremony of the Blessing of the Throats, when two unlighted candles are held against the necks of the faithful. In Ireland the church has ruled that this useful precaution against sore throats may also be administered to dairy cattle.

Which is, perhaps, one reason why the old men gave me such odd looks when I asked them about Blaise. At any rate I got bored with asking directions to something no one had ever heard of, so instead climbed the citadel and sat in a café. It was a beautiful evening. Only when you looked down on Sivas from above did you realize that it was an island. From the café you could see that it was a solitary green oasis, alone in the northern Anatolian plateau, separated from the arid flatlands around it by a rim of ash-coloured mountains. You could see neither the old men nor the gangster cars, nor the traps nor the horses, only an expanse of poplars and cypress, irregularly broken by the roofs of the old stone houses, the double brick minarets of the *medresse* (Islamic college), and the domes of the *hammam* (baths).

I got out the logbook and began scribbling. But it was cold and getting colder, and after a couple of pages I gave up and went out into the dusk to explore the town's Seljuk remains.

The Ulu Jami, the oldest mosque in Sivas, lay near the bottom of the citadel mount. It was a small, low-slung building with a corrugated iron roof and a tottering minaret. Prayers had just finished and the old men were hobbling out in order of seniority, which made for a very slow exit. As they left the prayer hall they fumbled around on the floor to try and find

89

their shoes. But it was dark and they were old. Long after the senior mullah had crossed the road and the crowd dispersed, three men remained in the porch with five odd shoes. At the other end of the courtyard the ablution fountain provided another focus of activity. Half of Sivas seemed to have converged around its taps, the women filling water bottles, scrubbing and cleaning, while their children played and the Geordies combed their beards.

Inside, the Ulu Jami was dark and cavernous. Like the crypt of a romanesque cathedral, it seemed built to bear an enormous weight. Its walls sloped inwards, and the great rectangular plinths, each as wide as a fully grown camel, sloped out. Built of massive blocks of dark, lead-grey stone, unornamented and without a break at the capitals, they rose into huge monolothic vaults. Threadbare carpets were spread out along the avenues of arches, and the mihrab, which was almost invisible, was hung with heavy crimson velvet.

Only in one corner, that nearest the porch, was there any noise. There a mullah was holding a Koran class. A crowd of little boys were kneeling in front of miniature wooden mosque desks, reciting from the strange calligraphy of classical Arabic with the speed and fluency of rote-learned multiplication tables. They were barefoot, and uniformed in white embroidered mosque caps, and as they recited they rocked backwards and forwards, backwards and forwards, in time with their chant. Slowly the pitch rose from the low hum of a chant to the wailing song of the muezzin. It was a strange and beautiful sound, and I drew nearer and leant against a plinth, listening.

When the lesson broke up, it was not yet dark, so I walked back behind the citadel to have a look at the Gok *medresse*. The college is only three hundred yards from the Ulu Jami, and was built less than one hundred years later, but a remarkable renaissance separates the two buildings. The restraint and dignity of the Ulu Jami gives way to an almost baroque richness of decoration. Nothing I had seen before in Islam prepared me for the sight. In the Islamic Art Museum in Istanbul I had walked around the collection of Seljuk *art mobilier* and I remembered thinking how ungainly it seemed: large pregnant-looking ewers, spiky candlesticks with stems like kebab skewers, a set of heavy brass mortars, lumpy with large protruding knobs. The pottery was repetitive and unattractive, and its figure work lacked precision, either in line or in colouring. Even the famous fourteenth-century wooden mosque doors from Konya failed to impress: they were pretty, like Iznik tile work, but were somehow tame, predictable.

The sculpture on the front of the Gok *medresse* was in a different class. It was wild, frenetic and restless – nomad sculpture; a star-burst of interlace and pattern sweeping out from the stalactite archway. Struggling out of two dimensions into three, the tendrils would suddenly erupt into high relief; jungles of acanthus and vine swirled, thrashed and clung. The sculptor was driven by the same decorative urge and *horror vacui* that motivated Anglo-Saxon artists, but here it produced sculpture at once more violent and barbaric than any Celtic decorative work. Commissioned in 1271, when the Mongols were threatening to swamp the Seljuks, this was the art of a people under siege, of a culture revitalized by the threat of extinction.

Whether there was more sculpture of this quality inside the *medresse*, it is now impossible to say. Most of the college was burned to the ground in August 1400, when Timur the Lame (the Tamberlaine 'scourge of God' in Marlowe) fell on Sivas and captured it after a week's siege. What happened then is unclear. According to *The Life of Timur*, a gallant attempt to whitewash the actions of one of the most unpleasant mass murderers in history, he spared the life of the Muslims in Sivas, and simply put to death the Christians, whose Sipahi cavalry had put up the most stubborn resistance. *The Life of Timur* is not, however, the most reliable of documents, as its subtitle (in the 1597 edition: 'A rare example of heathenish piety, prudence, magnanimity, mercy, liberality, humility, justice, temperance and valour') might lead one to suspect.

The Armenian historian, Thomas of Metsope, seems to have

given a more factual account. According to Thomas, on the first approach of Timur's army the people of Sivas sued for peace by gathering the Muslim children of the city in the plain in front of the city walls, each one bearing a copy of the Koran. Timur, who was not unaware of the attractions of little boys, was no doubt moved by the sight, but that did not stop him ordering that the children be trampled to death under the hooves of his heavy cavalry. He besieged the city for a week, mined the walls then stormed the breeches. The four thousand defenders who survived the ensuing slaughter were divided among his tumans (generals), and buried alive in specially dug pits. No less than nine thousand virgins (of both sexes) were carried off for the Imperial harem. Sivas was burned, and left empty.

The reason for all this, according to the *Life*, was Timur's problem with boredom. As he headed home to Samarcand along the shore of the Caspian, he passed his time, says the *Life*, 'in hunting and hawking, in order to try and make the journey a little less tedious. . . .'

Mr Orhan Ghazi (Prop., Manager and Rm. Service, Hotel Seljuk) woke us the following morning bearing not only our breakfast (comb honey) and two buckets of hot water, but also the good news that our Chevrolet was waiting.

After getting back from the Gok *medresse* the previous evening I had done some research. With the aid of an earnest engineering student (who spoke English) and a semi-subterranean *cay* shop full of old men (who did not), I had managed to establish that whatever was the case in Polo's time, there were no longer any Greeks or Armenians in Sivas. According to the old men they had all 'left' during the First World War (i.e. they had all been slaughtered during the 1917 massacres) and since then their churches had fallen into disrepair, and eventually had been swept away. The one near the citadel, probably the Armenian church of St Blaise, had been used as an army store, and when the roof fell in in 1953 it had been destroyed. The other, presumably the Greek church of St George, was knocked down in 1978 and its stones had been used to build a mosque. Both sites were now covered with blocks of flats. No one knew anything about the shrine of St Blaise which used to occupy a site on the citadel near the Gok *medresse*, but if it had not been desecrated before it must have been destroyed when the top of the citadel mount was bulldozed to make a park in the late 1960s. On one thing everyone was agreed: there was now no church in Sivas, no priest, and with the exception of one alcoholic Armenian tailor, no Christians. But according to the old men in the *cay* shop, carpet production had survived, not in Sivas itself but in the villages to the south of it, and for the price of a taxi ride from Chelsea to Piccadilly, a chauffeur-driven gangster car was mine for the day to go and look for it.

Mr Orhan Ghazi had already briefed the driver when we appeared at the doors of his hotel with our notebooks and cameras, and he saw us into the magnificent limousine with another of his Abyssinian bows. We sat dwarfed in the leather acreage of the back seat, sauntering slowly through the streets of Sivas, threading our way through herds of sheep and goats, past the shuffling sacks and their husbands, queueing up behind slow-moving processions of Geordie-crammed *dolmus* (minibuses). As we left the bazaar we narrowly avoided a collision with a cavalcade of cars going in the opposite direction. They honked their horns, and trailed bunting and streamers. They were returning, if I understood correctly the gestures of our driver, not from a wedding, but a circumcision: a great cause for celebration if you are a Turk (or rather for your friends and relations; less so, at least initially, for you yourself).

Then we left the shady avenues of cypress and were out in the strong white light and bleached flatlands of the Anatolian plateau.

I knew this landscape. For one month the previous summer I had trekked through it, following the route of the First Crusade, and I knew how soon the eyes tired of its great wide solitudes. It was not yet a desert; it was still intermittently, grudgingly fertile. Every so often you would pass a single, lonely farm with its cones of dung chapattis and whitewashed mud-brick byres. But then the sudden burst of colour would give way again to the monochrome plains and the road would stretch on, unwaveringly straight, into the dry heart of Asia Minor.

This plateau had once been the breadbasket of the Roman Empire, a kind of Imperial prairie, and its prosperous farms had for a millenium provided the backbone of the Byzantine army: the free peasant small-holders who had made up the regiments of *caballarii*. But when the pastoralist Turks swept into Asia Minor in the 1070s they left the fields untilled, and soon the irrigation systems broke down and the land dried up and salinated. When the armies of the First Crusade marched through Turkey only twenty years after Manzikert, they found that many of the Empire's most fertile *theme* (provinces) were already waste. In twenty years the Turks had killed the land.

We stopped at the oasis village of Sultanhani. After an hour of deadening plains it seemed a fine place. There were some new bungalows, some ancient mud-brick farms with walled gardens, several smart new tractors and a small filling station. Beside the filling station was a pond, with ducks paddling around in a sludge of old dogweed. At our approach two geese waddled off with the self-important swagger of a pair of portly Whig landowners. There was a slight scent of vegetation.

We sat outside a teahouse and drank some *cay* while the driver sucked at a *nargile*. Nearby were two policemen who looked grateful, in their boredom, to have something to be suspicious about. One, all peak cap and bristling moustache, possessed an air of casual brutality; the other, a smaller man, had the sad face of a First World War daguerrotype; he might have been a Balkan general or a Tsarist armament minister. They eyed us up and down, but it was too hot to be overly curious, and they soon returned to their game of cards.

We wandered over to the *han* which gave the village its name. According to an inscription, it was commissioned in 1230 by the Seljuk Sultan Keykubad I. It was a royal foundation, deliberately built to make any other caravanserai look small and provincial: a totally unembarrassed public demonstration of royal taste and, more importantly, royal wealth.

A broken-toothed ruffian sat at the gate by a rickety trestle.

'Good morning, Ingliz,' he said, inclining his head. 'Three hundred lira. Each.'

We payed the first entrance fee we had been charged since Jerusalem and the last until Peking.

The court of the *han* was larger than those of most Oxbridge colleges. On one side the dormitories, baths and bedrooms led off from the courtyard; on the other there were workshops, stores and a kitchen. At the far end a huge emblazoned gateway gave off into the stables, a vaulted cathedral with stalls on either side of its nave, impossibly large and grand for any except a race of nomads whose wealth and status depended on horsemanship. The plan was exactly that of the *medresse* in Sivas. Here were a practical people, only newly come to erecting buildings any more substantial than a nomad's tent. In the earlier *medresse* at Sivas, they had adapted to their needs a building plan (of ancient, probably Sassanian origin) and, that perfected, they saw no need to adapt it any further. It was a good plan, they seem to have thought, why bother to change it? Thus all Seljuk buildings surviving from this period share an endearing sameness. Their hotels look like their mental hospitals, their mosques like their stables; the exteriors of their schools barely differ from some of their castles and their minarets can be mistaken for burial towers.

Only in several minor details does the Sultanhani *han* diverge from the model of the Sivas *medresse*. The walls were made taller, thicker and more substantial, so as to be able to withstand the raids of bandits or Turcomen. The *ivan* gateway was made stronger and more imposing. Buttresses were added, as were lion's-head corbels, decoration perhaps thought unsuitable on the more serious walls of a religious college. A slatted cone the shape of a *yurt* was added onto the top of the stables to catch light for the horses. And most inspired of all, as if to offset the added bulk of the fortified walls, in the middle of the courtyard was raised a *mescat*, a floating pavilion-mosque of fabulous intricacy, suspended, as if levitated, on four delicate arches of apricot-coloured stone, as lightly and subtly carved as an inlaid jewel box.

The Seljuks did not invent the caravanserai. There were *han* and *rabat* all over Turkestan and Persia. But the Seljuks were the first to build a planned network along their trade routes so that ideally there was a caravanserai every eighteen miles, the distance it took a laden camel to travel in a day. In practice most trade routes went without rest houses, but the main roads were well provided for. According to the thirteenth-century Muslim traveller, Ibn Sa'id, there were over twenty *han* between Sivas and Kayseri, a distance of only seventy miles.

The *han* would have been forty years old by the time Marco Polo passed its doors. There is no reason to believe that he and his father did not spend the night here. I climbed up the flight of steps above the gateway and looked down over the *mescat* towards the great stable-hall. The *han* was well preserved, but it was as empty as any ruined abbey, and as difficult to fill with imagined inhabitants. What would Polo have seen when he walked within the gateway? I thought of the famous nineteenth-century description of caravanserai life given by Chateaubriand:

> Turkish merchants were seated cross-legged on carpets in groups round the fires at which slaves were busily employed in dressing pilau. Other travellers were smoking their pipes at the door ... chewing opium and telling stories . . . hucksters went about from fire to fire offering cakes, fruits and poultry for sale. Singers were amusing the crowd; imams were performing their ablutions . . . camel drivers lay snoring on the ground. . . .

Would it have been like this in Seljuk times? No contemporary accounts survive, and modern authorities disagree. Some historians pack the buildings with earnest craftsmen providing a while-you-wait veterinary and engineering service;

others envisage a more luxurious regime of pastry cooks, musicians and dancing girls. Certainly they were lively places, free to all merchants after payment of an annual trade tax, and seem to have been infinitely preferable to most of the hotels we stayed in – as, indeed, I said to Laura as we returned to the car to search for the village of Sarikli. It was here that the old men in the Sivas *cay* shop had suggested we might still find some carpet making.

The policemen pointed us back up the road to Sivas; the man at the gates of the caravanserai thought Sarikli lay somewhere in the opposite direction towards Kayseri. The pump attendant at the filling station had never heard either of Sarikli or of the manufacture of carpets. *'Yok,'* he said, in answer to all our questions, jerking his head skywards, a gesture which means something in between 'It doesn't exist,' 'I don't know whether it exists,' and 'I couldn't give a monkey's whether it exists or not.' Then Laura found a footnote in Yule which claimed that Anatolian carpet manufacture had died out before the nineteenth century, in which case, said Laura, it hardly mattered where Sarikli was anyway. Another glass of tea and we decided to follow the policemen's instructions and search for the carpets on the road back to Sivas. If they did not exist, at least we would be heading back towards the welcoming arms of Mr Orhan Ghazi, and the possibility of some of his comb honey for tea.

Things, of course, did not work out as we had planned. They rarely do in Asia.

I remember being directed off the main road, our sleek black Chevrolet bumping over hard, parched, stubble fields and fouling itself in a stream-side dung pile; I remember Laura predicting disaster and our driver's long, caressing first-aid to his ailing motor car on the far side of the river. And I remember the village idiot, and the punctures, both of them, and the slow, relentless fall down the slope and the impact into the shack at the bottom then the heroic attempts to keep believing in the carpets, and that long, circular conversation we had with the Turk who lived inside the shack.

WD:	*Hali?*
Laura:	Carpets.
Turk:	Car-pets.
Laura:	Do you speak English? Listen, William, this man speaks English.
Turk:	Car-pets.
Laura:	Yes, that's right. We want carpets.
Turk:	Car-pets.
Laura:	WE (*pause*) WANT (*pause*) CAR-PETS.
Turk (*nodding*):	Car-pets.

(*Driver here explains in Turkish that we are searching for carpets. Turk looks horrified. Then he says 'Yok'. We depart at 10 m.p.h. our ailing motor pursued by a jailbreak of shaven-headed children.*)

It got worse before it got better. We recrossed the river, had another puncture, and were forced to negotiate a new rate for the outing; I fought with Laura, who I suspected of plotting with the driver. Then we patched up a compromise. I was to be allowed to ask one more peasant for directions; we were to follow those directions for a maximum of quarter of an hour, and we were then to return home, with or without carpets.

The first peasant we came across was clearly a halfwit. He was sitting vacantly by the roadside wearing scarecrow rags, and had on his face that dim, incomprehending look which is unique to Turkish labourers. When asked the way to Sarikli he pointed first to the sky, then to the ground, and finally towards a field of hayricks in the near-distance. With unexpected fidelity to our arrangement, the other two agreed to go to the field and see if any carpets were being made there. There weren't, but from the field a track led off downhill towards a small group of huts, and as a last gesture towards compromise Laura and the driver agreed to go to the village, if only to get a glass of tea before heading back to Sivas.

That the village was Sarikli, and that one house still contained a loom on which carpets were still being made, took me as much by surprise as it did the others. I had long before given up hope of finding any carpets, and was continuing the search only out of a stubborn refusal to admit the foolishness of the expedition, and also out of a vague sense of loyalty to Trinity College, which had after all sponsored me to hire Chevrolets to dung-heap villages, searching for freak survivals of once-healthy cottage industries. What Laura and the driver had forgotten was that we were supposed to be pushing back the frontiers of knowledge.

Our loom lived in a large, two-storey mud-thatch house belonging to a small Geordie in a tea-cosy hat. He must have been a more potent gentleman than he looked, for he had a brood of children which rivalled that of our friend in the shack. They chased our car past the hayricks, past the duck pond and the fountain covered with climbing roses, past the donkeys and flocks of bantams until the Chevrolet drew to a halt outside the loom house. Their mother sat on the ground beating a pile of old goatskins with a heavy wooden stick. It was she who operated the loom, though clearly infrequently: it lay at the back of the room, behind bags of wheat, old twig brushes and a single, sleeping cow. Nor, in the event of the loom actually being used, did it produce carpets in the European sense of the word. The main frame of the machine was less than five feet wide, and it produced a piece of material about half that, a small gaudy rug of bright primary colours known as a *kilim*. Nevertheless, the loom did work and the woman did know how to use it.

While our driver disappeared under the bonnet of his car, Laura and I watched the woman at work. With unexpectedly nimble fingers, she passed different coloured threads of wool through the matrix of taut strings looped around the two rough-hewn wooden cross-shafts of the loom frame. She knotted the threads, cut them with a rusty dagger, then thumped the knot down into the main weft of the *kilim* with a heavy copper wool-comb. She continued in this manner, gathering speed as she went and working entirely from memory, until she reached the end of a line. Then she would pause, put down the comb and trim the pattern with a pair of long, Strewelpeter thumb-scissors. It was a hypnotic and strangely thrilling sight. This was certainly small-scale production, even by thirteenth-century standards, yet the techniques cannot have been any different from those witnessed by Marco Polo. Yule was wrong. If only on this much-reduced scale, carpet production had survived in the uplands of Anatolia.

Even the demand for double the agreed rate from the driver did not diminish the sense that, if nothing else, we had at least achieved something on the journey.

We walked through the lamplight as the last pony traps were rattling home along the cobbles. At the *kebabji* that evening forty Turks were watching one television. We sat down with a plate of shavings from the great elephant's-leg of doner kebab, and breathed in the bitter, acrid stench of *nargile*. The fat cook turned the doner spit. No one spoke. It was only after we had begun eating supper that we noticed that the programme was a Turkish-dubbed version of the BBC series *Little Lord Fauntleroy* and I sat for a while, writing postcards and trying to imagine what the Turks thought was going on during the scenes of village cricket matches and port-swilling country house dinner parties.

After a few minutes the two German trans-Andes bicyclists wandered in. They were wearing matching blue tracksuits, and they made a great show of looking for dirt on the seats before they sat down. After wiping the covers with Kleenex they settled at the next table to us. The man leaned over.

'How much are zay asking you for your rhoom?'

They converted the sum into Deutschmarks, and discussed it among themselves. Then:

'Zat is vehry good value. In Germany hotels are more expensive. But ze are clean. Zese are dirty. So dirty.'

I smiled and picked at the garnish of my kebab. The German leaned over again.

'You know in zis hot veather, it is very dangerous to eat ze salad. It is unhygenic. Maybe you should eat only ze cooked vegetable.'

'Maybe.'

There was a pause.

'You vill die.' said the German.

We meant to leave the next day, but could not bring ourselves to do so. We returned from supper to find that Mr Orhan Ghazi had filled our room with pot plants, drawn the curtains and folded back the top corners of our coverlets, like an unseen housemaid in a stately home. We decided to stay for at least one more day, and the next morning, before Laura awoke, I slipped out to explore.

Sivas is forced into compactness by its geology: the collar of mountains – pale blue in the morning, rather than the tired ashen-grey of evening – hunch their shoulders around the plain of Sivas, encircling it and forcing the streets into a tightly-knit grid of winds and lanes and alleyways. Yet its inhabitants maintain the ways of villagers, and have resisted the municipalizing forces thrust upon them. A few paces beyond the wide, asphalted main streets lies a network of separate self-contained villages with their own pastures and fields. Already, at eight o'clock in the morning, these villages were in the full swing of the agricultural day. Women were carrying piles of firewood towards their houses, while the men began solemnly to disembowel their tractors. Children were sitting on broken balustrades, watching the grazing sheep or throwing grain to the hens and the bantams. A few of the older ones rattled worry beads. In the tea gardens other families were picnicking. They sat in close little groups around boiling *demlik* (Anatolian samovars) reproducing in the open the *zenana* of the house: girls were tucked into neat semicircles around odalisque mothers, at a safe distance from the men.

Around these scenes lay the debris of the past. Near one tea garden stood a bulbous, low-roofed Ottoman mosque, hexagonal with a single squat minaret. Ottoman mosques have never appealed to me. Although the exteriors of the great Sulemaniye and Bayazit mosques in Istanbul are impressive, with their shady cloister arcades and ripple of cupolas, their interiors are always disappointing. They are simply pale imitations of Hagia Sophia, without the latter's perfection of colouring (imperial gold and purple) or form (perfect shapes: the square and the circle). Instead they are gaudy affairs of scarlet, copper-green and lavender, and to the Vitruvian shapes is added the pointed arch, an alien element which adds nothing to the design. The result is a pastiche, as uninteresting and derivative as Victorian Gothic, and as far from the perfection of Byzantine architecture as the Albert Memorial is from Chartres. If this is true of Ottoman architecture in Istanbul, it is all the more so of the millions of identical maquette mosques erected over the empire. The interior of that in Sivas impressed on me the heaviness of provincial Ottoman architecture: thick columns with chunky arches, heavy marble balustrades. There are none of the flutings or fantasies one expects in Islamic architecture, no development of the ideas of Seljuk architects, only an uninteresting, bastardized Byzantinism, lacking either the dignity or the grandeur of the original.

Much more intriguing was the nearby Seljuk Shifaiye *medresse*. In its day this was one of the greatest medical schools in the Islamic world. It had a magnificent library, available to both students and the staff, and its teaching combined practical work at the bedsides of the sick with more theoretical study in the classroom. Its staff included surgeons, oculists and specialists in internal diseases, as well as a pioneering group of psychiatrists whose cures for mental illnesses used the sound of dripping water, music and hypnosis. There was nothing remotely comparable in Europe, even at the outstanding Italian medical school at Salerno.

The Shifaiye *medresse* was built in 1217, and its façade is an obvious prototype for that of the Gok *medresse*. Like the latter it is covered with swirling interlace, but of much more primitive type, with far fewer, much cruder motifs deployed across the whole façade. In the Gok the interlace is limited to the *ivan* gateway and even here within sharply defined borders, emphasized by the strong verticals of the two minarets. These rise up from directly above the borders: two magnificent pillars of crisp, pink brick, inlaid with ceramic tiles the colour of lapis lazuli. In the earlier Shifaiye *medresse* there are no border panels and minarets. The interlace spills out unimpeded onto the retaining walls. It is a wilder creation than the Gok, but a less balanced and successful one.

However, there is the ample compensation in the surviving court – a quad of beautifully arcaded cloisters. The arches are high and narrow with tall spandrels springing inwards only at the very top of the horseshoe; the voussoirs are polychrome, made up of alternate black and white stones. I had seen such arches before, not in Islam but in a Christian church: the transept arches in Catania cathedral. They are eleventh century, and arguably the first pointed arches in Europe. Islam had used the pointed arch since the eighth century and it seems likely that it passed its discovery to Europe through the medium of Norman Sicily. Hence it spread to Monte Cassino, and through Benedictine architects to France and St Denis. The lovely cloisters in the Shifaiye *medresse* were unexpected confirmation that the origin of the pointed arch, the key feature of European Gothic, lay not in the Ile de France but, like so much of European culture, in the Muslim world.

It seemed an exciting discovery, and I sat contentedly in the sun, under the arches, writing it up in my diary.

To one side a gardener was digging the cloister garth. Apart from the noise of spade on soil and the cooing of doves, the *medresse* was silent. This perhaps was the Peace of Islam. My pool of sunlight had already turned to shade when I looked up to find a beautiful, dark-haired girl walking towards me. From a distance I thought she must be Italian, but when she introduced herself it turned out that she was Turkish. Her name was Kevser, and she had just come back from Germany where her father had been a guest worker. She had lived there for eleven years, but when her father died her mother had had to return. She did not know whether she would be able to go back. She had taken exams and if she passed she might be able to get a place at a German university; like me she was in the limbo state of awaiting results. When I asked which of the two countries she preferred her reply surprised me.

'I have lived two completely different lives for the last eleven years,' she said. 'Most of the time I have lived in Germany, but every summer I have returned here for the holidays. I have close friends in both places.'

She struggled for the right words.

'Technically life in Germany is much better. Life here is very hard. We have to go a long way for water, and sometimes we are hungry. There is no television, no music, no entertainment. There is only one post a week. And if I live here I will be very poor. But in some ways the people are luckier, richer. In Germany neighbours hardly talk to each other. They say "hello" when they pass in the street, but it is all small talk: they talk about the weather. Here people smile more. Really. They are happier. I am related to everybody near here, so I can go to any house. I can spend the night, sleep there and there will be no scandal. Some nights my cousins and I stay up all night talking. I have many close friends in Germany but we never do that.'

She shrugged her shoulders and smiled. 'It's hard to explain the difference.'

I asked her whether she did not mind the inferior status of women in Islam, and the fact that the two sexes were so segregated.

'It is different here from the rest of Turkey,' she replied. 'My family – many of the people of Sivas – came here from Russia, from the Caucasus, one hundred years ago. In some ways we behave differently from the Turks. Separating the sexes and making the women slaves is not Islam, it is Turkish. We are good Muslims. We pray, we read the Koran, we believe in one God – Allah. But we behave differently from the Turks. We speak our own language, wear our own dress, have our own folk dances where the girls and boys dance together. I have as many friends who are boys as girls. So, no, I don't have to behave very differently from Germany. And my status is not lower. The girls in my family have our own tasks, but we still have a big say in the running of the household. We have a good balance. In Britain I think your women have too much power.'

'Some British people would agree with you.'

'I have heard that in Britain your women go out to work, leaving the men to run the household.'

'It does happen.'

'Your women must be very tough.'

'They are.'

One of the toughest was waiting for me when I got back to Hotel Seljuk.

'Do you like it?' she asked.

'Why . . . well . . . it's. . . .'

'Is it so ridiculous?'

'It. . . .'

'You'll just have to get used to it. I'm going to be wearing it all the way through Iran.'

My travelling companion was dressed from head to foot in enveloping black wraps, like a vampire from a low-budget horror film. A black headscarf was lowered over her forehead to reveal her beady black eyes, hawk-nose and trireme chin. A black stormtrooper shirt gave way to an ankle-length dress of Victorian cut. Below the straps of her sandals I could see the familiar black socks.

'I rather like it. It's very . . . alluring.'

'You're always alluring, Laura,' I said, ever keen to please.

'Not too gaudy?'

'On the contrary.'

'Reliable sort of outfit.'

'Dignified.'

'Steady.'

'Understated.'

'Rather distinguished. . . .'

'. . . in an Islamic sort of way.'

Laura twirled in front of the mirror kindly provided for her by Mr Orhan Ghazi.

'Maybe it suits me.'

'Maybe it does.'

*   *   *

We finally left Hotel Seljuk the following afternoon. I could have happily stayed another week, but Laura was anxious to keep to our schedule and we were already behind. Mr Orhan Ghazi was there to see us off. He bowed a final bow and wrung his hands like a widow. It was an emotional moment.

'Friendship is a fine bondage,' were his words. 'By the grace of God you will come back.'

'By the grace of God we will.'

'Allah is merciful.'

'Let's hope so.'

'May his blessings always be upon you.'

'And on you. . . .'

Chivvied on by Laura, we reached Sivas station a full half-hour before the scheduled departure time. I had never before travelled by Turkish railways. From my experience of Indian trains I imagined overcrowded carriages, packed aisles and hawking vendors. But as far as hard, factual information went, I had nothing more up to date than the confident prediction I had read in the 1920 *Encyclopedia of Islam*: 'A new era will dawn with the construction of the Ankara–Sivas railway, already progressing fast thanks to the work of the Kemalist Republic's government. . . .'

As we were soon to discover, the construction of the Ankara –Sivas railway seemed to have done very little to alter anything. Despite our experiences on the overnight trip from Mersin, Turkey has always had one of the most reliable bus services in the world. As a result, the inefficient state-owned Turkish railways have never been used by anyone except those government servants who are given free tickets. At half past four, the scheduled departure time, the only other person on the platform apart from ourselves was the station master, and he was fast asleep. He was still snoring at six. At seven the light was beginning to fade and the station master was slumped forwards over a bench, snoring as before. He awoke at eight and took us off to his dimly lit office for a glass of tea. We were joined there by three soldiers at a quarter to nine. By twenty past there were eight of us packed in tightly around the station master's *demlik*. Someone produced two bottles of *raki* and one of the soldiers tried to teach the station master and me how to play a card game, a complicated cross between bridge, snap and pontoon. Laura, sensibly, did not join in.

We played two games and the station master won them both. We drank each other's health, and played another game. It was dark in the office and we could hardly see our cards. I suspected the station master of cheating.

Time passed; the *raki* bottles emptied steadily. We cannot actually have drunk very much but the whole evening assumed that air of guilty debauchery that always hangs over Muslim drinking sessions. A *birasi* with a handful of sober Turks drinking weak Efes Pilsen can usually be made to feel as wicked as the most degenerate bordello.

At eleven o'clock the train had still not come. It was stuffy in the room and smoke stung the eyes. Everyone was fairly drunk. Gradually the conversation became lurid.

'I am knowing Ingliz,' said one of the soldiers. 'I am knowing dirty words.'

'Which ones?'

The soldier paused.

'Shirt,' he whispered.

'Any others?'

He looked nervously around him, and brought his head closer to mine. 'Bigger.'

'That's a very dirty word indeed.'

He bit his lower lip, and the play continued in a hushed silence.

At the end of the game the station master persuaded me to play backgammon with him. Here too I suspected foul play. As he shook the dice he stared directly at me as if to distract my eyes, and he played his moves with dazzling swiftness. He moved his counters as soon as the dice settled. He never counted out his moves. I played different tactics: moving very slowly, tapping out my moves, trying desperately to find a way to double up my counters. But one was always left on its own, and it always seemed to be caught by the station master's pieces as they shot off for home on the wings of a double six. I was soon backgammoned.

Dizzy with smoke and *raki* and failure, I agreed to play another card game, some sort of Turkish strip poker. This did not go well either. I felt increasingly miserable, and when one of the soldiers knocked his glass of *raki* over me, I vented my frustration in a flash of temper.

'Look, is this bloody train going to come or not?'

'Oh yes. Train he comes. No problem,' said the station master.

'When?'

'Soon.'

'How soon?'

'Soon.'

'HOW SOON?'

'Maybe today. Maybe tomorrow.'

'You lose again,' said one of the soldiers, trumping my hand. 'Now, Mr William, you reveal yourself.'

'Forget the game for one second,' said Laura, creating a welcome diversion. 'I want to know if this train is going to come.'

'Yes, exactly.'

'No you worry, Missy, Sir,' said the station master. 'Train he comes. Choof choof. Very fast top class train.'

He beamed proudly: 'People of Sivas, much they like him.'

'Top rate,' said the first soldier.

'Fut fut fut,' said his friend.

'Choof choof . . . first class . . . whoosh whoosh,' echoed the others.

The train did come, but not for another hour. Humbled and exhausted, I followed Laura into one of the carriages.

Never have I seen a train less likely to raise the spirits. It could not have been further from an Indian carriage. There, for all the discomfort, the seats are packed with people busily unrolling bedding, setting up primuses, cooking supper and generally making themselves at home. Walking into an Indian train is like walking into an Indian village. Entering a Turkish train is like finding oneself in a solitary confinement cell. The empty carriages reminded me of the dowdy, unloved look of run-down hotel lounges in the Scottish Highlands. The plastic seats were torn, the windows would not open and there was a melancholy whiff of urine in the air.

We sat in a compartment beside a suicidal policeman returning to his posting in Erzurum after a holiday on the Aegean coast. His clothes were dirty and unwashed, and three or four days' stubble covered his face; he chain-smoked and spat on the floor. His mood reflected my own and I was wafted to sleep by a long lullaby of his woes:

'In Bodrum I went with bad womens. . . .

'Perhaps diseases. . . .

'My wife, once she pretty woman. . . .

'So many childrens. . . .

'Fat now like Bayyram sheep. . . .'

He droned on much of the night. I would wake up, find him still talking, make a few sympathetic noises, then sink back into a slumber. By three o'clock the policeman had finally fallen asleep, but I found myself wide awake. There were no curtains on the windows and outside Turkey was juddering past. You could feel it clatter by beneath the wheels: *Truckety-truck, truckety-truck, truckety-truck.* Occasionally the train would hoot to itself but that was the only noise to break the rhythm of its heartbeat. It was a comforting, umbilical sound and I tucked myself up into an embryo position and rested my head against a folded jersey. Exhausted, befuddled by sleep and the soldiers' *raki*, anaesthetized by the smell of sour urine, I sat looking out of the window, trying to forget the snoring police-man and the grimy, ill-smelling train. In the bright moonlight the landscape seemed surprisingly fertile. There were small cottage-garden fields scattered randomly around the track, and in some of them was a sheen of flood water. At the edge of the pools I could see the unmistakable silhouettes of water buffa-loes – the first I had seen since India – as big and leathery as tusked walruses, but sitting like kittens with their legs folded up beneath them.

This was good grazing land, the area Polo must have been

referring to when he wrote 'in the summer the country is frequented by the whole host of the Tartars of the Levant, because it furnishes them with such excellent pasture for their cattle'. I had read the passage in Sivas and had been struck by it: the dry flatlands there were quite unlike Polo's description, and it was difficult to imagine how those expanses of long-exhausted land could transform themselves into the pastures described in *The Travels*.

A few minutes later I saw the reason for the transformation. The train rounded a long curve and found itself in a broad, high-backed, deep-cut valley. The track stood on a raised bank surrounded by a moraine of pebbles, and on one side ran a wide, fast-flowing river. Surprised, I scrabbled around in the luggage rack above the policeman, and managed to find the map without waking him. Following the railway track east from Sivas I located the river. Its Turkish name, the Firat Nehri, meant nothing to me. Only when I followed the thin blue line down through Syria and out towards Baghdad, did I see the river's more familiar name – the Euphrates.

I grabbed my normally monosyllabic logbook and scribbled several pages of unusually emotional, florid prose – *pace*:

> The Euphrates! Is there another river which carries with it so many associations? How many times have I heard the name in church and at school? The river which ran through the Garden of Eden, one of the five rivers of the Apocalypse! Following its course on the map, its banks are littered with the names of the ancient cities it once gave life to: Mari, Nippur, Uruk, Larsa, Erdu, Kish. I think of all the hours I have spent in the Assyrian gallery of the British Museum haunted by the bas-reliefs and winged bulls brought back from Nineveh by Layard; now I am looking at the river its sculptors drank from! The same river cleaned the men who built the Ziggurat of Ur, watered down the wine in the goblets at Nebuchadnezzar's feast, and irrigated the Hanging Gardens of Babylon.... Et cetera, et cetera.

Despite the excitement I seem to have fallen asleep soon after writing this, for the next entry records that I was abruptly woken by the conductor shaking me by the shoulder.

'Eggspress, eggspress, change, change. . . .'

Trailing sleeping bags, water bottles and maps we were ousted onto a deserted stretch of line. No one had warned us that we were going to have to change.

'Eggspress he coming ten minutes,' shouted the conductor – unconvincingly – from the departing train.

It was still dark but you could smell that we had left the river behind. The ground around the tracks was hard and coarse, sprouting only litter and broken glass. Three other figures stood around silhouetted against the moon. We unrolled our sleeping bags, spread out the ground sheet and lay down beside the tracks, waiting.

We reached Erzurum at ten-thirty a.m., fourteen hours late.

It took several hours to walk across the town, a bleak expanse of bus parks, roundabouts and *kebabji*, as unattractive as Mersin, only larger. It is distinguished by its tiny university campus, possibly the only such in the world to be seasonally terrorized by wolves.

A lorry took us as far as the Seljuk bridge at Horassan, where the drivers stopped to swim in the Aras Nehri, a tributary of the Euphrates. They dived in fully clothed, stripped, and washed themselves, their hair and their clothes in an orgy of soap and splashing. Then they lay down, stretched, and dried themselves in the sun. When they were dressed, Laura was allowed out of the truck, and we sat under a clump of silver birch quartering watermelons and drinking the juice. We spent that night in the truck. After a breakfast of thin *chorba* soup we flagged down a *dolmus* heading for Dogubayazit.

It was a long journey, through wild, upland country. The ground and the stone was dark, black and volcanic and Yuruks were moving slowly across the planisphere flats, faces cast downwards, gypsy locks tied into buns and pigtails. Some drove cattle ahead of them.

We reached the town in a Neolithic late-evening gloom. Dogubayazit was full of sinister, swarthy Turks. A few had slit-eyed Mongol features. They wore ragged waistcoats and stared deadpan from open doorways. Tartar children were kicking a ball, wind raked along the street.

We found a hotel and lay flat on our beds. Sometime later the patron knocked on the door and told us he could rig up some hot water if we would like it. In so bleak an evening it seemed too good to be true. Unfortunately it was. When I got into the shower and turned the tap, the water spluttered, dripped, then gave up. I called Selim (we never discovered his real name, but named him after the manic Ottoman, Selim the Grim), and explained the problem. He fiddled around, banging the boiler and hammering the pipes. I stood by uselessly in my bath towel. He went off and returned with a spanner. He fiddled a bit more. Then he turned around.

'Wallah,' he whispered in undertaker tones, 'much hot, but no water.'

Laura tried to ring home from the post office; I sat in a café writing postcards to my friends and family. An air of terrible finality hung over that evening. Only a few miles away from Dogubayazit was the Iranian border. Tomorrow we would try and cross it. We had no idea what would happen. The officials at the Iranian Embassy in London had given us contradictory statements. One had said that we would be put in a bus and driven straight across the country. Another thought that we would be given a minder, our very own Revolutionary Guard, who would 'protect us' and keep us away from what the official picturesquely called 'sensitive areas'. A third diplomat who Laura confronted said what we would be left to our own devices – and the tender mercies of the Iranian people. It was difficult to know which of the options was the least appealing.

Our ideas of the country itself were little more developed. On the one hand we had seen perfectly civilized Iranians with our own eyes. But then again, we had seen the pictures: crazed revolutionaries burning effigies of Uncle Sam, incarcerating hostages and calling down hellfire on the Great Satan (Ronald Reagan) and the She-Devil (our own Prime Minister). The British Foreign Office was little more cheering. The man we had spoken to at the Iranian information desk had warned us that Britons were strongly advised not to visit the country. Two Englishmen, one a student, were languishing in Iranian jails on trumped-up charges of espionage, and a backpacker of our own age had been shot dead at the border. He was thought to have been carrying drugs, and to have panicked when they were discovered at customs. Then there were the reports of the Morality Police, the Islamic Secret Service set up by the Ayatollah Khomeini. They operated both in Iranian homes, through a network of informers it was said, and more publicly, through a fleet of plain-clothes agents. Men and women walking together in the streets could be stopped and asked to present a marriage certificate. If none was forthcoming, the Morality Police could order an instant public flagellation. They had similar powers in the enforcing of the Dress Laws. If anyone, men as well as women, were regarded as immorally dressed, wearing a T-shirt or simply revealing an ankle or a wrist in public, that person could be immediately arrested and flogged. Travelling unmarried with Laura was going to be risky, however much trouble we took with our dress. Finally there was the Gulf War and the dangers of bombing raids by the Iraqi airforce.

Laura did get through to her mother. Her news did not add to the general air of jollity.

'My mother says she has spoken to the British Embassy in Teheran.'

'Good. What did they say?'

'They say we are mad to cross the border.'

'Oh.'

'The Morality Police have stepped up their operations.'

'I see.'

'They've been ordered to double the number of public beatings every month.'

'Ah.'

'And apparently the Iraqis have been night-bombing Teheran and Isfahan.'

'Well at least we'll be able to sleep through that.'

'If we go.'

Neither of us spoke for several minutes. I sipped at my tea.

'My mother sends her love,' said Laura.

'How nice of her.'

I played with the tea leaves at the bottom of my glass.

'Have you written lots of postcards?'

'Lots.'

We sat in silence for another minute.

'Do you want some more tea?'

'No.'

'Well, what do you think?'

'What do you mean "what do I think?" '

'You know exactly what I mean.'

'What do *you* think?'

Laura considered.

'Well I think it would be a shame if we got killed.'

'So do I.'

'And I don't much fancy being flogged.'

'Not my idea of a good time either.'

'But I couldn't face anyone at home if we wimped out now.'

'So we go?'

I found a small-time crook in one of the *cay* shops. He had a
thin red scar under his right eye and he chuckled as he
changed our lira into Iranian rials at the black-market rate. He
put the lira under the label in his flat cap, winked, then slipped
out into the darkness.

Then we packed, set the alarm clock and went to bed early.

FOUR

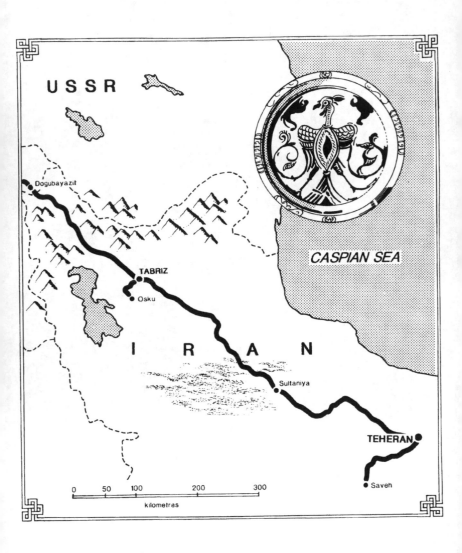

We were not a very cheery party in the bus the next morning. It had dawned hot and muggy, and the *dolmus* was two hours late. Laura and I sat in the middle row. Behind us were two families of grumbling Iranians. Ahead sat a solitary Japanese. His name, so he said, was Condom.

Laura had woken in a foul mood. She had snapped at Selim when he serenaded her with grisly stories of what Iranian Revolutionary Guards liked to do to immoral Western girls, then had sat in silence as she waited for the bus, staring pink and cross from her *chador* battle-dress. Ten minutes into the journey she had still not said a word.

'You're very quiet,' I said eventually. 'How are you feeling?'

Laura scowled from beneath her headscarf.

'Hot.'

'Never mind. Nearly there.'

'I know.'

'Happy?'

'No.'

Condom, I had already discovered, spoke no English. He sat picking his nails, staring out of the window. I looked at him. How could he be so clean, calm and neat-looking? It seemed as if hardly a speck of dust had fallen on him since he left Tokyo. He wore a white zipper anorak, dazzling in the sunlight; his mauve canvas slacks were neatly pressed and spotless. Even his rucksack appeared to have received a recent, energetic scrubbing. He did not look at all nervous. He looked bored. He was about to enter revolutionary Iran, a country ruled by religious extremists, but for all the apprehension on his face he might have been about to embark on a bus tour of the Home Counties.

I followed his gaze out the window. According to my guidebook, Mount Ararat and the remains of Noah's Ark lay to our left, but I could see only the ghost of the mountain's shape through the heat haze. I got out my pocketbook and began to quiz one of the Iranians on the basics of Farsi. I copied down the Persian for 'Yes' and 'No', and a few other essentials, then asked Laura what else we might need. She turned to the Iranian.

'What is the Farsi for "If you arrest me there will be a diplomatic incident"?'

The border post was a sprawl of concrete bunkers surrounded by barbed-wire fences. We passed the Turkish authorities without problem, and stepped through the border gate, beneath a huge portrait of Attaturk in a white tie. A Turkish guard gave me a reassuring pat on the shoulder.

'Iran good,' he said.

We found ourselves in a huge hall full of Iranian women in black *chador* attended by their menfolk. Many were sitting patiently on benches set along the walls while customs officials ransacked their cases. While we queued I asked my Iranian friend from the *dolmus* to guide me through the iconography of the Islamic Republic. We worked our way along the posters on the wall.

'That man is Ali-Akbar Hashemi-Rafsanjani, the Speaker in our Parliament. He is a very progressive mullah.'

'In what way?'

'He thinks we should conquer Iraq before we declare *jihad* on the satanic West.'

'I see.'

'Ah, this is Ayatollah Sadeq Khalkhali, the Judge of the Revolution. He is very good judge, very fast judge.'

'Very fast?'

'Oh yes, I have heard that once he sentenced fifty-six Kurds to death in one day.'

'Fifty-six? Are you sure?'

The man considered for a moment.

'Yes,' he said, nodding his head thoughtfully. 'I think fifty-six was the figure. Or maybe it was five hundred and sixty. It does not matter. They were not Shi'ites.'

He pointed to his left.

'These men here are Martyrs of the Revolution. You see that man? He was the leader of the *Motorihaye-i-Allah*.'

'What are they?'

'They are the Allah's Motorized Ones. In the Revolution they were fighting the Shah's army from their sacred motorbikes. This man was killed by the Shah's Zionist troops in the Jaleh Square Massacre. It was a black day for Islam.'

He went up to the next poster and studied the caption.

'This man here dressed up in women's *chador* for two years and was shooting policemen from beneath it. But he was caught by SAVAK, the Secret Police, and they killed him.'

'He should have shaved off his beard.'

'Perhaps. But we regard beards as very holy. The Prophet had beard and so all good Muslims grow one too.'

'Even when they wear *chador*?'

'Yes. Especially when they wear *chador*.'

After this the courtesy and charm of the Iranian customs officials was disappointing. Far from the beturbaned fanatics we had expected, they appeared almost embarrassed to have to search our rucksacks, and expressed polite approval at an illustrated book on early Islamic art they found in mine. No, they said, there was absolutely no question of being put in a bus and driven through the country, nor of being given an escort. The Islamic Republic of Iran was a free country. Where did we think we were? The Soviet Union? They all spoke perfect English, and seemed far more westernized than their counterparts on the Turkish side of the border.

The same was true of the Iranians we met outside. They were all returning from holidays in Europe and all possessed private cars, a luxury unheard of in Syria or Turkey. One family gave us a lift to the bus station in Maku, a few kilometres away. We sat in the back of their Alfa Romeo. Dariush had been at the Sorbonne, and now worked in a gum company. He expected to go on a business trip to England in a few months if he could get a visa. We swapped addresses. Dariush lived in Isfahan. If ever we were passing. . . .

As we sat waiting for the bus to Tabriz, the next town on Marco Polo's itinerary, we watched the mullahs speeding past in their sporty Renault 5s. Iran was proving far more complex than we had expected. A religious revolution in the twentieth century was a unique occurrence, resulting in the first theocracy since the fall of the Dalai Lama in Tibet. Yet this revolution took place not in a poor banana republic, but in the richest and most sophisticated country in Asia. A group of clerics was trying to graft a mediaeval system of government and a pre-mediaeval way of thinking upon a country with a prosperous modern economy and a large and highly educated middle class. The posters in the bus station seemed to embody these contradictions. A frieze over the back wall of the shelter spoke out, in the name of Allah, against littering. On another wall two monumental pictures of the Ayatollah were capped with the inscriptions in both Persian and English:

BEING HYGENIC IS DIRECTLY RELATED ON
THE MAN'S PERSONALITY.

and:

ALLAH COMMANDS THE RE-USE OF RENEWABLE
RESOURCES.

We had expected anything of the Ayatollah. But hardly that he would turn out to be an enthusiastic ecologist.

Tabriz, claims my ever-optimistic guidebook, has 'a slightly old-fashioned, early nineteenth-century atmosphere with a distinct Russian flavour'. In several hundred years of travellers' accounts these are the only words of praise I have been able to find for the town. No one seems to have liked Tabriz. Still less have they liked the Tabrizis. 'The people of the place are poor creatures,' says Polo, 'and the worshippers of Mohammet there are an evil race.' His Muslim near-contemporary, Ibn Battuta, reached a similar conclusion, although he admired the bazaar.

> Every trade is grouped separately in it. I passed through the jewellers' bazaar, and my eyes were dazzled by the variety of precious stones that I beheld. They were displayed by beautiful slaves wearing rich garments with a waist-sash of silk. They stood in front of the merchants, exhibiting the jewels to the wives of the Turks, while the women were buying them in large quantities and trying to outdo one another. As a result of this I witnessed a riot – may God preserve us from such! We went on into the ambergris and musk market, and there witnessed another riot like it, or worse. . . .

The reason for this volatile prosperity in the late thirteenth century was that the Mongol Ilkhans, the new rulers of Persia, had chosen Tabriz as their capital. From the time of Abaqa Khan, merchants flocked to its bazaars, where, in the words of a contemporary Tabrizi historian, they mixed with 'philosophers, astronomers, scholars and historians of all regions, of all sects: people of Cathay, of Machin, of India, of Kashmir, of Tibet, of the Uigur and other Turkish nations, Arabs and Franks'. The town must also have attracted to its slums the refugees left from a hundred cities destroyed by the Mongol conquests. Suburbs and buildings sprung up. In the single generation before Polo's visit, the city had doubled, tripled, quadrupled in size. Alone in the wastes left by the Mongol devastation, it had been possessed by a sudden burst of frantic, uncontrolled growth.

In this respect the atmosphere of Tabriz on our arrival exactly paralleled that at the time of Polo. The oil wealth of the sixties and early seventies had financed a population explosion in the town, and if the town had ever had an old-fashioned, Russian flavour it had certainly lost it by the time we visited. Like any other rapidly developing town in the Third World, Tabriz was surrounded by miles of ugly urban sprawl.

*   *   *

'*A une époque elle était très jolie. Mais aujourd'hui c'est plus la même ville.*' The Armenian pointed to a high-rise development facing his tiny bookshop. '*Ça c'était un jardin de thé.*'

His friend, a thin Armenian priest in his late thirties, nodded in agreement. He had done a PhD with the Dominicans at Blackfriars, spoke good English, and beamed when he discovered Laura was at Oxford.

'The Shah let them do this to the town. He allowed anything as long as it looked modern and Western. There used to be gardens everywhere, and rows of lovely merchants' houses. But at least people used to have fun in the Shah's days. You see that building?'

He pointed down the street.

'That used to be a cinema. Now it's another revolutionary lecture theatre. And over there. That used to be a bar. Now it sells non-alcoholic carrot milk shakes. You're not even allowed to play chess or backgammon any more.'

We had come into the shop simply to try and find a Farsi–English dictionary, but it quickly became clear we would not be let out without accepting a cup of tea. Tadios, the priest, led us into a room behind the shop where he lit a burner on the gas stove and put a small samovar onto the flame. He sat down at the table, knitted his hands, and began reciting a litany of disasters.

According to Tadios the economy was in ruins, the factories were all closed, there was massive unemployment and inflation was out of control. A kilo of butter apparently cost twenty thousand rials – nearly thirty pounds sterling. Sugar, meat and eggs were all rationed and because the mullahs spent all Iran's foreign currency on arms, imports had run out. It was impossible, for example, to buy light bulbs any more. Or paint.

'What about the political situation?' I asked.

'That's much more serious. Since the Revolution about forty thousand people have been thrown into prison for disagreeing with the mullahs. Many are just boys or girls. Thousands have been shot. Then there is the war with Iraq. So far about half a million people have been killed. Are you getting this down?'

He gave me a severe scowl as I scribbled the figures into my notebook. His initial light-heartedness had disappeared.

'We Armenians are not exempt. One of my brothers was killed fighting in the Ayatollah's war. Hundreds of our young have died. Yet do they treat us well in consideration of the Armenian blood they have spilled? No. I tell you, we are treated like fourth-class citizens. We are a cow, a donkey or a camel to them: they don't kill us but they beat us and make us work, using our skills for their ends.'

'Do they allow you to keep the churches open?' asked Laura.

'The churches, yes. But they have closed all our schools and clubs, stolen our lands and expelled our missionaries. We are powerless to protest. We have to put up with whatever comes, and make a show of supporting the regime. Conditions are very bad. Every day it gets worse.'

'Why do you stay?' I asked.

'Many of us have gone,' replied Tadios. 'As many as thirty thousand have fled, either to the USSR or to Syria. After the Jews were expelled our people were frightened. But most remain. We have to weather the storm. We Armenians have been in Tabriz for thousands of years, always ruled by others. We have suffered worse than this. We will survive. We are a resilient people.'

Tadios got up and poured three glasses of tea from the samovar. He put a sugar lump between his teeth and sipped the tea through it. When he had finished he continued.

'Sometimes I am worried, though,' he said. He spoke slowly, choosing his words carefully. 'For the last century or so there has been some sort of consensus across the world as to how civilized men behave. You know. There is agreement that men should not be killed for peacefully believing in an idea, that every man deserves a fair, impartial trial, that all men have a right to express what they think. Often these values have been ignored, but however evil a government may be, it has always paid lip service to them.'

He refilled our glasses.

'Well it's different in Iran now. The Ayatollah does not believe that all men are free or equal. He does not believe in human rights. He accepts only the morality of the Koran. For the first time in modern history a government has built as its bedrock the idea that all men are in bondage to Allah. That frightens me very much.'

The conversation in the bookshop left us in a gloomy mood. We wandered back to the hotel through pavements full of women in *chador* and khaki-clad Revolutionary Guards. On the street corners men were selling cassettes of the Ayatollah's sermons. Revolutionary tricolours fluttered half-heartedly in the breeze. On the way, we stopped in at the Azerbaijan Museum to see the famous gallery of Sassanian sculpture, but the display had been cleared away. The museum authorities had replaced it with a room full of line upon line of specatacles and false teeth. They belonged, so we were told, to the fallen 'Martyrs of the Revolution'.

The first time I awoke that night, the room was quiet, it was neither too hot nor too cold, and I could not understand what had woken me. Then, rolling over, I noticed the bump in the bed. It was not a wrinkled sheet. Nor did it seem to be the mattress. I felt under the bed. It was not a broken spring. I got out, turned on the lamp and lifted up the mattress. There lay an empty bottle of Glenfiddich whisky. I slung it away and went back to sleep.

The second time, I knew exactly what it was that had woken me. I sat bolt upright, muttered 'shit!' and streaked out of the room, up the corridor to the lavatory at the far end. I only just made it in time. It must have been the dubious chelo-kebab I had eaten the night before, or perhaps the cloudy water in the restaurant at Maku. When Laura awoke the following morning (predictably quite untouched by my bacillus) I was able to announce that I had 'been' seven times in as many hours. The news seemed to restore her spirits somewhat.

'You mustn't eat anything this morning,' she said. 'This afternoon you may have a small bowl of yoghurt. The bacteria in it will help fight whatever is in your stomach. On no account take any antibiotics. They will only weaken your resistance in the future and we can't have the expedition delayed any more than it is already.'

Laura spent the morning exploring while I trotted up and down the corridor. Languishing in bed I felt empty and weak and ill and sorry for myself. I wondered if I had a temperature. Perhaps I had dysentery. Perhaps I had caught one of those worms that you hear about in medical jokes. Some could grow thirty feet long; others made you go blind. To try and take my mind off my stomach I opened *The Travels*, but only found that Polo had suffered the same fate as I: 'The water causes violent and excessive purging,' he writes, 'nigh ten times a day.'

I turned to Robert Byron. *The Road To Oxiana* had done more than anything to lure me to Persia in the first place, and was always favourite reading in moments of depression. Tabriz, I saw, was the scene of one of Byron's funniest playlets (the Ghiboon! Ghiboon! muleteers), but the town of his description bore little resemblance to that I could see from my window. The 'plush-coloured mountains approached by lemon-coloured foothills' were now obscured by the decaying skyscrapers, windows boarded up with black eye-patches. The 'bronze statue of Marjoribanks in a cloak' must have come down with the Revolution, and disappeared along with the 'drinkable white wine and disgusting beer'. At least there was no sign of the athletic fleas which had disabled his companion, Christopher Sykes.

Laura returned at lunchtime. She marched over to my bed, felt the temperature of my brow and declared me cured.

'What you need,' she said, 'is some exercise. While you've been asleep, I have been doing some research. I went back to our Armenian friends and checked Polo's notes on Tabriz. The "charming gardens" have all gone, and according to Tadios the Armenians have given up weaving and handicrafts in favour of electronics and computers. But silk weaving still goes on in a village called Osku on the outskirts of town. Why don't you go off and discover it?'

'I'm not up to it.'

'You most certainly are. A little diarrhoea never did anyone any harm. Here, I've bought you some kaolin and morphine to keep you corked up.'

'Are you not coming too?'

'No. I thought I might stay behind and read. But make sure you are back by six. I've got tickets for the evening coach to Zanjan.'

On the bus to Osku, feeling like death and bunged up with enough kaolin and morphine to constipate the entire Iranian army, I cursed my weakness. Why did I always take the line of least resistance? But it was too late now. I arrived in Osku with an effective Persian vocabulary of one word. I got out of the bus and said it.

'*Abricham.*'

Around me were scenes of mid-afternoon torpor. Old men lay sprawled about in the shade of a tree. Some sipped tea through sugar lumps held in their teeth. It was very hot. A few of the old men looked up, but no one answered me. I took a glass of tea from a ragged *chai-khana* boy, and slumped down against the bark. Now was no time for battling against language problems.

An hour later the sun had sunk a little lower and I tried again.

'*Abricham,*' I said.

The old man next to me shrugged his shoulders.

'*Abricham,*' I said again.

This time, for some reason, it worked.

'*Abricham?*' said the Persian.

'*Abricham,*' I replied.

The old man muttered to his neighbour and a Chinese whisper passed around the tree. One of the younger old men on the far side of the trunk was deputed to guide me. The man got up, shook the dust from his flat cap, and led on through a maze of mud walls. I followed. After a few minutes we arrived at a small wicket gate set low in the wall. The old man knocked, waited, then knocked again. There was the sound of footsteps and the gate opened. A tall man in his late thirties came out. The old man rattled away in guttural dialect, pointed at me, shrugged his shoulders then grunted. The tall man smiled and extended his hand.

'How do you do?' he said. 'My name is Salim. I am the village schoolmaster. This old man says that you are a crazy foreigner who keeps repeating the same word over and over again. What do you want?'

'I'm looking for the silk farm. The word I kept repeating was *Abricham*.'

'*Abricham*?'

'*Abricham*. Farsi for silk.'

'Oh I see. I am sorry. You see most people around Tabriz speak Turkish. No one here understands a word of Farsi.'

Salim took me to the silk farm. It was another backyard affair, although by necessity a silk loom was a more complicated machine than the simple carpet loom we had seen outside Sivas. It lay in a small semi-subterranean mud-brick hut, attached to a courtyard house in a distant part of the maze. The silk was already wound onto seven weighted spindle whorls which Salim said came from a village nearby. The silk was spun out across the full five-foot width of the loom frame into a sheet of separate threads. At the far end a single man sat on a bench. He operated the entire machine. Two pedals alternately lifted and lowered two frames of tightly strung cross-threads. A chain shot a shuttlecock in between, across the width of the loom, carrying a line of silk alternately under and over the spread of silk threads. A comb then pulled the woven material towards the operator where it wound itself around a wooden roll.

The machine was completely unmotorized and apparently homemade. Its existence near Tabriz, where Polo talks of the weaving of 'many kinds of beautiful and valuable stuffs of silk and gold', again proves Polo's accuracy in all matters mercantile, although since the time of Yule that has never really been in doubt. I was shown the finished dyed silks and to the inexpert eye they looked exceptionally fine.

I was on the verge of haggling for a piece but, looking at my watch, I saw the time and rushed back to the square to catch the next bus back into town. It was never wise to anger Laura unnecessarily.

Sleep was impossible in the evening coach. We bumped along minor roads, stopping every half-hour at *chai-khana*. A sermon gabbled on the tannoy. We arrived at Zanjan thoroughly exhausted, well after midnight. Two hoteliers refused to take us; a third showed us to a windowless cubbyhole covered in graffiti. He said he had been to Aberdeen ten years before, and he smelt as if he had not washed since. To be fair to him there did not seem to be any provision for so doing in the hotel.

The next morning we rose early and caught a minibus filled with angry old women. Our destination was Sultaniya, now a deserted, crumbling spread of ruins, but once the capital of Mongol Persia. From it was ruled an empire which spread from the Oxus to the Euphrates.

When Polo passed through Persia on his outward journey the town had not yet been built and its site was still occupied by the cornfields of the Qongqur-Oleng, the brown meadows. But by 1324, when Polo died, the town had a population of well over a million. Sultaniya was built to the command of Ilkhan Uljetu, the great-great-great-grandson of Ghengis Khan, a Claudius-figure known to his family as 'the Muleteer' and distinguished in history books by his wide-ranging interest in religion. Born a Nestorian Christian and baptized Nicholas, he became in turn a Shamanist, a Buddhist and a Shi'ite Muslim, before finally converting to the Sunni faith. Having professed every available religion, he died of a digestive disorder in 1316.

Sultaniya was his great love. Much of his childhood had been spent hunting in its rich pastures, and in 1305 work began on what he intended to be the largest and most magnificent city in the world. Walls were built, 30,000 paces in circumference, and within, a network of streets rose up as if by magic. Nobles and officials were encouraged to build palaces for themselves and houses for their peasants. The vizier, the historian Rashid ad-Din, built a whole suburb which he modestly named Rashiddya after himself. It contained twenty-four caravanserai, a magnificent mosque, two minarets, a college, a hospital, fifteen hundred shops, over 'thirty thousand fascinating houses, salubrious baths, pleasant gardens, factories for paper and cloth-weaving, a dye mill and a mint'. Craftsmen and merchants were forcibly moved to the town, and each profession was assigned its own street. An idea was mooted to make Sultaniya a centre of pilgrimage. Uljetu began to build an enormous mausoleum in the centre of the town, intended for the bodies of the two most important saints of the Shi'ite world, Hussein and Ali. Only his conversion to Sunni Islam stalled the plan, which would have turned Sultaniya into a Shi'ite Mecca. The mausoleum became his own tomb.

Soon the place began to prosper. The historian Mustawfi said that nowhere in the world were there such fine buildings. The bazaars had no equal in the whole Mongol Empire.

> Everything imaginable could be found there. Precious stones and costly spices from India; turquoises from Khurasan and Ferghana; lapis lazuli and rubies from Badakhshan; pearls from the Persian Gulf; silk from Gilan and Mazandaran; indigo from Kirman, the wonderful textiles of Yazd; cloth from Lombardy and Flanders, raw silk, brocade, lacquer, oils, musk, Chinese rhubarb, Arab hounds, Turkish falcons, the stallions of Hijaz. . . .

There was even a Catholic archbishop.

Yet the prosperity was illusory. Magnificent as it was, Sultaniya was the creation of one man and it died with him. The day Uljetu was buried fourteen thousand families left the town. They had been forced to live there on the whim of a foreign ruler, and they took the first possible opportunity to leave.

Cool and pleasant in summer, it was unbearably cold the rest of the year. There was an inadequate water supply. It lay off the main Silk Route and was soon bypassed by merchants after they ceased to be forcibly rerouted there. Its star waned quickly. Uljetu's successors chose Tabriz as their capital. The population of Sultaniya drifted off; their mud-brick houses were washed away. It was not even a ghost town. The whole city simply disappeared. Only the vast mausoleum of Uljetu remained.

The first thing we saw was the great turquoise dome flashing in the early morning sun. It stood in the middle of an expanse of flat pastureland, completely alone, an artificial mountain of brick and tile. The minibus did not stop anywhere near it. It lay two miles off the main road and we had to walk.

The tomb would be an extraordinary building in any age, but as the first great monument to emerge from the ashes of the Mongol invasions it must rank as one of the supreme achievements of Mediaeval Man. The mausoleum was built only fifty years after the *medresse* at Sivas, but a great gulf separates the two. The architect not only equalled anything ever built in the Golden Age of the Seljuks, he completely surpassed it. He made the leap from the crude mediaeval splendour of Seljuk architecture to the subtle classicism that would reach its finest flowering in Mogul India. Already, in 1320, every idea in the Taj was fully expressed here in the plains east of Tabriz. The Taj is simply a refinement of Sultaniya; in its essentials it is restating an idea three hundred years old. Robert Byron wrote that the audacity of Uljetu's inventiveness made him think of Brunelleschi, but in fact there is no comparable leap in European architecture. It is as if St Peter's were to follow fifty years after Chartres.

The mausoleum is octagonal, rising to a parapet from which springs a crown of eight minarets and a bee-hive dome. The sides of the octagon are not equal. There is a main front, once the climax of the Mall of Sultaniya. On it a central doorway is flanked by six blind arches, three on each side, once filled with faience-work inlay. The wall of tobacco-brick rises up to an open, arcaded gallery. This, as Byron pointed out, is a façade, a new departure in Islamic architecture. It was built primarily to be looked at. Unlike almost all earlier Islamic buildings which were bounded by walls and faced inwards, the tomb of Uljetu is centred on the dome and looks out. It is a public building, built at the centre of an imperial capital, a concrete expression of the Emperor's power.

With its city decayed and its empire fallen, there could be something almost pathetic about so proud and vain a monument. Yet the building still retains great dignity and power. This is especially so of the interior. Nothing, except perhaps Hagia Sophia, prepares one for the sheer scale of the vast, unsupported, heavenward-thrusting dome. It encloses an enormous space, far greater than one would expect from the outside. It dwarfs the observer.

Because of this it is only gradually that one notices the fabulous detail of the stucco. Some of the colours and motifs are familiar from Seljuk tile work, yet as with the architecture the whole spirit of the design has been transformed. It is as fine and intricate as a lace ruff. In this subtlety, in the delicate pale colours and nervous, vibrant patterns, lies the key to the entire building. There is an unmistakable Central Asian or even Chinese spirit at work. Certainly those impulses are crossed with the native traditions, but their contribution is clear. For all the destruction wrought by the Mongols, *Pax Mongolica* allowed an unprecedented flow of artists and intellectuals over the length of the empire. When the apparently barren Mongol tree burst into flower in the early fourteenth century, it did so with a brilliance derived from cross-fertilization. It was from this fusion that all future Persian art would develop.

We wandered around the building all morning. To me, as remarkable as the structure itself was the eclecticism it revealed in the society that created it. As I circled beneath the dome I thought of the people who made up that world, who controlled the forces that must have been beginning to make themselves felt when Polo was here. Uljetu himself is a shadowy figure, clearly a great patron, but personally naive, even ridiculous. His vizier, Rashid ad-Din, however, can still be seen in sharp focus. Many of his writings and a large number of his letters have survived, and he emerges as a sort of symbol for the curiosity and·learning of his age.

Born of a Jewish family, he converted to Islam and entered the household of the Ilkhans. He gradually rose in the service and finally became vizier under Uljetu. The post gave him enormous power and extraordinary wealth: in lands alone his private empire stretched from orchards and vineyards in Azerbaijan, through date palm plantations in southern Iraq to water meadows and cornfields in Anatolia. But his letters do not reveal him to be an ambitious sycophant. He was above all an intellectual, and it is his love of learning rather than his statesmanship that emerges most clearly in his correspondence. For such a powerful man there is a surprisingly donnish tone to his letters. He writes to one friend from India thrilled at his discovery of spices unavailable in Persia. To another he extends an invitation to visit a garden he has just made at Fathabad. He sends 'fowls, honey and yoghurt' to a monastery and 'choice garments and a horse' to a scholar who has dedicated a book to him. To his sons he takes a sterner attitude. He writes to one regretting that the boy is occupying himself with astrology (Rashid had just appointed him Governor of Baghdad, and thought there should be more pressing concerns on his mind); another receives a sermon warning him against 'sloth, wine-drinking and over-fondness for music and dissipation'.

These warnings are mixed with passages in which he enthuses about his schemes to revive learning in Persia. For him much the most interesting aspect of Rashiddya was its college, and he writes regularly to his sons describing its progress. He took great pride in the number of Koran readers and doctors of theology, the 'fifty physicians from Syria and Egypt', the oculists and surgeons and bonesetters, and particularly the seven thousand students from all over the Islamic world. Many of these students he financed himself. 'It is most important that scholars should be able to work in peace of mind without the harassments of poverty,' he wrote. 'There is no greater service than to encourage science and scholarship.'

To large numbers, therefore, he gave not only houses but daily stipends, yearly clothing allowances and money for sweets.

It was to Rashid ad-Din that the Ilkhans entrusted the writing of the official history of the Mongol conquests. It was so well thought of that Uljetu went on to commission further histories, of the Turks, Indians, Chinese, Jews and Franks, along with a geographical compendium. It was planned to bind it all together into a single-volume world history, the *Jami al-Tawarikh*, a vast historical encyclopaedia, unique in the Middle Ages. The administration of the realm filled the day so the writing of the *History* had to be fitted in between sunrise and morning prayer. It took Rashid the better part of his life. Today it still makes fascinating reading. Particularly interesting is the *History of the Franks*, the only Islamic work on Europe to be written until the Ottoman period. His sources sometimes let him down (a papal text misled him into thinking that the Pope was in the habit of using the bent head and neck of the Holy Roman Emperor as a step to mount his horse), but on the whole it is as reliable as it is unique, and is full of surprising details: he knew, for example, that there were no poisonous reptiles in Ireland.

As a historian Rashid was well aware of the transience of human achievement and in his old age he became haunted by the idea that his life's work would be forgotten by posterity. He made elaborate arrangements for the preservation of his books, putting aside the vast sum of 60,000 dinars for their copying and translation, and for the provision of binding, maps and illustrations 'on best Baghdad paper and in the finest and most legible writing'. It was just as well. Rashid's enormous power and wealth could only create envy among his contemporaries, and at the death of his patron Uljetu, Rashid's enemies managed to secure his dismissal. Two years later the seventy-six-year-old man was summoned to court and accused of poisoning his former master. After a brief trial he was put to death. His head was carried through the streets of Tabriz with cries of: 'This is the head of a Jew who abused the name of God; may God's curse be upon him!'

His family was disgraced and their estates confiscated. Rashiddya was looted and burned. All the copies of his works that could be found were destroyed. Like a fallen Stalinist, he was airbrushed out of history.

But the memory of Rashid ad-Din was not extinguished. Copies of his work survived in translation in the libraries of neighbouring Muslim states, and while the names of his murderers are long forgotten, Rashid's life remains one of the most fully documented of his age. Along with Polo's *The Travels* his *Jami al-Tawarikh* is today the main historical source for Mongol Asia.

As we left Sultaniya the oasis gave way to a wasteland. It was not the romantic desert of Doughty, Burton or Lawrence and there were no dunes or camels or caravanserai. It was simply an arid flatland, a desolate, echoing emptiness.

There was virtually nothing to break the monotony: the odd, sad peasant working away in a tragic attempt to wring vegetable life out of the land, two marooned mullahs inexplicably throwing great stones at each other, a burned-out bus, a lost nomad on a scrofulous donkey. Through the middle ran the road, and from it the dust rose in clouds and swept into the bus, blinding the eyes and gritting the mouth.

As we drove on the landscape became harsher still. The scrub turned to sand and the shallow line of mountains that formed the horizon to our right dipped lower and lower and then hit the plain. There was a gap, a last craggy outcrop and then nothing. Never has a landscape filled me with such a sense of melancholy. It felt as if some terrible biblical disaster had taken place, that its inhabitants had been caught committing sodomy or castrating Israelites, whereupon fire and brimstone had rained down from the sky, leaving only a few dazed-looking nomads and an awful lot of sand.

Laura had fallen asleep soon after we left Sultaniya, so it was left to me to entertain our fellow passengers, who, with nothing to look at outside the window, had without exception focused their attention on us. Dirty and unattractive we might be, but in contrast to the wastes outside we were objects of considerable fascination.

'Where is your province?' asked a peasant across the aisle.

'Scotland.'

'They speak Farsi in Scotland?'

'Not as the first language.'

'And are there Mussulmans there?'

'There are some.'

'And Zoroastrians?'

'No, I don't think there are many of those.'

'In Isfahan it is the same: there are few Zoroastrians. It is a bad religion. They love fires too much.'

'The Scottish love fires but are not Zoroastrians.'

'By the holy Ka'ba! Your Scotland sounds a strange place!'

'Oh, it is. Some of the men wear dresses like women.'

'By Ali! Dresses? And a veil too?'

'No. But some of the women wear trousers.'

'You must take us to this province, Agah.'

'I would be delighted to.'

'Is many days' journey from Isfahan?'

'Many days.'

'Agah, that does not worry me. I do not mind long journeys. I once went to Teheran.'

When Laura awoke we wiled away the time reading *The Travels*. The next passage turned out to be one of the most intriguing in the entire book. Unusually, Polo's concern is not with the merchandise that can be bought and sold in some obscure burned-out caravanserai town. Instead, he tells a strange version of the story of the Three Wise Men:

In Persia is the city of Saveh, from which the Three Magi set out when they went to worship Jesus Christ; and in this city they are buried, in three very large and beautiful monuments, side by side. And above them there is a square building, carefully kept. The bodies are still entire, with hair and beard remaining. One of these was called Jaspar, the second Melchior, and the third Balthasar. Messer Marco Polo asked a great many questions of the people of that city as to those three Magi, but never one could he find that knew aught of the matter, except that these were three kings who were buried there in days of old. However at a place three days' journey distant he heard of what I am going to tell you. He found a village there by the name Cala Ataperistan, which is to say, 'The Castle of the Fire Worshippers'. And the name is rightly applied, for the people there do worship fire, and I will tell you why.

They relate that in old times three kings of that country went away to worship a prophet that was born, and they carried with them three manner of offerings, Gold, Frankincense and Myrrh; in order to ascertain whether that prophet were God, or an earthly King, or a Physician. For, said they, if he take the Gold, then he is an earthly King; if he take the incense then he is God; if he takes Myrrh he is a Physician.

Polo goes on to tell how the Three Magi arrived at the place where the child was born. They went in separately, and to their amazement each saw the child their own age: one found him young, the next in his prime, the third old and hoary. Then they all entered together. This time the child appeared its actual age, namely thirteen days old. No little impressed by this show, the Magi gave the child all three gifts. In return they were presented with a small closed box. There follows the strangest part of the whole story. In it the legend of the Three Magi is linked with what appears to be an account of the beginnings of Zoroastrianism.

And when they had ridden many days they said they would see what the child had given them. So they opened the little box, and inside it they found a stone. On seeing this they began to wonder what this might be that the child had given them, and what was the import thereof. Now the signification was this: when they presented their offerings, the child had accepted all three, and when they saw this they had said within themselves that he was the True God, and the True King, and the True Physician. And what the gift of the stone implied was that this Faith which had begun in them should abide as strong as a rock. For He well knew what was in their thoughts. Howbeit, they had no understanding at all of this signification of the gift of the stone; so they cast it into a well. Then, straightaway a fire from heaven descended into that well wherein the stone had been cast.

And when the kings beheld this marvel they were sore amazed and it greatly repented them that they had cast away the stone; for well they then perceived that it had a great and Holy meaning. So they took of that fire, and carried it into their own country, and placed it in a rich and beautiful church. And there the people keep it constantly burning, and worship it as a God and all the sacrifices they offer are kindled with that fire.

Such then was the story told by the people of that castle to Messer Marco Polo; they declared it to him for a truth that such was their history, and that one of the Three Kings was of that city called Saveh, and the second of Ava, and the third of that very castle where they still worship fire, with the people of all the country round about. . . .

At first sight the legend looks interesting, but wholly mythical. Reading it in the bus I thought it must have been an attempt by one of the last surviving Zoroastrian communities to give their cult a history that would fit in with the scriptures of the

Christians and Muslims who surrounded them. But one or two of the details in the story made me think twice about dismissing it in its entirety. According to Yule, the word 'Magi' used by St Matthew in his gospel does not actually mean wise men, as I had always assumed. The word is Persian, and so stands out in the Greek of the Gospel as a solitary foreign word. Its meaning is specific. It is the name of the ancient Zoroastrian priestly class. In all the elaboration that has grown up around the story in the Gospel, St Matthew's original meaning has been obscured. In the text the men who follow the star from the east are not the kings. Nor are they numbered or given names: this is all mediaeval legend. The Gospel text simply reads 'Some Magi came to Bethlehem from the East.' St Matthew's original audience would have understood that this meant a visit to Bethlehem of fire-worshipping priests from Persia.

As I read Yule's footnotes I remembered depictions of the Magi that I had seen on sarcophagi in the Vatican Museum and in the mosaics of St Apollinare Nuovo in Ravenna. The Magi are shown wearing trousers, tunics and pointed felt caps – the distinctive dress of the ancient Persians. This in turn reminded me of a story I had read the previous year in Runciman's *The First Crusade*. In the seventh century, the Persians had defeated the Byzantines and had swept through Palestine burning and pillaging every important building they had come across. Only one structure was spared: the Church of the Nativity in Bethlehem. According to Runciman, they made this single exception because over the doorway of the church was placed a huge mosaic showing the three Magi worshipping the Christ child. All three were shown in Persian dress. If the specifically Persian origin of the Magi is perhaps obscured today it was clearly understood into the early Middle Ages.

I had read Polo's story of the Magi before, but had never really taken it in. Now it suddenly seemed exciting and important. Most biblical scholars today understand St Matthew's story to be symbolic rather than historical. None of the other Gospels mention the visit of the Magi, and today it is generally

From the castle, Sis.

Cowherd, Sis.

Gunbad burial towers, near Erzurum.

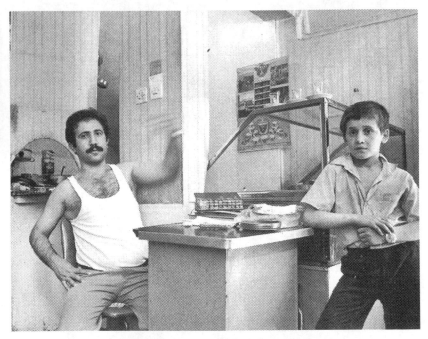

Mr Orhan Ghazi, Hotel Seljuk, Sivas.

Isaac Pasha Saray, Dogubayazit.

Goshawk, Erzurum.

Afghan shepherds, Quetta.

interpreted as a symbol indicating that all pagan religions would bow down before Christianity. Yet if it could be shown that the Zoroastrians had also maintained an independent tradition of a visit to Bethlehem. . . .

It certainly seemed worth investigating. According to my map, the town would be on the bus's route and we could at least find out whether the tombs described by Polo still stood. There was also the additional bonus, according to my guidebook, of 'a good *chai-khana* run by a retired Gendarmerie Captain where excellent Persian food and hard drinks can be obtained'.

We arrived at Saveh in the middle of a sandstorm. A high wind had sprung up and spiralling dust devils were raking the streets. We fled from the bus straight into the nearest *kebabji*, quickly abandoning any plans we might have had to search out the gendarme's *chai-khana*. Anyway, as Laura (somewhat heartlessly) remarked, the man had probably been shot for selling liquor and there was little point expending valuable energy looking for his widow.

The *kebabji*, like many other *kebabji* we visited, was a filthy, dirty place full of hungry-looking men. They munched chelo-kebab, and stared at us suspiciously. They stared all the harder when, having failed to find an English speaker, Laura and I began to act out the story of the Three Magi. Our mime-show was not a notable success. It soon became apparent that none of them knew the story. Nevertheless Laura's sketch of a *gunbad* (tomb tower) did provoke a reaction. There was a lot of nodding and murmuring among the kebab-eaters and a small boy was sent off to fetch a driver for us. While we waited for him to return we had lunch. We ate our way through four skewers, and as there was no sign of the boy we ordered four more. They arrived and we ate them too. There was still no sign of the boy. We debated ordering some more but in the end I was sent off to look for the boy instead. I left Laura deep in *Gone with the Wind*.

Outside, the sandstorm had died down. I walked down the gridded streets, searching either for the boy or a taxi driver.

Many of the shops and *chai-khana* were closed, and the midday heat had driven most of the people off the streets. Straight ahead, at the end of the main road, I saw a small crowd had gathered in the shade of a mosque gateway. I headed in that direction. Bound to be a taxi driver there, I thought. Always one near a mosque. Then I heard a voice behind me.

'Hey! You! What are you doing?'

I spun around. Behind me a man was getting out of an old mustard-coloured Mercedes. He was wearing khaki fatigues and on his head was perched a khaki pillbox cap. He was not smiling.

'Who are you? What are you doing?'

'I'm a tourist.' I said lamely, extending my hand. I knew from experience of Cambridge debauches that much the best way to deal with angry policemen is to smile innocently and say as little as possible.

'Passport!' said the policeman.

'I'm sorry but you see I've left it. . . .'

'No passport?'

'It's at. . . .'

'Get in!' said the policeman, pointing to his Mercedes. The seats were covered with furry pink material. I hesitated. The policeman put his hand on his pistol holster. I got in.

'It's really very easy to explain. . . .'

'No talking!'

We drove a short distance down the street, turned left and pulled into a small compound. I was marched out of the car and into the station. It was indicated that I should sit down. The policeman left me in a waiting room, watched over by a minion. I smiled at the minion. He stared glassily back.

I sat and waited for something to happen.

The minion continued to stare at me for a while. Then he stared into the middle distance. I noticed some ants on the floor. I became aware of the urge to pee. My mind whirred: *I've got a valid visa. I've done nothing wrong. Persians are nice people who have a reputation for hospitality. I'll soon be out. Might even make Isfahan tonight. Just think of those mosques. Forget that bladder. This man's got no right to keep me waiting like this. Why is he keeping me waiting anyway? Probably doing some work. Probably illiterate. Probably can't spell his own name. Probably. . . . Maybe these boys mean business. Stop thinking like this. It won't help. Think of something else. Think of sex. Not in Iran. Think of your family. You might never see them again. Stop this. You're upsetting yourself. Laura will come and rescue you.*

The policeman beckoned me in.

'You are from Britain?'

That's something, I thought. His English is quite good.

'Yes.'

'Britain is no longer the friend of Iran.'

'Oh you're wrong,' I said desperately. 'The British people love Iran. It's only Mrs Thatcher who is creating trouble. She's an unpopular, evil, repressive tyrant like the Shah.'

'You have purges in Britain?'

'Oh, yes.'

He looked justifiably suspicious.

'And you will have a revolution?'

'Soon. Tomorrow, maybe. Who knows?'

The policeman crushed his cigarette on the table top.

'Do you know what happened today?'

'What?'

'In Qom today five bombs went off in the market.'

'Oh,' I said lamely. 'I am sorry.'

'Maybe you are a spy.'

'Me?'

'You.'

'No.'

The policeman continued to look accusingly at me.

'NO. I AM NOT A SPY. Really. I am a student.'

'Maybe. Maybe not. How do *I* know?'

He shrugged his shoulders.

Then, in a flash of inspiration, I remembered my university library card. I fumbled in my inside waistcoat pocket, and found my card wallet.

'Look.'

'What is this?' he said. He looked at the card. Then he looked up.

'You are at *Cambridge*?'

'Yes.'

'Cambridge University?'

'Cambridge University.'

His expression changed.

'Oh, Agah,' he said. 'By the great Ali! This is the most famous university in the world.'

He examined the card.

'Ah, my heart! Look at this card. Expiry date June eighty-seven. Borrowing October eighty-six. Five vols. Oh, Agah. For me these are magic words.'

'For me too.'

'Agah. I am your servant.'

I sat up.

'Do you mean that?'

'Agah. You are a scholar. I am at your service.'

He did mean it.

Five minutes later we drew outside the *kebabji* in the policeman's limousine. A bundle of black silk crashed through the doorway.

'And where in God's name do you think you've been?'

'Reza,' I said to the policeman, 'meet my wife.'

After the ease with which we discovered carpets in Sivas and silk in Tabriz, we were almost surprised when we failed to find the perfectly preserved bodies of the Three Wise Men lying unmoved in their 'large and beautiful monuments, side by side'.

All afternoon, Reza drove us around the monuments of Saveh, but it was clear that none of the surviving buildings fitted Polo's description. There were several tomb towers. They were low and round, topped by saucer domes and stepped at the base like ziggurats. But they contained Muslim saints, and anyway were too young for Polo to have seen. The nearest contender was a *gunbad* on the outskirts of the town. It was called the Imamzada Sayyid Ishaq, and centred on a three-tiered brick burial tower. Around it an arcaded court and a honeycomb of minor tomb houses had grown up. The site was still being used for burial purposes, and it was clear that a lot of rebuilding had taken place, including the addition of a flanged, onion-shaped dome. Nevertheless we were just beginning to believe that the older part of the complex could have been the mausoleum described by Polo when Reza discovered an inscription. It dated the tower to 1277 – five years too late.

By the evening we had discovered that there were only two structures in Saveh which could have been standing in 1272. Both were minarets. They were extraordinary structures: wonderfully primitive and squat, ribbed by bands of crude but very striking brick-work patterns of Stars of David, angular floral motifs and scarcely readable kufic inscriptions. They reminded me more of Irish round towers than of the needle-like minarets of later Persian architecture. In one, that attached to the Masjid-i-Maidan, the bricks were so eroded that they had melted into one another, like chocolate running in the heat. Later I discovered that these were indeed the two oldest minarets in Iran, both dating from the early years of the Seljuk conquest: 1061 and 1110 respectively.

After six o'clock, when the sun began to sink, we rested beneath the pomegranate trees planted within the court of Masjid-i-Jumeh. Looking at the ancient minaret standing at the far end of the mud-brick boundary wall, I had the same feeling of discovery I had felt first on the hilltop above Sis. In their own way, the two towers were as remarkable works of art as the couplets of Omar Khayyam (their exact contemporaries) or, for that matter, the poems of the European *Vagantes* or the Troubadours. Yet how many people in Europe have ever heard of the Seljuks? Their obscurity adds to their glamour. The academic machine has never been able to subject them to the learned overkill that has taken the joy out of so much Western art. Long may it stay that way. Sitting in the shade of the pomegranate tree, watching the great red sun set over the desert, we agreed to give up looking for the tombs of the Three Wise Men. We thanked Reza and apologized for wasting his time.

This was not in fact the end of the search. One day after I returned to Cambridge I found myself in the University Library with nothing to do, so I set about researching the early historical references to Saveh. Strangely enough it appeared that until it was burned down by Ghengis Khan, the town was the site of one of the most important astronomical observatories in Asia. It is first referred to by the chronicler al-Muqaddasi, but the fullest account appears in the writings of his successor al-Khazwini. Khazwini says he saw rooms full of astronomical instruments, globes and telescopes as well as a vast specialist library. In other words, if the Magi had been watching out for a new star anywhere, it would have been in Saveh. The more I read the stranger the coincidences became, and it became increasingly tempting to see some sort of historical event linking the two legends of the Magi – the one written down in Palestine around AD 80, the other preserved in a Zoroastrian community in Persia as late as 1272.

Certainly it seems that St Matthew's original Gospel story is informed with a knowledge of Zoroastrian beliefs and practices. The Zoroastrian Magi were astronomers and did interpret dreams. Like the Jews, they believed in the coming of a Messiah. This was Shaoshyant, the son of Zoroaster, whose virgin birth, announced by a bright star, would herald the beginning of the reign of justice. It was thus quite reasonable for St Matthew to send some Magi to Palestine to look for a Messiah. More telling still is the fact that there is no precedent for gold, frankincense and myrrh being grouped together in the Old Testament. The three gifts are, however, often recorded together as Persian temple offerings. In the Gospel, St Matthew's Magi do in fact present genuine pagan offerings at the crib.

But it is the *significance* of the gifts in Polo's Magi story that is one of the strangest aspects of the whole legend. In the West, the gift of myrrh has long been interpreted as a symbol of

Jesus's mortality. This does not derive from any explanation in the Gospel, but because in the Old Testament myrrh is mentioned as an embalming herb. In Polo's story, however, myrrh is not presented in homage, as a symbol of Christ's humanity, but as a test. If the child accepted it, he would not be a king or a god but a physician. This idea makes perfect sense in a Zoroastrian context, for Zoroaster was seen as the Divine Healer. His earthly representatives, the Magi, developed this idea into a system of supernatural alchemy, practising medicine alongside their priestly functions. What is interesting is that the early Christian East also understood myrrh as a symbol of healing. While the Western Church went on to develop the concepts of Christus Rex, Christ the King, the Eastern Churches retained the old idea of Christus Medicus, Christ the True Physician. Polo's story appears to have retained the original, authentic symbolism of the three gifts, a symbolism which was very early rejected in the West – but miraculously retained by the fire worshippers near Saveh. Is it possible that Polo's story may thus preserve elements of an early Christian tradition of which St Matthew has given only an abbreviated version?

This passage of *The Travels*, above all others, cries out for proper scholarly investigation. What was the building that was described by Polo? Its significance was not understood by the local population, which suggests that it was not a Muslim building. Zoroastrians do not bury their dead (they leave them on Towers of Silence to be consumed by vultures), so it cannot have been any normal Zoroastrian monument. Was it once a Christian shrine? This, like many aspects of the story, raises far more questions than it answers. Nevertheless, the remarkable story told by Polo must at least open the *possibility* that the visit of the Magi to Bethlehem was an historical event, that these Magi came from Saveh and that an independent tradition of their visit to Palestine was maintained in the observatory town from which they set off, and in which they were eventually laid to rest.

FIVE

I awoke the following morning to find that Laura was up and dressed. She had her back to me and was poring over the map and her diary, tut-tutting to herself. Hearing me stir, she turned around.

'We're behind schedule,' she said. 'Look.'

She pulled the map on to my bed.

'It's taken us nearly four weeks to get this far.'

She drew her finger over the black line that represented our route.

'We're barely halfway to Lahore and I've got to be back in Delhi within the week. It's at least one thousand five hundred kilometres. If there's to be any hope of us making it we must leave this morning and travel nonstop for the next six or seven days.'

'Nonstop?'

'Yes. Nonstop. Day and night.'

Laura always struck the fear of God into me at moments like this.

'In other words I suggest you get up immediately. I'll be downstairs and am going to set off in three minutes.'

She swept out. For a few seconds I toyed with the idea of letting her go, but decided against it and dragged myself out of bed. I pulled on some clothes, dashed downstairs and caught Laura just as she was marching off towards the bus station.

The place was crowded with piratical-looking Afghans. Given a few peg-legs, eye patches and macaws they could have happily stood in as extras for *Treasure Island* or *The Pirates of Penzance*. Yet although they all shared a look of unmistakable villainy, they were otherwise a remarkably diverse bunch. The most imposing was a six-foot-five giant who squatted against a wall of the bus station latrines, combing his flowing beard and peering down his long, aquiline nose at a tiny Iranian who was sitting nearby, nervously guarding a pile of belongings. He wore a smart double-breasted waistcoat, a voluminous *charwal chemise*, and over his shoulder he had draped a thick, brown *patou* blanket. He reminded me of woodcuts of young Hercules in the ancient Latin text books at school. Nearby stood a blue-eyed Rasputin with a shaven head, a thick, tangled beard and a malevolent grin. To his left were three much younger Afghans. They gathered around a large flap of bread, munching loudly and chattering away in guttural Farsi. They had downy, embryonic beards and all wore a style of *charwal chemise* that I had not seen before, buttoned at the shoulder like a dentist's smock and obviously *de rigueur* among the young bloods of the expat Afghan community. They differed only in their headgear. One wore a conventional turban of white muslin, another a wrap of brightly coloured printed cotton, the third an embroidered filigree cap, its front cut away in the shape of a double-cusped arch. I left Laura in their midst, looking after the rucksacks, while I went to find out about bus times.

My enquiries led me to the station manager's office, where I found a small officious man, his legs up on a table, reading a newspaper. Above him hung an outsized Ayatollah. He spoke perfect English.

'There is nothing going eastwards until tomorrow,' he told me without lowering his paper, 'but there are some Afghans who have chartered a bus to Zahedan. They are leaving this afternoon. You could try them and see if they have room for you.'

He lowered the paper to reveal a balding head and a pair of steel-rimmed spectacles.

'Personally I wouldn't recommend it. Afghans are animals. I would wait until tomorrow. Quite apart from the smell, those barbarians are more than likely to rob you of everything you possess.'

'You don't like Afghans?'

'No, I don't like Afghans.'

He raised the paper.

I returned to find Laura sitting on my rucksack, her hands folded purposefully on her lap. The group of young Afghans who had been sitting beside her had moved off to a safe distance, and it suddenly occurred to me how well her black uniform suited her. It brought out her more Victorian qualities. I debated whether to tell her so, but decided against it and instead reported the station manager's recommendations.

'William, you know very well we are not in a position to pick and choose our transport. These Afghans look perfectly nice and even if they didn't we would have to use their bus anyway. You don't seem to understand the timescale we're operating on. Go and ask the mullah over there if he'll take us; he appears to be in charge.'

The decision made, I trotted off obediently. The mullah was a smaller man than many of his flock, and on his nose perched a pair of enormous black spectacles. I addressed him in my best Farsi.

'I . . . we . . . *bus* . . . Zahedan.'

'Do you speak Turkish?' asked the mullah.

I repeated the request in pidgin Turkish. He looked me up and down.

'Where are you from?' asked the mullah. 'What is your job?'

'I am from Scotland and I am a travel writer.' I replied.

'What is Scotland?' asked the mullah.

'It's a bit like Inglistan.'

This caused much excitement. The Afghans who had gathered around the conversation bobbed up and down crying, 'Inglistan! Inglistan!' in a loud stage whisper. But the mullah had not yet finished his interrogation.

'What is "travel writer"?'

In Turkish, travel writing sounds a very sinister occupation.

'It's a man who travels for his living,' I said.

'Like a bus driver?'

'Yes, like a bus driver.'

The mullah translated this for the Afghans. This went down well too; perhaps Afghans have a special regard for their bus drivers. There was a gleeful chorus of 'Bussyman! Bussyman!' from their ranks.

'Come with us,' said the mullah. 'Our bus welcomes you.'

Then they were upon us. With excited cries of 'Bussy! Bussy!' Rasputin and another Afghan with Mongoloid features hoisted me up in their arms and carried me towards the bus, and I had a last blurred vision of Laura fighting off a similar welcome before I was whipped up through the doorway, along the aisle and deposited in a window seat. Laura joined me seconds later. At least they were not expecting me to drive the thing.

It was a rather comfortable bus and the seat coverings were decorated with pictures of a single pink rose and a jumbo jet taking off. Proud Afghan faces beamed at us from all sides.

'I have never seen so beautiful a bus in Scotland,' I said.

They looked delighted. From a bus driver it was indeed a compliment.

The whole troup poured in, and while we waited, the mullah led a series of prayers. The men who recently looked as lawless as the Wild Bunch suddenly became as pious as a coachload of nuns. Bearded faces were lifted heavenwards and the bus echoed with the sound of 'Al Hamdulillah! Praise be to God! Allah Akbar! God is all-powerful!' They then embarked on a spirited rendering of the Kalimeh, a short chant that sounds more like a rugby song than the Credo, its nearest Christian equivalent, and off we set into the dismal wastes of Baluchistan.

The atmosphere in the bus was as friendly as the desert outside was forbidding. A crescent of wide-eyed Afghans stared at us curiously. I smiled back for a while, gesturing amicably, then looked out of the window and finally fell asleep.

When I next awoke the bus was deserted; it was pitch dark and very cold. There was no sign of Laura. I pulled on my jersey and set off to see what had happened. It suddenly occurred to me that she might be in trouble. I remembered the station manager's warnings. While I had slept she might have been stripped, robbed or abducted. She might even have been raped; stranger things had happened, and after all she was the only woman on the bus. For a second I panicked. How could I have allowed myself to sleep with so dangerous a crew of cutthroats all around us? How would I possibly explain to her mother, an even more formidable lady than Laura?

My worries proved needless. Jumping out of the bus I saw Laura's hooded form standing a short distance away in the sand. Hearing me behind her she turned around and hissed at me to keep quiet.

'Shshsh.'

'What's happening?'

' "Songs of Praise".'

Twenty yards away, in a swirling desert wind, in the pitch dark, a long straight line of Afghans lay prostrated, face down in the sand. They howled the *Kalimeh* to the directions of the mullah who stood facing them with arms raised. The performance lasted over twenty minutes, until the worshippers were driven back into the bus by a sandstorm. We set off and didn't stop again until we drew in to eat at a restaurant standing beside the road, alone in the billowing desert wastes.

We arrived at Zahedan soon after dawn, and spilled out into the bus station feeling cold, dirty, exhausted and bad tempered. There was little about Zahedan to cheer us up. It is a shabby place, built of sand, sand-coloured, surrounded by sand and subject to a sand desert's impossible climate. Like Dogubayazit, the last town in Turkey, it exists only as an overnight stop on the way to the border, but unlike its Turkish counterpart it is a relatively recent creation. Historically, there was never a major trade route leading from Persia south-east towards India, for the dangers of the Afghan Pamirs and the Hindu Kush have always been considered less formidable than those of the shifting sands of Baluchistan. Only those unable to take the northern route from Meshed through Herat to Kabul and Kandahar – such as the Mogul emperor Humayun fleeing to Persia in 1542 from an invasion of India by an Afghan army – attempted the southern crossing.

But now, perhaps for the first time in a thousand years, the northern road has been closed. Entering Afghanistan from Iran became difficult after the Soviet invasion of 1979, but after the construction of a high tension fence and a formidable minefield running the entire length of the border in 1985, crossing has become virtually impossible, even for the Afghan *mujahedin*.

Even if we had had unlimited time it is extremely unlikely that we would have succeeded in following Marco Polo through the minefields into Afghanistan, and in the circumstances there was no alternative but to miss out that stretch of his journey and make a long detour through Pakistan. It would not be until Tashkurgan, the first town in China, that I would rejoin his route. Thus, during the night, we had for the first time since Ayas left the main Silk Road. About one hundred kilometres after Yazd it turns north towards Meshed, and instead we had continued south-east.

Nothing about Zahedan indicates that it now commands the only open road linking Europe with India, China and the East. It has only one, sordid, hotel, the eighty-four-kilometre road to the border post at Taftan is unmetalled and unused, and no bus service plies the route. We prowled around the bus station for half an hour looking for transport and were eventually directed to the office of a Baluchi businessman at the far end of the town.

'We want a bus to the border.'

'Oh, Agah! This is a sad day for me!'

'Why?'

'Because there is no bus.'

'There must be some way of getting to the border.'

'Agah! Praise be to God! There is!'

'Well, what is it?'

'My brother has a humble mini-transit.'

154

'Can we hire it?'

'By the beard of the prophet, Agah, that is a difficult thing that you suggest.'

'Seems perfectly simple to me,' said Laura.

'The Queen is wrong. To take the mini-transit to the border is a difficult thing. Many bad mens are along the way. They are not developed mens. They have guns, Agah. They want baksheesh. It is an expensive business.'

'We have money. How much will it cost?'

'God is my witness! Eight hundred rials.'

'Eight hundred rials? Are you mad? Eighty you mean.'

'Agah, eight hundred rials. I tell you only correct price. You want tea? Mozaffir Baroum? MOZAFFIR BAROUM? Bring tea for our guests.'

'To hell with tea, we want to get to the border.'

'God has sent you to me this day, Agah! Our friendship is ordained by heaven! Eight hundred rials.'

'That is a ridiculous price.'

'Oh, how can you say this thing?'

'Because we could buy a mini-transit for less.'

We haggled for half an hour but the man did not alter his figure. We made for a restaurant nearby and decided to wait for some other travellers with whom we could share the fare. It was a small, stuffy room with stained walls, flaking, stripy wallpaper, striplights and a sawdust floor. There were three rows of tables and chairs, and a television was raised on a bracket on the far wall. It was empty except for the owners, two ill-tempered Baluchi brothers, probably twins, with long Assyrian beards and mountainous turbans. On their feet they wore black and gold plastic sandals with raised platform heels. We ate several little omelettes with onion and chillies in them, and sat and waited. We ordered some more chilli omelettes. We sat and waited a bit longer. I began to moan about the heat.

'Oh, William, do stop complaining.'

'Why?'

'It could be worse.'

'How?'

'Well,' said Laura, thinking hard, 'you could be ill. You could have really bad diarrhoea.'

'I have got diarrhoea.'

'So have I. There is no need to make so much noise about these little crosses. And anyway, if you have got such bad diarrhoea you shouldn't be eating so many omelettes.'

We sat waiting; I reread *Crime and Punishment* while Laura read *Gone with the Wind*. We had only been in Zahedan five hours but already we were desperate to leave. It felt like the tenth circle of hell. Slowly a trickle of other passengers joined us there: Joe, a Ghanaian engineer, on his way to a new job in Japan; Ramesh, a westernized Pakistani studying Islamic law in Teheran; Nazir, an unhappy-looking Iranian surgeon practising in Pakistan. Everyone was in a hurry to leave Iran; but none of us was prepared to pay eight hundred rials to do so. We ate some more chilli omelettes and cursed the brigand who owned the mini-transit.

'Dat mun is a bum,' said Joe.

'A bun?' said Nazir.

'No, a *bum*. B-U-M. No-good mun. Bastard.'

'Really something bastard,' agreed Ramesh.

'He has no religion,' said Nazir.

We sat complaining for half an hour until we all got bored of that, and then Joe fell asleep, Ramesh went off to shave in a basin at the far corner of the room and Laura disappeared to go and harass the mini-transit owner. When she had gone Nazir leant over the table and whispered to me.

'Sir, are you married to that beautiful lady?'

'Yes,' I said, out of habit rather than any particular wish to deceive. 'My wife and I have been married three years.'

'And you have children?'

'Sadly not.'

'You are lucky fellow to be married,' he said. 'But to have no issue is a terrible curse.'

'I have high hopes,' I replied. 'My wife has good child-bearing hips.'

156

'I want to marry Europe girl. Does Europe girl like Iran man?'

'I'm sure she does.'

'I have big moustache.'

'Very big.'

'I want Europe wife who is good Muslim and has – how do you say? – big hip. But is very difficult to find. Very difficult indeed.'

'Yes, I can imagine.'

'Your wife is follower of Jesus?'

'I'm afraid so.'

'Once I met Europe girl. She was follower of Jesus. Very tall. Big hip. I asked her to marry me.'

'Did she say yes?'

'No.'

'I am sorry.'

He picked at his chilli omelette. It had gone cold, and had congealed into a heavy lump on his plate. Resting beside it on the table was Joe's head. He was snoring loudly.

'She was good lady,' said Nazir. 'She would have borne me many childrens. Now she is gone and I am alone.' He shook his head, paused and then continued: 'Today I go to Pakistan. I have no friends there, no relations. The Pakistan men they say, "This Iran man he is bad fellow," and they do not talk to me. The Pakistan women they do not look. Sometimes I wonder if God has forgotten me.'

'It can't be as bad as that.'

'It is. Maybe it is worse. I have a little surgery in the desert south of Quetta. The people are Baluchis and always they kill each other. Always they are giving grenades to each other's houses. To be a surgeon in the desert south of Quetta is a terrible thing. For me they are dark days.'

'Well, why don't you stay in Iran?'

'Iran is worse than Pakistan. In Iran I was sent to the front and made to – how do you say – amplify?'

'Amputate?'

'Yes, I was made to amputate. They say to me – "Nazir you

must take this finger, or Nazir you must remove noise. So all day I am cutting noises and always there are more noises to cut. And all the time the guns are going BAM BAM BAM, and my scalpel it trembles. I would prefer to die alone without wife and without issue in Pakistan than to stay at front. But either way my life it is lived in shadow.'

Nazir poured out his heart until well after noon. He was like a character escaped from a terrible nineteenth-century German novel: the sort of manic who totters from disaster to disaster through books one, two, three and four, only to commit suicide on page nine hundred and eighty-seven. Like his German counterparts his melancholy was contagious. After a couple of hours I too believed that I would die alone and without issue, in Zahedan, surrounded only by snoring Ghanaians and half-eaten chilli omelettes.

He was still describing the amputation of Baluchis when a party of twenty Afghans wandered into the room. Their leader walked up to Nazir and asked him a question. It was the one occasion I ever saw him smile.

'What did he ask?' I said.

'He says he is looking for some men to share a mini-transit to the border. They want to leave immediately.'

The words fell like manna from heaven.

The next few hours were dreadful. The stuffy morning had turned into a suffocating afternoon. The journey was slow and the mini-transit was hot and our shirts stuck to the plastic seats. On a good day, in a good vehicle, along a good road, you could cover eighty kilometres of desert in forty minutes. On that day, in the mini-transit, it took an hour and a half to get the engine started and well over four hours to drive the thing to the border post. The problem did not lie with the mini-transit itself but instead with the Baluchi, who forgot to fill its tank with petrol, and with the Afghans, who did not have a single passport between them.

At the first checkpoint we were held up for two hours in a thicket of limp barbed wire, while the Afghans argued with the Revolutionary Guards and waved a grubby identity document. The document was written in Pushtu and the Revolutionary Guards spoke Farsi and they were bored and had nothing better to do than argue. At the second checkpoint, the sun throbbed down and the Guards leant on their Kalashnikovs. All they wanted was a bribe and we were only held up for thirty minutes. But at the third checkpoint the Revolutionary Guards were officious teenagers, anxious to prove themselves. We left the Afghans there, barely half a kilometre from the border, kneeling down to pray in a barbed-wire pen, while the teenagers looked on, tittering like schoolchildren.

In a few minutes we reached Taftan, the border post. On one side a mange-struck dog lifted its leg on a 'Death to America' mural, opposite a bitch lay in the shade, sunk in a coma of inanition. The customs hut reeked of stale urine and something else dead. One guard wore a string vest, another, the customs officer, sprawled over a wooden desk, amid passport stamps, ink pads, half-used biros and an old safety razor. He was dressed from neck down in khaki. Above him hung a framed picture of Khomeini, Khamanei and Rafsanjani, the Trinity of the Islamic revolution, with an English caption, 'We don't want anything except the establishment of Islamic rules and laws all over the world.' Ramesh and Joe sat outside, Laura leant against a doorjamb, and I stood behind Nazir as he discussed the 'present' necessary to 'reopen' the border. The customs officer burped, studied Laura and myself, and then remarked perceptively, 'I suppose you two are Europeans.' We discussed a price, had our rucksacks checked, paid an additional 'departure tax' and then waited while the guards sent away a Baluchi tribesman and his goat. It took half an hour to find a key to the border gate. At just after seven-thirty we walked into Pakistan.

*   *   *

It was like coming up for air. I rolled up my shirtsleeves for the first time in over a fortnight. Laura whooped, tore off her black headscarf, tossed her black stockings over the barbed wire, and danced a jig on her *chador*, to the delight of the Pakistani customs men. After the Iranians they seemed as unthreatening and familiar as Dixon of Dock Green. All around lay objects that I hadn't seen for three years, since I had left India. The customs officers sat on rope-strung *charpoy*, drinking little white china cups of milk-tea. Two sandalwood incense sticks were burning beside the immigration ledger. A bicycle leant against the outside wall.

'What is your good name, sahib?' asked the customs officer 'and what is your mother country?'

I told him. They were the old familiar Indian questions. he took down a few more formal details.

'Are you wod?' he asked.

'What do you mean?'

'Are you and lady wod?'

'That's not English.'

'You do not speak English, sahib?'

'I am English.' There didn't seem any point in muddling the issue by bringing in Scotland.

'You have some words of English?'

'Yes, a number. I AM AN ENGLISHMAN.'

This was an aspect of India that I had forgotten.

'Are you and lady *wod*?'

He made an obscene gesture with the first finger of his right hand.

'Wed! Do you mean are we wed?'

'Yes, are you and lady wod?'

'No.' It was the first time we had admitted to not being married since Dogubayazit.

'Not wod?'

'NO I AM NOT WED.'

'I am sorry, sahib. I am not understanding your English. I think perhaps that you are not speaking English good. Sahib, may I ask what is your mother tongue?'

'I've told you that. I am an Englishman and I speak English extremely well. Jesus Christ.'

'Jesus?'

'He is calling on his God,' explained the second customs officer.

'You are angry with me, sahib?'

'No, I am not angry with you, I just want to get on.'

'Sahib, just one question.'

'What?'

'You like bottom?' He pointed at me.

'I look like?'

'No, no sahib. You *like* bottom? I like bottom.'

'I don't understand,' I said. I really didn't.

'Bottom, bottom,' he said wiggling his head from side to side in the Indian manner. 'I like bottom. I am bottom fan. You like bottom?'

'Well, I like some bottoms,' I said.

'You do like bottom? You are bottom fan?'

'Yes.'

'All English people like bottom.'

'Oh yes,' said the second customs official. 'All Pakistani people like Imran Khan, all English people like Botham. He is your famous English cricketer.'

The guards let us change in their hut. I wore a blue *charwal chemise* that I had bought that morning in Zahedan, Laura her beloved pink T-shirt and flowery Laura Ashley trousers; she put on two pearl earrings and made a neat little bonfire of her *chador* and veil. When she was ready we set off with Ramesh, Nazir and Joe to find some transport. Thanks to the delays of the morning we had missed the weekly bus by seven hours and the next train did not run until Sunday, three days away. We agreed to club together and hire a taxi to take us the six hundred and fifty kilometres to Quetta.

The village of Taftan lay half a kilometre from the customs compound, and we smelt our way towards it following the odour of spicy cooking in the evening breeze. After the horror of the desert heat, that evening's reprieve was especially lovely. The sun sank huge and red over the Koh-i-Sultan, and in the villages the people were lighting their lamps and squatting outside their houses cooking over sweet-smelling dung fires.

The village was poorer than any we had seen in Persia, but to European eyes it was infintely preferable. The faces of the men were craggy and rugged, and had none of the effeminacy of the Persians. There was a restrained dignity in their bearing. They regarded us with only casual curiosity and with none of the self-demeaning humility of most Indians. They wore long flowing *charwal chemise*, of a more generous and baggy cut than those of the Afghans, and many of the women had their heads uncovered.

Nazir led us through the alleyways of the village. While the women worked slaughtering chickens and thumping grain in great granite querns the size of boulders, the men sat around in groups of three or four smoking *bidi* cigarettes and staring silently into charcoal braziers. Others engaged in less peaceful pursuits. We were still in a Muslim country, governed by strict Islamic law, but judging from the shrieks of Baluchi laughter that emerged from some huts there was a lot more alcohol around than we ever saw in Iran.

Without warning Nazir dived ferret-like into one such hut and from within we could hear the sound of haggling. He emerged with a very wobbly-looking Baluchi youth. 'It is settled,' he said. The youth tottered off and we followed, intrigued as to quite what it was Nazir had succeeded in settling. We were led along several more dark pathways between groups of huts, and finally drew to a halt in an enclosure at the far end of the village.

In the middle something large and rectangular crouched beneath a covering sheet. Laura and I looked at each other, baffled. Then, with a single movement, the Baluchi hauled back the tarpaulin and unveiled a pristine new Toyota pick-up truck.

After days of venerable, crowded buses which had lost their last shock absorber long before the Revolution, the pick-up smacked of wicked luxury. The Baluchi caressed its bonnet lovingly, then produced a cloth from his *charwal chemise* and wiped clean the spot he had just touched. It was a magnificent vehicle. Its speedometer promised wild, illegal speeds, its two rows of oatmeal-covered seats looked more welcoming than any double bed. There was a cavernous boot. A heater which worked. A reliable-looking engine. A radio. We loaded up our luggage with the same excitement as a child putting batteries in a new toy at Christmas. The Baluchi hiccupped and turned the ignition. The pick-up purred into life. We set off.

There followed one of the most exhilarating hours of the entire trip. We shot crazily through the crowded streets of Taftan, pursued by a pack of hobbling beggars, before tearing off into open country, raising half the Baluchistan desert into a thick cloud in our wake. The road was terrible, reflecting the state of Irano-Pak relations, but that only added to the excitement. The Toyota nose-dived into great potholes then lurched out again to the accompaniment of drunken cries from our driver and equally enthusiastic cheers from ourselves. We would cruise along for a few minutes, then down we would plunge into another wadi or a deep wind-eroded shell-hole before emerging into the open desert and the moonlight. All the time the radio blared loud music from Indian films which the Pakistanis enjoy just as much as their Hindu neighbours:

Verse 1:

> Ek, do, wail, wail, wail
> Teen, char, wail, wail, wail

(screeching instrumental interlude)

Chorus:

> Shriek, shriek, HOOEE, HOOEE
> Shriek, shriek, HOOEE, HOOEE

(another painful instrumental interlude)

Verse 2:

> Pange, che, wail, wail, wail
> Sart, arht, wail, wail, wail

> (third instrumental interlude)

Chorus:

> Shriek, shriek, HOOEE, HOOEE
> Shriek, shriek, HOOEE, HOOEE

> (more terrible instruments)

> > *(Repeat for half an hour*
> > *getting ever louder, and*
> > *more piercing.)*

Already the tedious wastes of southern Iran seemed worlds away. There the tarmac roads, the regular bus services and the taped sermons which are played during them, had largely anaesthetized any sense of adventure. This was very different. Careering at breakneck speed along a route distinguished from the open desert only by the odd, ambiguous marker-stone and the faint tyre-tracks of previous vehicles, with our safety in the hands of a drunken psychopath, we felt just as much at the mercy of fate, fortune and the elements as any Bedu caravan of Doughty.

This was, however, more of a recommendation to Laura and me than it was to the others, and after a few hours they looked distinctly raddled. Ramesh and Nazir had both made the journey many times before, and for them, as Nazir frequently pointed out in funereal tones, the journey was not an adventure, merely an irksome necessity. He treated us to a long monologue on the subject of Pakistani backwardness and corruption – there was some story of millions of Iranian rials given by the Shah for the rebuilding of the road disappearing after the Revolution. Ramesh took offence and sunk into an irritable nationalistic grump. Perhaps it was just more uncomfortable in the back. Joe's spirits had sunk, too, which was not really surprising as his head kept hitting the roof, and his growing misery channelled itself into a violent dislike of Psycho. He became convinced that 'dat mun is snoozin' at de wheel' and to keep him awake began insulting him and poking him in the ribs. The driver took revenge in the only way he could, by speeding up and making the going as rough as possible, swerving into potholes, bumping over marker-stones, and turning up the din on his radio.

Laura tried to soothe them by suggesting they look forward to the delights of Nek Kundi, the first settlement marked on the map. It was, she said, probably full of charming little res-taurants offering the very best in Baluchi cuisine. That only made it worse when we arrived. As the only settlement for four hundred kilometres, the cartographer who created our map had given it the status of a provincial capital with print bold enough to imply a thriving town with hospitals, schools, cinemas and shops. Nek Kundi in fact consists of six sheds, one tea house and a *charpoy*. There was no restaurant and the inhabitants refused to sell us any food. We sat in a circle on the carpet of the tea house and dipped some bread we had bought in Taftan into a tin of cold baked beans belonging to Ramesh. A little boy threw stones at us. It wasn't quite the feast we had hoped for. Laura called to Psycho that he should join us for *cay*.

'Leave him,' said Ramesh. 'He is bastard.'

'He is driving, he needs *cay*.'

'He is bastard. Really he thinks something dirty.'

'Mun's a bum,' agreed Joe. 'He snoozin' at de wheel.'

'Really bastard,' said Nazir. 'When we say go fast, he go slow. We say go slow, he go fast. We say drink *cay*, he go piss.'

'Really something bastard.'

They got back into the pick-up with the same enthusiasm as three convicted criminals being led to the scaffold. Although sleep was impossible, Laura and I sank into a state of exhaus-ted, befuddled semi-consciousness, and thereafter the night took on a confused and even surreal quality. Sometime soon after midnight, we ran into a herd of camels. There must have been nearly a hundred of them and the first thing we saw was the dust cloud they raised looming ahead of us in the head-lights like a bank of swirling sea fog. They were running towards us along the road and when we slowed down, you could hear the thundering of their hooves on the ground long before you could see the camels themselves. Then they were all around us, banging into the pick-up, muzzling its sides, lolloping along aimlessly with the whole desert to wander in, yet pressing around us as closely as a herd of cows in a Dorset lane.

Then, at about three o'clock in the morning, in the middle of the Baluchistan desert, we ran into a speed trap. Psycho was jolting along at one hundred kilometres an hour when from behind a sand bank a police Jeep pulled out and drove into the middle of the road. We braked and the pick-up skidded to a halt only a few inches from the police vehicle. There was no question of a speeding ticket and a telling off; while we sat watching, helpless, four policemen seized Psycho and set about him with *lathi*. They beat him down onto his knees, delivering terrible blows to his ribs, his shoulders and his hands, which he clasped about his head. The violence took place in complete silence; there was no explanation from the policemen, no cry from Psycho, no protestations from us. Then they doffed their caps at Laura and I and returned to their Jeep. Psycho was on the ground, sobbing. Then as we looked on, he got up, wiped away the tears with the back of his hand and drove on. For two minutes no one said anything, then Laura, through Ramesh, asked whether he was all right.

'Why did they do that to you?'

'Because I am a Baluchi.'

'Aren't they?'

'No Baluchi is a policeman. The police force is Punjabi.'

'And they do that to all Baluchis?'

'Not all.'

'So why to you?'

'Because I haven't got a driving licence. Every time they beat me.'

'It's happened before?'

'It happens every time.'

166

'Then why don't you get a driving licence?'

'I cannot afford it. It costs much baksheesh.'

The Baluchi shrugged his shoulders and drove on.

Just after dawn we hit a tarmac road. It was cold. All night we had been so shaken and jolted that we had hardly noticed the temperature. Now, on tarmac, we felt the chill and huddled up, hands in our sleeves, shivering. The morning light was brittle and steely and in the silence it lit up a depressing landscape of bleached, white solitude; wadis, hills, cliffs and, everywhere, sand.

Then, as the sun was beginning to rise, we turned a corner and there opened up before us an extraordinary vision: a caravan of two hundred camels, winding their way to Quetta along the dip of a dry water course. In the lead was a huge Afghan, and behind him another, bearded like an Old Testament prophet, with a hooded falcon on his wrist. Some of the animals were loaded with tents and possessions, while one carried a woman hung from head to foot in gilded silk, with a grille for a face, sitting as upright and proud as a duchess in a landau. Behind the camels trailed a string of goats and sheep, and behind them a pack of little boys, ragged and dirty, chased the sheep with sticks and brought up the rear.

Two hours later we arrived in Quetta. After the camel caravan the desert had slowly sprung to life. At first we had come across a few temporary groups of black, felt *kibitka*, the deserted tents of Afghan shepherds, and after that some large white marquees belonging to relief workers. The black tents stood in groups of four or five, randomly placed in the middle of hillsides; the white ones stood singly in the valley bottoms surrounded by pens of barbed wire and besieged by small armies of Afghan refugees. The roads began to fill with trucks, brightly painted and inscribed in English: PUBLIC CARRIER–HORN PLEASE O.K.! USE DIPPER AT NIGHT. The letters were surrounded by medallions of Urdu calligraphy and flourishes of arabesque, broken into small fields of bright primary colours, like enamel inlay in cloisonné jewellery. After that came water buffaloes, plodding bullocks, *tonga* pulled by blinkered horses, and swarms of yellow autorickshaws squealing like kicked pigs. There were the film hoardings, with the stars bathed in gaudy blue and inferno orange, and there were the buses, all filled with luggage, leaving the people to spill out onto the roof. We passed posters of a man in a lambskin hat, and a small political rally led by a tractor and two Baluchis. They were carrying a banner and shouting. We saw peasants leading flocks of sheep to market, and a trailer piled high with farm workers carrying embroidered bags, sacks of grain and big tin pails of thickly set curds. There were no Sikhs, and the women wore heavy white *chador*, but otherwise the scene was instantly recognizable: it was a typical, busy, noisy, dirty, stinking, bustling, loud, hot town in north India. It was like a homecoming – a sight which I knew well, and loved, and had not seen for three years.

We dropped Ramesh and Nazir at a hotel, and got back into the pick-up. Ramesh went in to look for a room, but Nazir came up to the window, and clasped our hands.

He said: 'I will never forget you.'

'It was good to meet you, Nazir.'

'You do not know what it is to me to have met you. Really you do not. Never has anyone cared so much about my life and my misfortune.'

'It was a lot of fun listening.'

'I have little joy now.'

'We'll go for another nightmare drive sometime, don't you worry.'

'You cannot know how much I enjoyed talking to you.'

'I enjoyed it too.'

'Always I will remember.'

'We'll organize a reunion in Zahedan and eat some more omelettes.'

'May Allah protect you.'

'Good luck in Baluchistan.'

'Write to me.'

'I promise.'

We shook hands one last time and Nazir kissed me on the cheeks. We drove to the station and paid off dear old Psycho. It was all curiously moving.

We bought tickets to Lahore. The train did not leave until mid-afternoon, but exploring Quetta was out of the question. All we were capable of was collapsing. But before I did so, I had another promise to fulfil. Leaving Laura and Joe in the waiting room, stretched out on Bombay Fornicators (ingenious Anglo-Indian wicker chairs with extended arms on which you can put up your feet), I set off to find the telegraph office. Here I sent two telegrams, one to my parents to tell them that I had left Iran, another to my great aunt to tell her I had arrived in Quetta. In the late twenties and early thirties Quetta had been her home for nearly a decade while her husband was the Commander of the Western Command, India. She had been swept off her feet by a General in the Coldstream Guards and after her marriage was suddenly transported from a large, cold country house in Norfolk to the wilds of Baluchistan.

She managed the transition effortlessly. She was in many ways the conventional English memsahib, but bothered to learn fluent Urdu, and, teaching herself to paint, began wandering around the bazaars in a long white muslin dress, with an easel and a box of water colours. For years she worked away and produced a whole series of small, precise paintings of tribesmen and traders, always against the same copper-green background, always the same handsome, rugged faces wrapped in great swathes of turban, rising from a grey *charwal chemise* or the stiff-necked jackets of the Muslim League.

Before the war, she returned to England, and when her husband died she moved to the Suffolk coast, where I used to visit her from Cambridge. She would sit, engulfing a chintz-covered armchair, chins wobbling, and while describing her golden Quetta days and the breaks for the Simla season, she would quietly drink me under the table. She had pickled herself, and this was the secret of her great longevity. Before luncheon, sipping at glass after glass of very strong gin and Dubonnet, nibbling at Bombay Mix, she would sink into paroxysms of giggles from which it might take five minutes to disentangle her. Then without warning her head would suddenly drop to one side, and she would fall fast asleep, snoring loudly. Often she would not wake until teatime. She got my telegram, and wrote a letter home thanking me for it in large, spidery writing, but I never saw her again. She died a fortnight after I returned, and at her funeral they draped a Union Jack over the coffin. As the body left the church they played 'Land of Hope and Glory'.

By two-thirty, after a snooze, a shower and a curried mutton cutlet, we were ready to fight our way onto the train. We came out of the half-light of the waiting room, and blinked at the dazzling brightness of the platform. It was roofed with whitewashed planks and lined with elaborate fluted columns of Sheffield steel. The roofing cast a little shade onto the platform, but it was hot and light and noisy after the waiting room, and hard on the eyes. Everyone was on the move. Scarlet-coated coolies tottered past with great mountains of luggage on their heads. *Cay* wallahs pushed trolleys along the platform and shouted *'Garam Cay! Garam Cay!'* The trolleys contained great gleaming Thermos vats, and looked like the hair-growth shells from *Heath Robinson at War*. Men selling samosas passed along the windows shoving their greasy triangles through the bars, and other salesmen passed after them offering combs, Korans, digital watches, shaving brushes, worry beads, scissors and sunglasses. There were uniformed policemen swinging *lathi*, soldiers with bulging kitbags, boys with jars of water, mullahs, groups of their pupils, sleeping-car attendants with white jackets and gleaming brass buttons.

And in the middle stood the train. The carriages looked as if they were born long before Independence, perhaps in Crewe or Derby, and had seen better, grander days. But it was impossible to believe that they had seen busier ones. Laura, Joe and I had between us good experience of Third World rail travel, but none of us had ever seen anything like the 15.30 Lahore Mail. It was far worse than the usual, mildly irritating discomfort one expected: it called to mind the total chaos of the Partition trains. It wasn't a matter of finding a seat, that was a hopelessly optimistic dream. Nor was there any point in fantasizing about snuggling up in that last unused bit of luggage rack. On this occasion one simply hoped to get onto the train. Already the corridors, loos, doorways and running board were all packed. We walked up and down the length of the train looking for a point of entry, then spotted a single window which had lost its bars.

We heaved Laura up on our shoulders and precipitated her forwards into the train. She fought her way in, flaying like a Saracen. Once she had established a bridgehead, we followed. A coolie passed up our rucksacks, and we manoeuvred ourselves over legs, shoulders, tiffin cans, sacks, tables and benches, until we found ourselves above the central passage. Then we burrowed down. Within a few minutes we had reached the floor, and seconds later had excavated enough space to place our rucksacks down on it, and ourselves on them. We looked at each other and beamed with satisfaction at our achievement.

Then the beggars appeared. How they got to us confounded all known laws of physics; some strange miracle of agility transported them. But they appeared with the speed and appetite of ducks to breadcrumbs, hobbling, shrieking, tapping, circling above our shoulders, hands extended downwards. They hovered above Laura and me, peering down into our faces, then they noticed Joe. They stopped, cocked their heads, and looked back at us.

'What is this?' asked one in English.

'He is from Ghana,' I replied.

'A Ghana,' he whispered to his companions.

'Ghana, Ghana, Ghana,' they echoed.

'Name's Joe,' said Joe.

'He speaks,' said the first beggar.

'Yeah, and a whole lot else besides,' said Joe.

'Listen!' cried the beggars.

Claw-like hands caressed Joe's hair. A leper's stump felt his gleaming, matt-black skin. One woman cackled.

'Hey, get out of heah!' said Joe. 'Yeh, get, shoo.'

He rose to his full height, and brushed them away. They scuttled out of the carriage, but were still taunting him from the window when the train pulled out at 15.30 exactly.

'Damn animals,' said Joe. 'Dat's wad de are. Damn animals.'

I read a bit more of *Crime and Punishment*. I had just got to the bit where Raskolnikov axes the old women, when I felt completely and utterly exhausted. I curled up on the rucksack and fell fast asleep. There, lying in the middle of the corridor, with half the population of Quetta stepping over me, poking, asking the terrible monotonous round of oriental questions (Who? Where? Why? Oh Sahib, just one more question, How?), I fell into a deep sleep, and did not wake up until nine o'clock the following morning.

Everything was green. After days of sand, shale and desolate aridity, the colour was almost violent to the eyes. The railway was raised on a bank, and all around us stretched the rich expanse of the Punjab. Even the word implies fertility: *pange ab* are the five waters, Chenab, Ravi, Jhelum, Sutlej and Indus; between them they made the Punjab into one of the great cradles of civilization, the Mesopotamia of Middle Asia, and still the breadbasket of India and Pakistan.

It was the monsoon season, and the first rains had already passed. Out of the window I could see paddy fields stretching away on either side. Villages were everywhere, and seemed to grow organically out of the soil, to be part of the teeming, procreating richness that formed so complete a contrast with the lifeless half-continent that separates the Punjab from the Mediterranean. Only after passing through Turkey, and the terrible wastes of Persia, can you fully comprehend why the Islamic paradise is a garden, a green dream of fertility.

The day passed uneventfully. After four days and three nights of nonstop movement I ached to stop. I fantasized quietly to myself: in my mind most of that day was spent having long, hot baths, rolling in cold, clean sheets, putting on new underpants, things like that. I longed to be on my own for a moment, to bask in just a few seconds of privacy. But it was not to be. As ever the peasants kept their distance; the problem lay with the pseudo-Europeans. The first to intrude on my dream world was a dowdy creature, who sat nursing an engineering textbook on a seat a short distance away. I could see him eyeing me up for a while before he actually put down *Elementary Engineering Drawing*, and came over to me.

'*Crime and Punishment*,' he said. 'What is this?'

'It is a novel,' I said.

'You are studying this book?'

'No, I'm reading it for pleasure.'

'Why pleasure?'

It was a good question. It wasn't one of those novels that particularly improved on third reading.

'Well, I suppose I rather enjoy reading novels.'

He eyed me suspiciously.

'What,' he asked, 'is your qualification?'

The blind spot.

'I haven't got a qualification,' I said.

He gave me an I-thought-as-much look, and returned to his seat.

We passed more paddy, edged by a slow-flowing irrigation channel. It was almost empty of people; only one or two men stood, bent over the plants, knee-high in water, picking, or perhaps grafting the young shoots. Then we left the paddy and passed drier fields of date palms and banana groves before returning to the thick clumps of boggy marsh grass and the jungle-book green of further fields of ripe rice. I remember passing a level crossing: a herd of elephants stood queueing behind the barrier as nonchalantly as a line of Ford Escorts would behind a similar barrier in England.

At Multan the train stopped for an hour and we all left the carriage to look for lunch. We ate another plate of curried lamb then returned to the train, where we fought to retain our places. I snoozed for a while, then awoke and got into conversation with Firdausi, a young Pakistani lawyer. His family were *Muhajir*, refugees from India, and before Partition had been wealthy Delhi-wallahs, merchants in the Chandi-Chowk, where they had cornered the Delhi end of the jute trade. He was very handsome, with dark intelligent eyes.

'Of course,' he said, 'to be a lawyer is not the most interesting of careers.'

'Really?' I said. 'I know some lawyers who love their jobs.'

'Oh don't be absurd,' he replied. 'Everyone knows lawyers are the dullest people in the world. The only thing to be said for it is that it pays well.'

'Is it easy to get a job?'

'Yes, quite easy. In Pakistan there is much crime, especially in Lahore. There is a lot of work for lawyers.'

'What sort of crimes? I thought Lahore was a stable city, very prosperous and clean.'

'No, no,' he said, his face lighting up, 'it's full of crime: murder, robbery, rape. Especially rape. There is more rape in Lahore than any other city in Pakistan.'

'Really?'

'Oh, yes. Last week in my street a fourteen-year-old girl was raped. She was a pretty girl. Educated. Would have been very beautiful. But her face is now badly scratched; she will find it hard to get a husband.'

'How horrid. I always thought rape was a Western disease.'

'Oh it is. But we're very westernized in Pakistan.'

We arrived in Lahore at five o'clock, and took an autorickshaw to the house of a Pakistani friend from Cambridge, Mozaffar

Quizilbash. Mozaffar was an Eton-educated aesthete, a kind of Muslim Harold Acton, who lived with his canvasses and library in a palatial house in Shah Jamal, a leafy suburb in the north of the town. We were greeted warmly.

'William, darling, how wonderful to see you. But, my dear, you're absolutely *filthy*. And why are you wearing those beastly Paki clothes?'

He rustled his silks.

'When you've washed you can come and see my new painting. I've been agonizing over it for a week. It shows Love struggling, hopelessly, against Desire.'

SIX

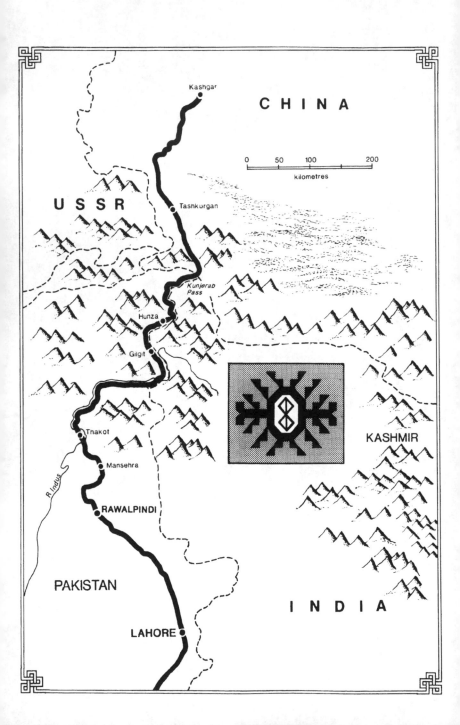

From the logbook

Lahore
26.vii.86

Too much food, too much tea, too much lying in bed, too many baths.

I'm writing in the icy air conditioning of Mozaffir's drawing room. Mozart is playing, I am wearing clean clothes and the logbook is resting on a Louis Quatorze bureau. Mozaffar is lying on a divan at the far side of the room. Occasionally he reads out snippets from his paperback: Freud's *Leonardo da Vinci*. In this unlikely setting the last week has been spent in relaxation. It seems onerous even to have to walk outside to the swimming pool. Any whim is attended to by Mozaffar's servants, who exist here in almost Victorian profusion: bearers, drivers, *derzi, mali, dhobi*, cooks and chauffeurs.

A bewildering hierarchy serves to create employment for this household. If the Begum Quizilbash wishes to buy a chicken from the bazaar a complicated ritual is enacted. She must first summon the bearer who will take the order. The bearer will send the cook's boy to the secretary who will give him the appropriate number of rupees. The cook's boy will then approach the sweeper who will approach the *mali* who will be sent off to the bazaar to negoitate the purchase with his cousin who keeps the bazaar hen-coop. At this stage the Begum might remember that she has guests and will tell the bearer that she wants not one but three chickens. The cook's boy will be sent for again. He will re-approach the secretary and then find the sweeper who will find the *mali*'s boy and send him off after the *mali*. Finally the Begum will remember that the Indian Ambassador is a vegetarian, the previous two orders will be countermanded, and the *mali*'s other boy will be sent to fetch back his colleagues while the *chowkidar* will go off and buy some *dal*, rice and potatoes.

Such pampering is fast softening any resolve to continue the journey. The day of departure has already been put off twice. Lahore is one of the most beautiful towns I have seen: if it were not teetotal I would see very little reason ever to leave it.

Yet amid all this luxury I am like a spoilt child who has lost his nanny. Laura left yesterday, on the midday flight to Delhi. Having travelled overland this far, she discovered that the Indian border was closed because of a Sikh uprising in the Punjab. Her first impulse was to attempt to cross illegally with the camel-trading nomads who live in the desert between Baluchistan and Rajasthan. We eventually dissuaded her from this, and instead Mozaffar took her to the Pakistan Airlines office to buy a ticket home to Delhi. On being told that all the places were booked she displayed a last flash of the spirit that got us this far, safe, and two days ahead of schedule. According to Mozaffar she assaulted the unfortunate airline official threatening him with a diplomatic incident and telling him to pull his socks up. She was off at noon the following day, welcomed onto the plane by a delegation of Pakistani officials. They seemed to be under the impression that she was a member of the Royal Family.

When travelling with her I could never decide whether she reminded me more of Boadicea or Joyce Grenfell, but now she has gone I find that I am already missing her. It was she who propelled me this far, and now I do not know what are the chances of reaching Peking without her. Louisa, my companion for the rest of the journey, flew in two nights ago, dressed as if for the King's Road.

She is much easier company, but is made of different, slighter stuff. She is beautiful, delicate and fragrant. In the mornings she sleeps late (now, though it is nearly noon, she is still slumbering) and when awake she moons around only semi-conscious of the Begum and her household. The reason, I fear, is that she is in love – and not with me. Those days are gone for ever. Her new boyfriend is Edward, and he has already been sent two ten-page letters; (I cannot remember ever receiving more than three pages).

But there are other more serious problems facing the expedition. We simply do not have the necessary permits either to go up the Karakoram Highway or to cross into China over the Kunjerab Pass. The Pakistani Embassy in London told us that the former document could be arranged, with difficulty, but according to the Chinese Tourist Service ('service' here being a poetic euphemism) the latter permit is almost unobtainable: it can only be authorized by Peking, takes at least six months to arrange, and then is generally granted only to groups of octogenarian Americans.

All, however, is not lost. Before we left Britain Laura wrote to enlist the aid of the Permanent Under-Secretary at the Foreign Office. I have the reply in front of me. It is written on a piece of thick, heavily embossed paper with a lion and unicorn at the top right-hand corner. From it, it would appear that the Permanent Under-Secretary is a personal friend of Laura's. It also appears that the embassy in Peking has been instructed to contact the Chinese Foreign Ministry to arrange an express permit, and that the embassy in Islamabad is waiting to help us with the Pakistani Civil Service. Of all the wonders I have seen Laura work over the past few weeks this must be the most spectacular. I have one other letter in front of me. This I organized (although acting on Laura's instructions). This second letter is written on paper so thick it almost approaches parchment and bears the great crest of Trinity

College, Cambridge. If it is to be believed any obstacle to our expedition could well prove a major blow to the study of the Orient as we know it:

To whom it may concern:

This letter introduces William Hamilton-Dalrymple, a scholar of Trinity College Cambridge who has been researching the journey of Marco Polo and the conditions of China at the time of Kubla Khan. Currently he is completing his research by following Marco Polo's journey to Peking.

Mr Hamilton-Dalrymple's expedition was carefully scrutinized by a committee of academics at Trinity, and he was given a large grant by the college to undertake it. As a representative of that college I am happy to vouch for the academic objectives of the expedition and for the personal qualities of its members. The expedition's results will issue in work which we much hope will considerably enlarge the knowledge of the history and culture of the People's Republic of China in both Cambridge and England as a whole.

I hope that Mr Hamilton-Dalrymple will be granted such permissions as he may require to continue and complete his remarkable and important journey. On behalf of Cambridge University, I should like to express gratitude for whatever assistance you may be able to afford the expedition.

Simon Keynes

(Dr Simon Keynes MA
PhD, FSA, FRHS
Fellow of Trinity College,
University Lecturer.)

And this, God bless his soul, from a man who received five essays from me in an entire academic year, and they on the Anglo-Saxons. The Begum Quizilbash in her capacity as Minister of Health, Special Education and Social Services, is also contributing a letter to my collection. She promises that it will outline how any obstacle to the expedition could well endanger the Pakistani Health Programme. The trouble is that the Chinese cannot possibly be taken in by this nonsense. Reading these letters they will expect a one-hundred-man team of wizened professors, veteran Sinologists and a whole United Nations health delegation. They certainly won't believe it when Lou and I turn up at the Islamabad Chinese Embassy in our rags, without a single word of the Chinese language and only the most superficial grasp of Chinese history. They might even rescind our visas.

The Begum has just swept in and announced that lunch will be ready in quarter of an hour. I had better wake Lou.

When I think back to that time in Lahore, in my mind's eye I always see the town at twilight. It is the best time of day. The great Indian sun hangs over the domes and the *chattri*, and it is then that you notice the smells: the sweet, heavy scent of dung fires, a whiff of monsoon-wet casuarina, the odour of sweating coolies. In the bazaars the barbers are shaving the businessmen and the *derzi* are bent over their sewing machines. There are garish film hoardings at the corners and beneath them there are men selling samosas and men selling fruit. There are quacks and cobblers and women in black calico cowls. There are children, everywhere and all about, flying kites and playing cricket, scuttling after the bullock carts and chasing the pidogs. Most evenings we would wander through these bazaars, or perhaps visit the Shalimar gardens. I would sit and write my logbook while Mozaffar would tell us the names of the trees: the eucalyptus, the banyans, the deodar and the mulberries. Lou would sketch.

But the place that interested me most was at the far end of the Anarkali bazaar, beyond the madness of rickshaws and the terrible, crashing traffic. The Ravi flowed there, and on its banks, within a walled garden, there stood the tomb of the Mogul Emperor Jehangir, the World Seizer. It interested me not because it was a particularly fine tomb (although it was) nor because Jehangir was a particularly important emperor. My interest derived from the works of one of my travel-writing heroes, Tom Coryat. The 'Odcombian legge-stretcher' as he liked to be known, was a buffoon, a figure of fun at the court of James I. He was renowned for an 'irrepressible loquacity' and according to one contemporary 'he carried folly in his very face'. But he was an astounding traveller, and he is the first Englishman known to have visited Asia purely for pleasure. 'I have an insatiable greedinesse of seeing strange countries,' he wrote, 'which exercise is indeed the queene of all pleasures in the world.'

Coryat discovered his love of travelling during a quick trip around Europe in 1608 which he wrote up in *'Coryat's Crudities, Hastilly gobbled up in Five Moneths Travells. . . . Newly digested in the hungry aire of Odcombe in the County of Somerset, and now dispersed to the nourishment of the travelling Members of this Kingdome'*. Despite its title the book was a bestseller, and was celebrated for its revelations into the many strange sights of the continent (including a famous passage on the ostrich at Fontainebleau: 'it is a very foolish bird: for whereas hee doth sometimes hide his necke behind a bush, he thinks that nobody sees him, though indeede he be seene of every one'). Having published a supplement to his *Crudities (Coryat's Crambe Now Served as a Second Course to his Crudities)*, Coryat set off with the intention of walking overland to the court of the Great Mogul and there riding upon an elephant. He 'traced all this tedious way afoote with no small toyle of body and discomfort', living 'competentlie for a penny sterling a day'. He crossed the Indus ('as broade againe as our Thames at London') and finally entered the dominions of the Great Mogul sometime in the spring of 1613. His reward was a view of Lahore in its Golden Age. 'It is one of the largest cities of the whole universe,' he wrote, 'for it containeth at least XVI miles in compasse and exceedeth even Constantinople in greatnesse.' Agra he thought 'in every way inferior'.

For all his buffoonery Coryat was a perceptive observer, and it is his mix of humour and accurate detail that makes his account so riveting. His description of Jehangir is typical:

> This present prince is a verie worthy person. Hee is of complexion neither white nor black, but of a middle betwixt them. . . . He is of seemlie composition of bodie, of stature little unequal to mine, but much more corpulent than myselfe . . . it is said that he is uncircumcised, wherein he differeth from all the Mohometan princes that ever were in the world.

On his 'exoticke wanderings' Coryat picked up Arabic, Farsi, Urdu and Hindu, and it was his skills as a linguist that enabled him to include the spicy details of bazaar gossip that enliven his picture of Mogul India. It brings the Emperor and his court far more vividly to life than any of the formal histories which have survived:

> One day in the yeere, for the solace of the King's women, all the trades-men's wives enter the Mahal with some-what to sell, in the manner of a faire. The King is broker for his women and with his gaines that night he makes his supper, no man being present. Now observe that whatsoever is brought in of virill shape, as instance is reddishes, so great is the jelousie, and so frequent the wickednesse of this people, that they are cut and jagged for feare of converting the same to some unnaturall abuse. By this meanes hee attaines to the sight of all the prettie wenches of the towne. At such a kind of faire he got his beloved Normahal.

Nur Mahal, the Light of the Palace, was a famous beauty and an exceptional and talented woman. She was an accomplished poet, an influential designer of carpets and a good shot (she hunted from a closed howdah on the back of an elephant). She also appears to have been a faithful and loving wife. But she was as ambitious as she was beautiful and had no qualms about using her influence over her husband for her own ends. According to Sir Thomas Roe, the English Ambassador, 'all justice or care of any thing or publique affayrs either sleepes or depends on her, who is more inaccessible than any Goddesse or mystery of heathen impietye'. When her influence came to an end at Jehangir's death, she occupied her retirement by building her husband's tomb in the centre of the lovely Mogul garden which then, as now, must have been well outside the bustle of the town. She may have been involved in its design: it certainly has very similar lines to the other tomb that she commissioned, the mausoleum of her father Itmud ad-Daula, which lies upstream from the Taj Mahal in Agra.

The Itmud ad-Daula was the first Mogul tomb that I ever saw. I was seventeen, and the spring morning that I spent looking at it inspired in me the love of Islamic architecture that has propelled me around the mosques and tombs of Asia ever since. Driving out of Lahore towards Jehangir's tomb, I became worried that in comparison with the great buildings of the Seljuks, Saffavids or Ottomans that I had seen since, the brilliance of Mogul architecture might pall. But it was like a homecoming. Jehangir's tomb was a fine building, set in the middle of a Mogul garden, the climax of a symmetry of pools and canals and long, worn, redbrick paths. As the first great building that I had seen since leaving Iran, what struck me was its simplicity, both of design and material. In shape it is a low, plain rectangle, arcaded on all sides, centred on an unpretentious *ivan* gateway and flanked by four minarets. It is built of brown stone inlaid with white marble. There is no tile work, no fussy detail, no extravagance. Only the cenotaph itself is at all elaborate, inlaid with semi-precious stones and covered with kufic designs listing the Ninety-Nine Names of God.

Like its European contemporary, Baroque, Mogul architecture represents only a variation on an old, familiar theme. But while Baroque saw a swing towards extravagance, the Mogul architecture of Lahore represents a retrenchment, a reaction against the tendency to ever-greater scale, ever-greater luxuriance and ever-greater detail. Combined with the Mogul genius for landscaping, the result is not grand or sumptuous, but instead something dignified, and – in the case of this tomb – something surprisingly humble and human. It is immensely accessible architecture.

Leaving the gardens we came across what seemed to be a changing of the shifts in the beggar community at the gates. One group got up and walked towards the tea stall, while another party took its place. Having finished his cup of tea, one of the off-shift came over and half-heartedly tried his luck with us.

'Oh sahib,' he wailed. 'My father has ill, my mother is disease.'

I was just about to give him a coin, when there was a howl of outrage from the gate. The beggar scuttled off. Union regulations, it seemed, had been broken. In India I had heard stories of such things (it was said that the Rajasthan beggars flew up to Ladakh for the summer season; only the hippies underwent the four-day bus journey from Delhi) but until this moment had never believed them. The beggars reminded me, however, of the fate of Tom Coryat.

Having finally reached the Mogul's court he found himself almost destitute. Although he had found travelling in Asia very cheap, he was 'cousened of no less than ten shillings by certaine lewd Christians of the Armenian nation', and he was forced to come before Jehangir and make a begging speech.

'Lord Protector of the World,' he said. 'All haile to you. I am a poore traveller and world-seer, which am come from a farre country, namely England . . . queene of all the ilands in the world. . . .'

Jehangir took him for a holy man and gave him only one hundred rupees, thinking that he, like the Indian *sadhu*, had voluntarily renounced wealth. Coryat set off back for England, but before he had left India his health broke down. He finally got to Surat but there drank 'a surfeit of sack' given him by the English merchant community. This aggravated his dysentery and he fell into a fever. He died a few days later. His letters back to England were printed as soon as the news of his death was announced. But it was tragic that he never lived to write what would certainly have been his most remarkable and – if Sir Thomas Roe was to be believed – most voluminous book:

'With his most unwearied legges . . . [he has collected] notes already too great for portage . . . [some] he left at Aleppo, some at Hispan – enough indeed to make any stationer an alderman that merely serve the printer with paper. . . .'

I had been eight days in Lahore before I finally roused myself into action over the permits. We decided that we could prepare the ground for the assault on the Kafkaesque bureaucracy of Islamabad by telephone from Lahore. A couple of phone calls, we hoped, and the field could be open for us to flash our letters, collect the permits and set off up the Karakoram Highway to China. But we had forgotten the joys of the Pakistan Telecom network, and not yet met the Chinese brickwall approach to relations with foreigners.

The Begum's office contained three telephones and an angry secretary. He had black spectacles and effused boredom and irritability in about equal parts. Although the Begum had warned him the day before that I would be coming, he much resented my invasion. 'Sahib, do not put your letters on my table,' he said as I sat down. I apologized and tried dialling the number of the British Embassy. I failed to get through. I tried again. Brrrrrrrr, said the telephone. Out of the corner of my eye I could see that the secretary was watching me. After three further attempts he took the receiver from my hand with an I-was-doing-this-before-you-were-born look on his face, dialled the operator, spoke to someone he knew, and was put through first time.

I spoke to a weary Scots Consul whose job, so he said, now consisted in arranging for the corpses of mountaineers to be returned to England. He had received the Permanent Under-Secretary's letter and said he was happy to help us as long as we promised not to go climbing. He put me through to a liaison officer who listened to an account of our problems and agreed to telephone the Chinese Embassy. I next rang the Pakistan Ministry of Tourism. For a while there was no answer, then a bad-tempered voice rather resentfully asked what I wanted. I asked for Mr Muneeradin, the name I had been given by the embassy in London. The voice said Mr Muneeradin was on holiday. When would Mr Muneeradin be back? I asked. The voice said it did not know. Did no one know? I asked. No, no one, said the voice. For the third time that morning, but not the last, I explained the problem. Why didn't I try the Ministry of Sport? suggested the voice before somewhat abruptly hanging up.

At that moment the liaison officer rang on the second phone. The man I wanted at the Chinese Embassy was a Mr Qiu. He was waiting for me to call. In the meantime, said the liaison officer, he would contact the Pakistani Civil Service. I thanked him and rang the Chinese Embassy. I got through on my second attempt, but of a Mr Qiu the embassy denied all knowledge. That was the *Chinese* Embassy? I asked. And there was no one with a name even approximating that of Mr Qiu? No, said the embassy receptionist, there was no Mr Qiu, there had never been a Mr Qiu and as far as she knew there were no plans to employ a Mr Qiu.

I considered the options. Assuming a French accent, I again tried the Chinese Embassy, asking for the visa section. I explained what I wanted. Was it a tourist visa that I wished to apply for? No, it was a Kunjerab permit. What was my group? I did not really have a group; I was part of a two-person expedition from a British university. Ah, said the visa official, in that case I needed to get in touch with the Cultural Mission. Then he too rang off.

I continued the battle after a siesta. First the Chinese Cultural Attaché was asleep. Then he was in a meeting. I finally cornered him that evening. He would love to help, he said, but if it was a permit for the Kunjerab that I wanted then the man I should speak to was Mr Qiu at the embassy.

The Pakistani Sports Ministry proved equally elusive.

Eventually the Begum put me through to the Minister himself. We had a long and friendly chat. What was my good name? Cambridge University? How lucky I was. Was I an old friend of the Begum? She was a remarkable woman. Perhaps I might be so good as to give the Minister my address? He was planning a little trip to England to visit a cousin. Perhaps we could meet if ever he found himself in Cambridge? We swapped addresses and vowed eternal friendship, but as to a Karakoram Highway permit, he was very sorry. He knew nothing about such permits. Had I tried the Ministry of Tourism?

Three days later the secretary managed to get hold of Mr Qiu and Mr Muneeradin. Both said the same thing. Permits were not necessary either for the Karakoram Highway or the Kunjerab Pass. The fools in London knew nothing. Pakistan, China and Britain were old and valued friends. Their peoples were brothers. I could go wherever I liked.

I did not believe a word that either man said. But there now seemed no choice but to attempt to reach China and see what happened.

That evening the Begum asked her bearer to arrange two bus tickets to Islamabad. The bearer approached the cook's boy, who approached the secretary, and then disappeared off into the garden. We returned to our bedrooms after supper to find our bags packed and a small envelope containing two tickets sitting on the bedside table.

It was a cool, sharp evening when Louisa and I arrived in Mansehra. The town sits at the top of a small ridge in the foot-hills of the Karakorams, hemmed in by slopes of spruce, fir and birch. As far as Abbotabad we had ridden on top of the bus, but as the road rose into the hills, the temperature had dropped steadily. It was cold in the nights in the hills and already the tribesmen were huddling around the roadside braziers.

Mansehra was a wilder place than any I had yet seen. We had left the easy plains of the Punjab behind us and were now in a landscape of narrow valleys and steep, wooded slopes. The change in the human geography was even more dramatic. The neat, civilized Punjabis who had filled the bazaars of Lahore were nowhere to be seen. Instead we were surrounded by some of the most frightening men I had ever laid eyes on. Towards the end of the journey I had looked under the bottom of my book and noticed the size of a tribesman's feet. They were vast. But then everything about these men was outsized. They had big hands and big noses. Their beards cascaded over their chests. They grunted at each other with deep, resonant voices that any Welsh bass would have been proud of. They were, as Louisa remarked admiringly at the time, Real Men.

'You wouldn't find of these boys nancying around reading books or learning English,' she said as we got out the bus, and was soon proved right when I failed to get anyone to understand my request to be directed to a hotel.

We did find a hotel, eventually. It lay hidden behind the bus station and you entered through a narrow wicket gate which led into an open courtyard. The hotel was built of wood, and the upper storey of the building was ringed by a wooden balustrade. It looked a fine spot, and we decided to take a room. Then we met the owner. He was a Pathan, one of the biggest we had yet seen. I filled in the register, then timidly asked if he would send a pot of tea up to our room.

'No, sahib,' he replied. 'This hotel is self-service.'

'Self-service?'

'Yes, sahib.'

'So we can't have a pot of tea?'

'No, sahib.'

He gave the key to Louisa and I followed her up the stairs. She unlocked the double doors and looked in.

'Willy, I know I'm awfully stupid, but don't Pakistani hotels normally have beds in them?'

'Yes, of course they do,' I replied, rather enjoying the role of Experienced Traveller that I had assumed since Laura left.

Then I looked in the room. It was, as Louisa had indicated, quite bedless. I trotted down the stairs, back to reception.

'Excuse me,' I said. 'I don't think there is a bed in our room.'

'No, sahib.'

'There isn't . . . meant to be a bed in our room?'

'No, sahib.'

'I see,'

The Pathan stroked his beard.

'Uh . . . I'm sorry to . . . be a nuisance or anything, but what do your guests . . . normally . . . do?'

The Pathan considered for a moment.

'They hire mattresses, sahib.'

'Terrific. That's terrific. Um . . . where do they hire mattresses?'

'From me, sahib. Ten rupees extra.'

'Good. Well could we have two?'

'Yes, sahib.'

'Any time you've got a moment just bring them up. No rush or anything.'

The Pathan knitted his outsized brows.

'No, sahib,' he said in a voice that indicated lost patience.

'What do you mean?'

'Sahib, this hotel is self-service. I have told you this thing before. Mattresses are over there.'

He indicated a dank corner of the courtyard near the open drain. I paid twenty rupees. The Pathan watched while I selected two damp mattresses and dragged them upstairs.

At supper that night we shared a table with a reassuringly small Punjabi. He had just finished a term teaching English in the hills above Swat and was heading back to Lahore as fast he could.

'Oh gentleman-sahib, these Pathans, they are barely human,' he said. 'They have no civilization. They are not using right thinkings.'

'What do you mean?'

'Gentleman-sahib. They are Junglies.'

192

'Nothing wrong with that,' said Louisa. 'They're just natural. Unspoilt. Noble.'

'Oh missy-sahib. You do not know what you are saying. The things I have heard. The things I have seen.' He wobbled his head from side to side. 'There are wicked mens in the hills. Always they are singing and dancing and making sexual intercourse. Missy-sahib, they are not Muslims.'

'What are they then?'

'Oh missy-sahib. I am telling you. They are worshipping goats.' He leaned across the table, eyes wide with horror. 'I'm am not making joke. Really. I have seen them. Among them there are many witches.'

'Witches?'

'The Pathan womens. They are more wicked even than the mens. If a Pathan witch-lady is wanting to go to see a friend she climbs up a tree and she flies this tree wherever she wants.'

'But you don't believe that nonsense, do you?'

'No, sahib. But many wicked things are happening and sometimes I am thinking: what are these things?'

'Tell me some more of the wicked things,' said Louisa.

'Oh missy-sahib. What can I say? Last term a policeman died and he was buried. Two days later his grave was found dug up and his body gone. Now this man – he was having many enemies. Always he was telling these Pathan-fellows: you must not do such and such. Maybe his enemies thought, let us dig up this man and then we will revenge ourselves. Maybe this is what happend. But there were other stories in the bazaars.'

'What sort of stories?'

'The Pathan women are of . . . a very lusty nature. Excuse me, missy-sahib. Now it is said that if a witch-woman is feeling of lusty inclination towards a man, and she wants to make sexual intercourse with this fellow, then she will go to a burial place and dig up a newly buried body.'

'How does that help?' asked Louisa.

'Missy–sahib, I am telling you. It is said that a witch will hang up the dead body on a tree and pour water over its head. She then collects the water dripping off the feet and takes a bath in it. The witch becomes very beautiful and no man can resist her.'

'And this sort of thing still goes on in Swat?' I asked.

'Sahib. By my word.'

'But Swat was where all the British officers used to go duck-shooting,' I said lamely. The Wali of Swat was famous for his house parties.'

'Sahib. No longer.'

'What do you mean?'

'Sahib. The Wali of Swat was hacked to pieces by some Pathans last year. Now he is no longer alive.'

We walked back to our hotel that night, our ears still ringing with the dangers awaiting us up the road in Gilgit and Hunza (where, according to our friend, the Pathans were notable for infanticide and cannibalism). More immediate horrors awaited us in our hotel room, however. Darkness had brought with it the local cockroach population and we found a number nesting contentedly on our mattresses. We spent half an hour in slaughter, but were still woken intermittently by their long cat-like feelers brushing our faces. The one consolation was that the cockroaches seemed to discourage the fleas, and, at eight thousand feet, we were now too high for mosquitoes.

We were woken by a volley of throat-clearing sounds from the balcony. Other splashing and gargling noises wafted up from the courtyard. Ablutions are an important and apparently enjoyable occasion for a Pathan, as for many peoples of the subcontinent, and they are entered into with great gusto. Phlegm is cleared from the throat, noses are blown, wind is broken. Then it is time to approach the tap. Every part of the body that can be cleaned, modestly, without removing a *charwal chemise*, is cleaned, particularly, for some reason, the back of the ears. Teeth are scrubbed with a twig, then picked with a toothpick. Finally the moment has come for the Pathan to comb his beard. This takes a very long time: a Pathan's beard is a manifestation of his virility, and is treated with the respect due to such. Great pride is taken in its trimming, curling and dyeing (orange seemed to be *de rigueur* while we were there). As anyone who observes a tribesman at his toilet will learn, there is a surprisingly dandyish element in the Pathan character. Some even use eye shadow.

We checked out of the hotel and, having found that no bus was expected until evening, we decided to hitch on up into the hills. But before we left, I wanted to see the rock edicts carved on two great boulders outside the town. They were put there in the second century BC by the Maurya emperor Ashoka. In the century following Alexander, Ashoka created a vast empire which included all of Pakistan and most of India. Sickened by the bloodshed he had caused conquering his dominions, he was converted to Buddhism and established the faith as the cornerstone of his empire. All over the subcontinent edicts were carved promulgating the new laws based on the principle of non-violence. It is all strangely familiar: Ashoka has a ring of Gandhi about him, over two thousand years before Gandhi was born.

The edict starts with a declaration of vegetarianism:

> Formerly in the Royal Kitchen every day many thousands of living creatures were slain to make curries. At present only three living creatures, one peacock and two deer, are killed daily . . . even these three creatures shall be spared in future.

Then follows a more ambiguous passage:

> Moral policemen, censors of the laws of piety, have been appointed to inculcate obedience, liberality, and avoidance of excesses among all classes of the Empire. For a long time past business has not been disposed of, nor have reports been received properly or at once. This laxity will cease in future. All work shall be for the public benefit. There shall be no other end than this.

On the smaller boulder, Ashoka declares that he will tour the Empire 'proclaiming the law of virtue' and banning 'corrupt and worthless ceremonies'. Sitting peering at the almost invisible hieroglyphics, I wondered what Ashoka's regime would have been like to live under. H. G. Wells in his *History of the World* wrote that it would have been paradise, and that Ashoka was the wisest emperor in all world history. But then H. G. Wells approved of totalitarian government. In the 1930s he was one of the first Western intellectuals to follow André Gide and proclaim the virtues of Stalinism. For all their touching vegetarianism, Ashoka's edicts do have a worryingly puritanical, authoritarian ring to them.

To my mind a more sympathetic character than Ashoka is the original translator of his edicts, James Prinsep. Prinsep was the secretary of the Royal Asiatic Society in Calcutta where he fought a rearguard action against the growing tide of Raj bigotry which in the early 1800s was threatening the whole study of Indian culture. The British at that time were just beginning to encourage the westernization of Indians rather than the orientalization of Englishmen which had been the keynote of British policy in the eighteenth century. Prinsep was the last of the great tradition of 'Brahminized' Englishmen who treated Indian civilization as the equal of that of Europe. Henceforth the coming of the memsahibs and building of the clubs and the civil lines would draw the two races apart and lead to the neglect of Indian history until Mortimer Wheeler in the twentieth century. Prinsep was an engineer who worked in the Calcutta Mint and became interested in oriental culture through his study of ancient Indian coins. He is remembered today largely for his work in translating two forgotten Indian scripts: Gupta Brahmi and Ashoka Brahmi, the script of the rock edicts. At the time, however, he was at least equally famous for his rust-proof treatment for steam boats and his design for the Calcutta Ice House, a project in which he co-operated with an alcoholic named James Pattle, my great-great-great grandfather. The Ice House was Calcutta's first experiment in refrigeration, and the day the first cargo of ice arrived from America a public holiday was declared. 'All business was suspended until noon. . . . Everybody invited everybody to dinner to taste claret and beer cooled by the American importation.' Pattle served 'tip-top champagne'.

Despite this public-spirited act both men came to sticky ends. Prinsep fell ill from overwork trying to translate the Ashoka Brahmi and after four years, having finally cracked its secrets, he developed 'an affectation of the brain'. By the time he was bundled aboard the *Hertfordshire* his 'mind was addled'. He reached England, but never recovered his sanity 'lingering a year until relieved of his sufferings' in 1840. His old partner, James Pattle, fared no better. 'The biggest liar in India', as he was known (with justice; one of his claims was to have rowed across the Atlantic in a hen coop), drank himself to death, and was put in a cask of rum to preserve him during the voyage back to England. His wife had the cask placed outside her bedroom door. In the middle of the night there was a violent explosion, and when the widow rushed out into the passage she found the container had burst and her husband was stuck half in, half out of the barrel. 'The shock sent her off her head then and there, poor thing, and she died raving. . . .' But the worst was yet to come. The cask was nailed down and put on board ship. Sometime after the boat had set off, the sailors guessed that the cask was full of liquor, bored a hole into the side of it and began to get drunk. The rum continued to run out, caught fire and set the ship ablaze. While the drunken sailors were trying to extinguish the flames, the ship ran onto a rock and blew up. So it was that Pattle was cremated rather than buried in England, as he had wished.

Mulling over whether there was perhaps a moral in this story, Louisa and I set off up the Karakoram Highway. It was a beautiful day and even the warnings of our Punjabi friend – that if we were not eaten alive we would certainly perish in a rockfall – did not lower our spirits. We were soon picked up by a road contractor. He was making repairs to the highway sixty miles further up and said he would take us as far as he was going.

197

The Karakoram Highway was built as a joint venture by the Chinese and Pakistanis in the 1960s when the two countries were thrust together by mutual hostility to India. It was planned as a military road, strictly closed to foreigners, but in May the Pakistan Government announced that it would be opened. This was the catalyst which led us to plan our expedition, and we were thus among the first Westerners ever to see the highway. The Begum had given us an unreadable publicity pamphlet about it before we left Lahore. If the brochure was to be believed, the road was eight hundred kilometres long, involved blasting some thirty million cubic yards of rock and claimed over four hundred lives during the twenty years it had taken to build.

Leaving Mansehra we snaked upstream along river valleys, high above the rapids. The mountainsides were covered with wild flowers. The upper slopes were wooded. There were some wattle huts built beside the road and in them tribesmen were selling melons. The road rose and the air grew colder. Then, suddenly, the spaces widened, and we found ourselves in a hanging valley, ablaze with the violent green of ripe paddy terraces. In the Punjab, all the rice fields had been full of villagers grafting and tending the shoots. The Pathans seemed to take a more relaxed attitude to agriculture. They sat on their *charpoy*, as immobile as the water buffaloes beside them, and waited for their rice to grow. One village made cricket bats, but despite a small pile of finished bats propped up against the wall of one hut, no one seemed to be too busy there either. When we stopped for *cay*, the male villagers were kind and relaxed and cheerful. They squatted on their hams and offered us dried apricots. We saw few women in these villages.

As we drove on, the valley narrowed again. The villages became fewer and the houses fuller and stronger. The walls were mud, but they were lined with timber, and their windows were narrow. At one such village we gave a lift to a family of Pathans. The father of the family was a fierce orange-bearded tribesman who held a machete in one hand and a live chicken in the other.

Sometimes, the contractor would ask one of us to take over the driving, but for most of the journey Louisa and I sat in the back. I browsed through the translated memoirs of the first Mogul, Babur, one of a number of books I had been lent by Mozaffar (in return he took my much-thumbed and very dirty *Crime and Punishment*). Babur was the great-grandfather of Jehangir, but lived in the very different, more precarious world of early sixteenth-century Transoxiana. He spent much of his youth throneless, living with his companions from day to day, rustling sheep and stealing food. Occasionally he would capture a town (when he was fourteen he took Samarkand and held it for three months) but generally he lived out of a tent, a peripatetic existence that appealed little to him. 'It passed through my mind,' he writes in the *Baburnama*, 'that to wander from mountain to mountain, homeless and houseless, had nothing to recommend it.'

What appealed to me, reading the book as we passed through the valleys of Bafa and Battagram, was the similarity of the landscape I was passing through to that described by the Mogul nearly five hundred years before. Of his home province of Ferghana he writes:

> It abounds in grain and fruit and its grapes and melons are excellent and plentiful. In the melon season it is not customary to sell them at the beds: passers-by eat them gratuitously. . . . The district also abounds in birds and beasts of game. Its pheasants are so fat that it is said that four persons may dine on the broth of one of them, and not be able to finish it. . . .'

It could be Battagram he was describing. It did not take much imagination to see in the turbaned valley tribesmen the bearded faces which fill the court scenes of early Mogul miniatures.

Having dropped the Pathan family in a fortified village, we stopped for lunch at roadworks forty miles north of Mansehra. About two-thirds of the width of the road had crumbled down onto the paddy terracing below, and with it had fallen a small

Toyota pick-up, the double of our own. The contractor took great pleasure in pointing it out to us as we sat on a *charpoy* at the edge of the precipice.

'Toyota with Australians,' he said with a cheery wave in the direction of the pick-up. 'All now deads.'

The food that his friends cooked for us was equally unsettling. At meals Pakistanis manage to produce pieces of meat from perfectly normal animals, sheep or chickens, that bear no apparent relation with the meat served up from the same animals in Europe. What part of a sheep was given to me that lunchtime I have never discovered. It was soft and flexible and covered with grey rubbery meat that tasted a little like gum Arabic. Worse still was the alcohol that was produced from a tent to celebrate our arrival. Pakistan is a teetoal Muslim country so all alcohol must be produced illegally. The contractor proudly told us it was made by a friend of his who worked in a hospital. It was stored in a little clouded-glass bottle, the sort used for cough medicine. He carefully mixed it with a sickly-sweet bottle of Cola, then decanted it into dirty tea cups. Louisa was sitting the far end of the *charpoy* to the contractor and was able to pour her cup down the precipice without being noticed. I, however, was forced to drink the whole measure: it was horrible stuff. The effect of drinking it was half anaesthetic, half disinfectant, but it did at least take away the taste of the gum Arabic.

Feeling distinctly unwell, we carried on up the highway. The contractor was in fine form after his fix of disinfectant and he drove on at a terrifying pace. He seemed to take particular pleasure in near-misses with juggernauts heading in the opposite direction, after which he would turn around and grin at us. Often this would lead to yet another even closer miss which would in turn cause ever greater outbursts of high spirits. Pakistanis believe illegal drinking to be rather chic, and will go out of their way to show quite how drunk they are. We closed our eyes, but were still haunted by premonitions of imminent disaster. Then it happend. We turned a sharp corner and suddenly in front of us, far below, we saw the Indus curving around the foot of a great mountain. The contractor looked around to point it out. There was a sickening jolt. I saw a cow take off, fly across the road and achieve a remarkable all-fours landing on the verge. Without so much as a look at us it continued to munch the grass, apparently unmoved by its brief flight. But the Toyota was a write-off. The front radiator had completely caved in on one side, and water from it was forming a large puddle on the road.

For a while we all stood around hopelessly. The contractor sobered up and examined the damage. We tried to look sympathetic. Lou helped the contractor to raise the bonnet. I tapped the radiator in an authoritative manner. Lou pointed to the puddle. The contractor nodded. He fiddled with the battery. He spun the fan. He got onto his back and wriggled under the radiator. He shook his head. The cow tore at a tuft of grass. I removed the rucksacks from the back. It was clear that the pick-up was not going anywhere, at least not in the immediate future.

The question was what to do next. The contractor decided to walk back to his friends at the roadworks and try and get them to help. We decided to walk on. We pushed the truck onto the verge, shook hands and set off in opposite directions, leaving only the cow to keep the pick-up company.

Ahead of us the gorge opened up into the main valley of the Indus. Here the river was about half a mile wide: a great swathe of stone-grey snowmelt cutting through the mountains. A small sidetrack led off the road to a solitary white bungalow on the riverbank. The bungalow was surrounded by mown lawns and hedged with conifers. It was now late afternoon and we had made no plans as to where we would spend the night. We stumbled down the track, and were met at the bottom by a *chowkidar*.

'Sahib,' he said, bowing slightly. 'This is an inspection bungalow. It is sadly reserved for the servants of the Government of Pakistan.'

I had seen these *dak* bungalows before in India. Officially they were open only to circuit judges, postmaster generals, brigadiers and the like, but occasionally an appropriate gesture (i.e. a bribe) to the *chowkidar* could secure a bed for a single night. I was just about to enter negotiations, when I heard Lou pipe up beside me.

'We *are* servants of the Government of Pakistan,' she said.

I looked round at her.

'Aren't we, Willy?'

'What?'

'We are the official Anglo-Pak Marco Polo expedition,' she explained to the *chowkidar*.

'Oh that's absolutely right,' I said, catching on. 'We are the official Anglo-Pak Marco Polo expedition. That's exactly what we are.'

I found the Begum's letter and gave it to the *chowkidar*. The man looked at it, bowed again, and led us into the bungalow. Lou winked at me, then followed the *chowkidar* inside. We were given a room looking out onto the Indus. In it were two magnificent four-poster beds equipped with elaborate canopies of mosquito netting. There was a clean, European-style bathroom. There was even a roll of soft loo paper.

The evening got better and better. Not only did the bungalow have an attentive staff which rivalled that of Mozaffar's palace, but it turned out that the mountain on the other side of the Indus was Pir Sar. According to a framed notice hung on the wall, this was the site of Aornus, the last citadel captured by Alexander the Great before he turned back westwards to die in Babylon. Alexander was a childhood hero of mine and the previous year on the route of the First Crusade, I had slept a night in an excavation trench on the hill of Pella, Alexander's birthplace. This was like completing a circle.

For two hours I sat inside and wrote up the logbook. Then I showered, drank a pot of tea brought to me by a bearer, and went out into the garden. Beyond the lawn of the bungalow was the riverbank and then the river. The bank was littered with smooth round boulders. The evening light played on the eddies on the surface of the river, and the sound of the running water echoed around the valley. As the sun sank behind the

Rasputin, Saveh bus station.

Kurdish *hoja*, Erzurum.

Sergeant Major, Mansehra.

Mad mullah, Mansehra.

Cynic, Mansehra.

Punjabi children,
outside Lahore.

Fruit seller, the market, Kashgar.

Old men on their evening walk, Keriya.

Uighur children, Keriya.

peaks a mullah came and prostrated himself on a stone on the riverbank. He touched his head against the stone and through the roar of the river you could hear the sound of the Kalimeh: *'La Allah illa Allah, Mahommet Resul-allah.'*

I found Lou perched on the lower branches of a tree on the riverbank, putting the finishing touches to a sketch of the Indus. She had spent the evening reading *Lolita*.

'It's a filthy, dirty book,' she said.

'You're not enjoying it?' I asked.

'No, I'm loving it.'

Sitting bird-like on her branch, Louisa looked even more alluring than she normally did. The sun had begun to darken her skin, emphasizing the blueness of her eyes and the fairness of her hair. Despite the rigours of our journey she was still immaculately turned out, and her art-nouveau bracelets glinted in the light. As I talked to her I took in her neat figure. She had such intelligent curves.

'What are you thinking about?' she asked, presumably noticing the glazed look in my eyes.

'Oh. Nothing.'

'Would you mind if I drew you?'

'No, go ahead.'

I struck an attitude on the riverside, with my legs dangling becomingly in the river. While Louisa sketched she talked, largely about Edward and his many fine qualities.

'I think I'm in love, Willy.'

'Who with?'

'Edward, of course.'

'Oh.'

'You don't mind me telling you all this, do you?'

'No,' I lied. 'Why should I?'

'I just thought you might be a little jealous, or something.'

'Me? Jealous?'

'It was just a thought.'

'Jealous? Not at all.'

I got up. 'Come on. Let's go in and get some supper.'

'Wait. I want to tell you more about Edward.'

'Go on. Tell me.' (About the little bastard.)

'Well,' she began. 'For a start he's absolutely gorgeous. You have no conception of what handsome means until you meet Edward.'

'I've met him.'

'So you have. But not properly.'

'No.'

'And . . . well, he's very well dressed.'

'*Very* important,' I said. 'Does he talk?'

'You *are* jealous.'

'Just interested.'

'Well, to be honest he doesn't say much. But he's very kind, very loving. I think you would really like him if you got to know him.'

'Sounds just up my street. Come on. Supper.'

We ate a meagre curry, then, while Lou finished a letter, I sat outside on my own on the verandah, and sought solace in the *Baburnama*.

The tribesmen who live on the slopes of Pir Sar are not Pathans. They are Gujars, relations of the Kaffirs of Nuristan. They are high-spirited and warlike. They have fair skin and their hair is sometimes blond. The Pathans dislike them intensely. Partly the enmity may originate in the Gujars' animism – they were only recently converted to Islam, and their allegiance to the faith is shaky. But mostly the Pathans resent the Gujars' height, strength, and good looks. Victorian explorers in this area thought the Gujars were descended from the stragglers of Alexander's army (did they not wear a woollen headdress similar to the *kausia* of the Macedonians?), but the Pathans have other theories. They trace the Gujars' descent from the irregular copulation of a Pathan witch and an excitable Indus water buffalo. The Indus still forms the frontier between the two tribes.

When, at breakfast the next morning, I mooted the idea of crossing the river into Gujar territory and climbing Pir Sar,

Louisa was less than enthusiastic. She had found Pakistan hard going and said she was feeling tired and frail. She did not feel quite up to climbing mountains.

'Don't come then,' I said eventually. 'Anyway the Gujars developed a taste for memsahibs during the Raj. You wouldn't be safe.'

'What about you?'

'No one will rape me.'

'No. That's true.'

The bungalow *chowkidar* was equally unimpressed with the plan.

'Oh sahib, sahib, these people are wicked mens,' he moaned. 'Do not cross the river, sahib. It is not safe. These Gujar fellows are robbers and murderers.'

I did not listen. There was barely a single place on the journey where we had not been told this of the next town. It was always full of deviants and perverts, mother-rapers, father-slayers and worse. It was always madness to go on. The *chowkidar*, however, proved more resolute than most of the Prophets of Doom we met. Having failed to dissuade me from climbing Pir Sar, he did his best to sabotage the attempt. He insisted on escorting me on the twenty-minute walk to the ferry point and there negotiated with the ferrymen, a villainous bunch of Pathans in charge of an equally unreliable-looking raft. This consisted of four water-buffalo hides, sown up and stuffed with chaff, inflated then strapped together with a fragile framework of wooden stathes. To my surprise it proved fairly safe. It was, after all, one of the most ancient and well-tried methods of river-crossing known to man. There are sculptures of similar rafts on seventh-century BC Assyrian bas-reliefs, and it was this method that carried Alexander and his army safely across the Danube and Oxus. Thanks, however, to the efforts of the *chowkidar* this raft failed to get me across the Indus, at least initially. Following the directions that they had been given, the ferrymen pushed the raft off into the river and steered it a mile downstream. They beached it just below the bungalow. To their bemusement as much as mine, I was deposited on a patch of sandy riverbank, and helped ashore by Lou and one of the bungalow bearers.

It took thirty minutes to explain that no, I did not just come for a joy ride, and that yes, I did actually want to cross the river. We spent another hour dragging the raft upstream to the crossing point, and a further thirty minutes reinflating the skins. This involved blowing through what had once been the buffalos' ankles, then sealing the legs with garden twine. It was virtually noon before we finally set off into the current on the short journey across the river. One ferryman, naked except for a loincloth, waded into the river pushing the raft in front of him. The passengers – elderly tribesmen clutching rifles and umbrellas – huddled together at one end of the raft. Suddenly we were caught in the flow. The raft shot off downstream, pirouetting in irregular circles. We hit some rapids and water cascaded over the boat. On we went, spinning and turning, eddying backwards and forwards. I bent over my camera bag, cursing that I had been stupid enough to bring all my film. But the raft was not out of control. At the far end sat two ferrymen. They clutched a pair of sturdy poles each strapped to wooden uprights. These they used as oars. Every time the ferrymen's backs faced the far shore, they heaved at the oars and the raft shuddered off in the right direction.

Only one old man looked at all worried. His tiny granddaughter was crooked under his arm and the child was sweating feverishly. Her hands hung limply from her wrists, and her hair was damp and matted. From the breast pocket of the old man's *charwal chemise* I could see the top of an unopened bottle of medicine, perhaps the reason for his journey across the river. The medicine was Benylin cough mixture. It looked a very inadequate cure for the girl's fever.

The ferrymen pulled the raft onto a mud flat at the foot of Pir Sar, two miles downstream. Alexander arrived here in the summer of 327 BC. Aornus was unfortified, but was still almost impregnable: its sheer height and gradient made it a far more formidable obstacle than any fortress. Pir Sar was the capital of the Buddhist Kingdom of Udyana, and all the fugitives from

Alexander's previous conquests had fled to it. A rumour went around Alexander's camp that the mountain was so high that 'even Herakles, the son of Zeus had found it impregnable'.

Siege was impossible, and the terrain limited the strategies open to Alexander. He had no choice but to fight his way painfully up the mountainside. The first assault was a disaster. The thirty hand-picked advance guards were crushed by boulders rolled down from above; Alexander himself only narrowly escaped death. For two days and two nights the Indians beat drums to celebrate the victory, but they recognized that the Macedonians would eventually break through. Sending envoys to negotiate a surrender, they played for time while organizing a secret evacuation of the hilltop. Alexander realized what was happening. Scaling a rock face with the aid of a rope, he led seven hundred of the Shield Bearers into the attack.

> The Macedonians climbed up after him, pulling one another up, some at one place, some at another. At a prearranged signal they turned upon the retreating Barbarians and slew many of them in flight; some others retreating in terror flung themselves down the precipices and died. Alexander thus became the master of the rock which had baffled Herakles himself. . . .

Alexander and his Macedonians had to cope with the local barbarians; I found it hard work climbing the mountain even without opposition. The hill rises steeply from the Indus and, failing at first to find a track, I battled my way up through the cultivation terraces, scrambling over ditches and dykes, brushing my way through the narrow strip-fields. The terraces contained thick plantations of maize, wheat, and marijuana. After a difficult climb of an hour I came across a track, a holloway sunk between two dry stone walls, perhaps the very 'stony path cut by the hands of man' used by the Macedonians. It was clearly very ancient: it was cobbled with massive slabs of limestone and these had been worn completely smooth with the passage of feet. The track led a winding course up the hill, past line upon line of neatly kept terraces, giving off to other less substantial goat trails. It was exhausting work. The chill of the previous day had gone and the temperature had risen. The midday sun beat down through the rarified air, and I could feel the weakening effects of altitude. After another hour I was parched. I left the main track and wandered along a trail to a mud-walled enclosure.

There I found a flat-roofed wattle and daub tribesman's house, a separate cooking hut and a courtyard lined with *charpoy*. Its only inhabitants were some sitting cows, a clutch of chickens and a few plump, contented-looking babies. Too exhausted to be polite, I keeled over onto a *charpoy*. A minute later, when I opened my eyes I found myself surrounded by an arc of wide-eyed children in embroidered caps, an orange-bearded Gujar in a dirty *charwal chemise*, and, further behind, some women in brightly coloured prints. Embarrassed by my rudeness, I smiled and introduced myself. After less than a minute I exhausted my Urdu pleasantries and we sat in silence staring at each other. The women built a fire and made some tea, whilst the eldest son was sent off to find a maize cob, which he brought to me still hot from the fire. When I finally got up to go, the boy insisted on accompanying me up the hill and he leapt up the path ahead of me. As agile and foot-sure as an ibex, he seemed not to notice the gradient and could not understand what was slowing down the sweating asthmatic behind him.

The regular terracing soon gave way to rough undergrowth, and the path became slighter, frequently splitting into several smaller tracks. Every so often we came to a hut and each time my friend would sit me down on a *charpoy* and ask the women to bring chapattis and fresh water.

We climbed for two hours before we reached a spring gushing out of the rock. Here the path finally gave out and my friend would go no further. After trying to persuade me to come down with him, we shook hands and he disappeared round the corner. As soon as he had gone I began to regret my decision. It was after four o'clock and there now seemed little chance of reaching the peak and getting back to the ferry by nightfall. Anyway, as Sir Aurel Stein's investigations had shown, there were no visible remains on the hilltop other than a couple of large stone slabs (which the great archaeologist had somewhat imaginatively identified as the altars raised by Alexander to Athena, the Goddess of Victory). There was a disconcerting silence on the mountainside: a stillness with no wind, no birds and no distant roar of the river. For a while I picked my way along the trail, but it soon became impossible to distinguish real paths from those imagined. Parted undergrowth powdered with dust from passing feet would lead forward, then suddenly give out. Retracing my steps, I would again confuse paths and end up out of sight of the river, facing blank rock walls. Once, not looking where I was going, I found myself tottering on the edge of a precipice. I attempted to trek vertically down the mountainside in the hope of regaining the main path, but only succeeded in cutting my legs on thorns. Beginning to panic I quickened my pace, and managed to twist an ankle.

I sat down on a stone. I was exhausted. My ankle was aching and leg muscles that I never knew existed were beginning to complain. The sun was casting long shadows and the silence worried me. There was no sign of the path, and no other trail looked at all convincing. I could not see a single house, there were no familiar landmarks, and the Indus was only a glinting trickle far below. I felt tired, miserable and slightly frightened. I sat for ten minutes without moving, unsure of what to do. All options seemed equally unappealing. Then, immediately above me, I heard gunshots. On other occasions the noise might have been sinister. Now they seemed welcoming, almost homely. I clambered upwards, and soon found a track. Following it around a bluff of rock I saw the source of the shots: a village of half-timbered huts clinging to the sheer hillside.

I walked into the village along a terrace. The alleys were deserted but from the far side I could hear other noises behind the volleys of shot: clapping, drumming, and singing.

Intrigued, I followed the sound. Passing under an intricately carved lintel, I peered into the courtyard beyond. Women and children dressed in coloured silks were dancing around a smoking wood fire, while their menfolk lined the walls howling, and occasionally letting off their guns. I had interrupted a Gujar *shin*, the pre-Islamic animist ceremonies still known to take place, but rarely witnessed by Westerners. I watched for all of ten seconds. One of the women screamed and pointed in my direction. Immediately the singing stopped and the women fled inside a hut. The men jumped up from the ground and came towards me with pointed guns. I could not run away so instead I stepped towards them, trying to appear unflustered. I extended my hand, lamely indicating friendship. No one shook it. I was led outside at gunpoint, and escorted up to a flat roof where there stood a single *charpoy*. The Gujars motioned that I should sit. They stood around me, guns still pointed, scowling. I had wrecked their party and Gujars, it seemed, were not of a forgiving nature. They were tall, thick-bearded and heavily-built. They wore Palestinian *keffiyeh* rather than turbans, and their *charwal chemise* were of a different, tighter fit than any others I had seen in Pakistan. One man stuck out from the crowd. His face – vaguely Germanic, I thought – was flat and skull-like. He had cold blue eyes and huge hands. He wore an Afghan chapatti-cap and you could see that he was either bald or shaven-headed.

I tried a little Urdu. None of them understood. I smiled. They continued to scowl. I tried looking arrogant. No change. Then I tried expressing interest in their guns. This was quite an obvious conversation point since about fifteen of them were pointing directly at me. Nevertheless it was a break-through. My enthusiasm for one rusty old rifle stirred up jealous competition from the owners of several others. Four or five apparently identical guns were proudly presented for me to admire. No, I maintained, the first rifle was definitely the one for me. The smoothness of its barrel. The length of its stock. The workmanship on its breach. There was nothing to compare with it anywhere in Inglistan. I must have a photograph.

I arranged its owner next to the *charpoy* holding the gun in front of him. He beamed and I snapped. This caused uproar. Everyone wanted their photograph taken. The men lined up, and stiffened as if at attention. The German demanded an individual portrait, but two friends barged in at the sides. I took family groups, I took cousins. I took the children. I took all the rifles lined up in a long row against the *charpoy*. I took a picture of the rifles without the *charpoy*, and of the *charpoy* without the rifles. Someone fetched me some food, a ghastly confection of sticky rice and goat's leg. The German fetched some even rustier rifles for me to inspect. We swore brotherhood. By the time I got up to go, fully equipped with a teenage guide, the wrecked *shin* was completely forgotten. Thanking God for getting me off Pir Sar alive, I set off down the slope at a trot. Despite the tender ankle, I made it down in less than two hours.

One interesting angle on the *shin* emerged only when I returned to England and set about reading Robin Lane Fox's definitive *Alexander the Great*. It appears that Alexander himself may have witnessed a similar ceremony during his passage through the Karakorams. Certainly the chronicler Arrian records that immediately before Alexander began besieging Pir Sar, a rumour circulated in the Macedonian camp that the tribesmen of the area had been settled by Dionysius, and that their town was the sacred sanctuary of Nysa. Many of the Greeks twined ivy into wreaths, sang hymns and were 'promptly possessed by the God and raised the call of Dionysius, running in his frantic rout. . . .' This incident has long baffled scholars. The nearest god to Dionysius in the subcontinent is Shiva, and during the last century it was presumed that the Macedonians came across some Shivaites on their passage along the banks of the Indus. It is a convincing explanation, but there is a small problem. The Gujars were never Hindus and they never worshipped Shiva. The only possible solution is that the Greeks must have come across a *shin*, and equated one ecstatic cult with the other. There is a further link: the worship of the goat. The cult of Dionysius included the killing and eating of an ibex, an equally important part of the Gujars' *shin*. It is an interesting thought that I may not have been the first Westerner to be presented with a goat's leg by the Gujars. It could well be an honour that I unwittingly shared with Alexander the Great.

That night the sky towards Swat was illuminated with bright flashes of blue lightning. The storm grew slowly nearer, rain began to fall and the electricity in the bungalow flickered and died. The next morning the road was wet and glistening. We pulled on our rucksacks and set off up the track. If we did make it to the border, we would try to cross into China, link up with Polo's route, and push on to Kashgar. There we would put up our feet and make merry for two weeks. That, at any rate, was the plan. It did not get off to a good start. It was hot and humid and we trudged five miles without a lift. The rucksacks seemed miraculously to have doubled in weight since Mansehra. We were soon sitting on the verge waiting for a truck.

We were picked up by nine Afghans. They had hired a Datsun truck in Peshwar, and were driving it to the Chinese border. They claimed they were *mujahedin* on holiday, but this I think was more fiction than fact. Plump, lazy and well-educated, none looked remotely warlike and during the two days we were with them we did not hear a single campaign story.

The back of the truck had something of the all-male atmosphere of a Yorkshire pub. At one end, amid a divan of quilts, *kilim* and sheepskins, sat a sanctimonious old man and his two silent sons. They wore white skullcaps and shared their father's long, basset-hound jowls. They did not look happy about the two strangers joining them, and at first studiously ignored us. The others were three brothers, and were more of a rowdy nature. They made room for us by dangling their legs over the side, quite a hazardous undertaking considering our speed, the narrowness of the road and the recklessness of drivers heading in the opposite direction. They were bare-headed and far removed from the noble Afghan of travel books. They did not talk of gardening or Persian poetry; instead they questioned us closely about the West:

'Is Inglistan better than Pakistan?'

'In some ways.'

'Pakistan is a country of dogs.'

I painted a very romanticized picture of Cambridge, and they promised to come and visit me.

'Is it far to drive?'

'Very far.'

I thought how they would look driving down King's Parade in their truck; we could take them punting. Then the eldest of the brothers brought his head close to mine and whispered something. I missed it and he repeated it louder.

'When I come to Inglistan will you take me to a club?'

'What sort of club would you like to go to?'

'There are many kinds of club?'

'Very many: sports clubs, dining clubs, nightclubs.'

'I mean the club where a man. . . .'

He made a small but graphic gesture with the index finger of his right hand.

'Oh. I see. You want a brothel.'

The Afghan nodded enthusiastically.

'Brothel, brothel.'

The old man was less appreciative company. When Louisa took out her Sony Walkman he glared at us both, then, using his son as interpreter, he said:

'That is not good.'

'I'm sorry?' said Louisa.

'That is not good. Your gramophone is not allowed.'

'What do you mean?'

'Your gramophone is not allowed in the Law of Islam. You must put it away.'

The old man was not yet finished. Was our trip for religious purposes? Not exactly, I replied. What did I mean? I was hoping to write a book, I said. A book of the Christian religion, he supposed. No? Of what religion then? Not a religious book? What other kind of book was there? I showed him *Lolita*. He studied the cover photograph, and flicked through the book from the back forwards. Then he informed us that the Prophet had also forbidden the works of Vladimir Nabokov. This seemed more reasonable, but equally unlikely.

Despite this, we were in high spirits. It was exhilarating to be moving again. We stopped occasionally, to pray or pick flowers, and at Chilas we ate some lunch. While we waited for the old man to return from the mosque, the Afghans broke into a chorus of contented flatulence. After that the landscape changed rapidly, and the mountains closed in around us. The cultivation began to recede, and the grey hillsides were now covered in jagged scree. The tops of the mountains were dusted with snow. The Afghans were happy:

'When the *Shuravi* invade Pakistan we will fight in these mountains too.'

To pass the time the three brothers tried to teach me Dari. The old man and his sons snoozed or mumbled their prayers. When the father was asleep one of the boys plucked up the courage to ask to listen to the Walkman. He tapped his feet through one Prince song, then glanced at his father and returned to his devotions. We drove on, higher into the Karakorams. We passed a broken-down bus full of Uigurs from Chinese Turkestan. They were on their way back from the annual *Hajj* to Mecca. The men had narrow eyes and long, silky beards. They wore khaki frock coats and green and black embroidered skullcaps. These were the first Uigurs we saw.

Towards evening we rounded a corner and saw in front of us a roadblock. Two guards stood beside it holding Lee-Enfields. The guards signalled that Louisa and I should get out. My heart sank. It had been too easy up to now. We had failed to get our special permits and now we would have to retrace our steps to Islamabad and try again. The guards took our passports and led us inside. The more senior of the two grunted something in

Urdu. He was presumably forbidding us to continue. If only Laura were here, I thought, she would get us through. Then something in me snapped. I was not going to be sent back without a fight. No, I said. Certainly not. We were not going back. No way.

I was just getting into the swing of things when I noticed that Louisa was giggling. We were about to be sent back, the whole expedition put in jeopardy and all Louisa could do was giggle. I glared at her.

'He only wants you to sign the register,' she whispered.

I looked around and noticed for the first time that the guard was pointing to a ledger. His other hand held a pen.

Louisa sat down and filled in the details.

'Thank you,' said the guard. 'Gilgit welcomes you.'

The guards raised the barrier, and we drove on. Mr Muneeradin had not lied. The highway was indeed open for its full length. We drove past Gilgit and made camp in an orchard in the Hunza valley.

Never sleep with an Afghan. They snore, and they rise inde-cently early. It was still dark the following morning when I heard the old man intoning his prayers. Someone rebuilt the fire, and a kettle was fetched from the truck. It dawned dull and overcast. Before long it began to drizzle. Hunza, a hanging valley of orchards and asphodels, looked that morning a little like the Scots Borders in February. Only the old man spoke. He seemed to find comfort in everyone else's gloom, announcing, 'It is man's destiny to be wet,' and 'The Prophet commanded rain.'

The people of Hunza are Isma'ilis. For generations they lived by robbery and slave trading and they are still supposed to practise infanticide. They are renowned for their longevity and their taste for butter buried in the ground for one hundred years. Huddled miserably in the back of the truck we left the valley and entered a harsh landscape that reminded me of the wastelands of Arthurian romances. We crossed a wide, deserted plateau, flat-bottomed and covered in sand dunes. White outcrops rose from the granite slopes, riddled with holes like diseased teeth. Then we turned into the valley of the Gilgit River and the road became lost in the pebbles of the alluvial plain. The truck skidded on the rocks and splashed through tributary streams. Twice we passed side valleys blocked with the white mass of unmelted glaciers. It grew increasingly cold, and the drizzle changed to half-hearted gusts of snow.

The Pakistani border post was as desolate as the landscape around it: a group of windswept huts and a few miserable-looking tribesmen, shivering under their *patou* blankets. There was no colour. The scene was entirely monochrome.

We said goodbye to the Afghans and had our passports stamped. Lou found a post office hut to post a letter to Edward, then we hiked eight miles over the Kunjerab Pass to the Chinese border. We crossed a mountainous no-man's-land: high, wild, dreich country, all rock and ice.

The Chinese immigration officials were dressed in green military uniforms. They grunted at us in an incomprehensible Chinese version of Urdu. We sat on a bench with a dozen Punjabi businessmen and filled out in triplicate the forms handed to us. The official copied the details into a set of huge ledgers, and stored the forms away in separate files. We were made to line up and come forward individually. Our visas were checked for irregularities. The details of our health certificates were scrutinized. They carefully studied our pass-port photographs and when it came to changing travellers cheques, they resolutely denied the existence of the National Westminster Bank. Never have I seen men who derived so much enjoyment from the administration of bureaucracy. When they had finished we were marched outside into the blizzard. There was no bus, and we had no option but to sit and shiver until one came. We were not the only ones who were stranded. A party of *Hajji*, all octogenarians or older, sat beside piles of their belongings, wrapped up in blankets, overcoats and quilts. Some were obviously very ill. They had been wait-ing two days.

A 'bus' did turn up, sometime towards evening. It was a preposterous vehicle, a mere skeleton of a charabanc, with torn seats, shattered floor and gaping, glassless windows. A yak skin acted as a windshield over half the front window. The officials demanded that we, as foreigners, use it in preference to the poor *Hajji*. We bumped off along the road. The much vaunted Karakoram Highway, built by the Chinese at huge cost as a symbolic as well as physical link between the two countries, came to an end at the border post. To reach Tashkurgan, the first town in China, we had to travel along an unmetalled track riddled with potholes.

To our surprise the bus only broke down twice on the way to Tashkurgan. The engine overheated and the driver had to pull to a halt, stop the engine, fetch some cold water from a distant farmstead, then douse the radiator. It delayed us for as little as four hours. There were no punctures, the chassis did not give way, and occasionally the headlights worked. We were less lucky on arriving at Tashkurgan. The hotel had closed up for the night and refused to admit us. The driver took us to a disused caravanserai and there we fought for floorspace. There was no water, no food, no loo and no beds. But we had crossed the border and were now in Chinese Turkestan. Kashgar was only a day's journey away.

Or so we thought. The next morning we awoke to find that our bus had disappeared. The Pakistani businessmen were milling around in a state of profound depression. No transport was expected for four days. We were stranded.

Anyone who has studied the Silk Road might expect Tashkurgan to be a rather exciting place. It was the ancient gateway town to China, the junction point of the Silk Roads leading north from India and east from Afghanistan. All merchants travelling overland to China would have had to pass through it. It is the easternmost place marked on Ptolemy's map of the world and he describes it as the entrance to Seres, the Land of Silk. Traders from the classical West came here to exchange their goods for the mysterious 'down' that they genuinely believed grew on trees. Pliny was typical. 'The Seres are famous for the wool of their forests,' he wrote authoritatively. 'They remove the down from leaves with the help of water. . . .' This was at least one step nearer the truth than the other contemporary theory that silk was really a vegetable, possibly a distant cousin of the cabbage family.

The dot on our map seemed to imply that today Tashkurgan was a substantial provincial town, and I was expecting something about the size of Berwick. Instead it turned out to be a single street, dwarfed by mountains and lying on the edge of a featureless plain. Cold winds blew down from the mountains, raked along the pavements, then gusted out onto the steppe. It looked neither beautiful nor exotic. It was certainly not the sort of place one would wish to spend four days. There was a blacksmith, a *cay* shop, a man selling watermelons, another selling bread, a few labourers gawping at the Pakistanis and doing nothing in particular, a post office, a school, a hotel, a line of ragged poplars and on them a few blaring loudspeakers. From these issued stirring military ditties and what sounded like news reports. Few were listening to the music and none was able to understand the news. It was in Chinese and the people of Tashkurgan spoke only Turki.

In Tashkurgan we were back on Polo's trail for the first time since Yazd. He arrived here from Afghanistan sometime in 1272–3, having spent a year recovering from an illness that he caught in the High Pamirs. He disliked the Afghans: 'They are an evil and murderous generation, whose great delight is in the wine shop; for they have good wine (albeit boiled), and are great topers; in truth they are constantly getting drunk.' The Uigurs of Chinese Turkestan were little better. 'The natives are a wretched, niggardly set of people,' he wrote. 'They eat and drink in a miserable fashion.' Polo, however, did not see either race at their best since when he passed the two were busily trying to wipe each other out. Kubla Khan was facing a challenge from his cousin Khaidu Khan and Chinese Turkestan was the battlefield. It was never a particularly good idea to get in the way of a Mongol army, and to be caught between two was even less advisable.

Tashkurgan may thus have been an even less jolly place to visit in 1272 than it was for us in 1986. Some things, though, would have been the same. Polo, like Lou and me, would probably have been faced with his first pair of chopsticks, and for the first time would have to drink his tea from a bowl rather than a cup. He would have found a country in which garrisons of troops from the East kept watch over a strange mixture of peoples: Tajiks, Kazaks, Uigurs, Uzbecks, refugee Persians, Tibetans, and Han Chinese as well as the odd Pathan who had strayed from the hills beyond. Today this racial mix is dominated by Islam and the totalitarian ideology of Mao; then Polo would have come across an amazing eclecticism of thoughts and ideas. There were Nestorian Christians who believed in another world for animals where they would be free from enforced labour; there were Persian Manicheans who believed that Satan was as much Lord as the High God; there were sun-worshippers and fire-worshippers; Hindus; Buddhists and Muslims; there were ancestor-worshippers who used to fill their temples with life-size effigies of the dead and ring their bells night and day; there were Uigurs who used to drown unwanted female infants, and kill off the old people by force-feeding them over-greasy food.

Polo would have recognized only one building in Tashkurgan today. This is the fort, the Stone Tower which gives the town its name. It stands on a slight rise and is a square structure with double castellated ramparts. It is built of stone and faced with mud brick. It has an impressive gateway which overlooks a stretch of flooded pastureland. The shattered ruins of the old silk town lie beyond.

With that half-hour visit to the fort we exhausted the sight-seeing possibilities of Tashkurgan. We returned to the one street and began searching in earnest for a way out of the place. At the caravanserai there was no news, at the post office no attendant and at the school there was no English-speaker. There was nothing to be done. Reconciling myself to spending the next week in Tashkurgan I dug in my rucksack for something to read. In Lahore, Mozaffir had allowed us free range in his library, but it did not contain much in the way of holiday reading. Shelves of black Penguin classics reflected his fondness for unreadable nineteenth-century philosophers: Hegel and Nietsche rubbed thick spines with Schopenhauer and Kierkegaard; Freud was the only concession to the twentieth century. I longed for an Agatha Christie, but found nothing more lightweight than *The Mayor of Casterbridge* and *The Idiot*. Neither was at all what I wanted, but I sat down on the steps and made a start to the *Mayor*. A crowd gathered to watch, and Lou sketched them. The day passed slowly.

By evening I had sunk into a deep depression. I wandered around Tashkurgan in the gathering gloom thinking black thoughts. There are moments in all long journeys when the whole business of travelling seems utterly futile. One feels homesick, tired and above all bored. Nothing pleases. Everything palls. For me that moment came in Tashkurgan. The town was ugly and cold, the people were gawping morons and the nearest off-licence was in Kashgar. The caravanserai looked and felt like a refugee camp, which indeed was exactly what it was. I wanted to be anywhere, anywhere but not Tashkurgan. Someone suggested that I pray.

The next day I awoke to find the Pakistanis squatting in small groups around the caravanserai court, moaning and wringing their hands. A few were boiling pans of *cay* over small primus stoves. One complained of having been bitten by a rat. I lay in my sleeping bag until after noon, paralysed by despair. Lou seemed to have a higher boredom threshold than I, but to compensate for this Fate had given her a lower resistance to bacilli. That morning it struck her down with terrible diarrhoea. From my worm's-eye view on the floor I could see her dashing off outside every few minutes clutching her precious roll of loo paper. She would limp sadly back munching diocalm tablets. 'My bowels have died,' was her one contribution to the morning's conversation.

Then, at two o'clock, a bus drove into Tashkurgan. For a

moment I thought it was an hallucination. But as it drew nearer I became sure that I was not delirious. It was a bus. I was certain of that. And compared to the ancient charabanc that had brought us to Tashkurgan it was a modern vehicle and fitted with such rare luxuries as windows and seats. There was only one problem. It was packed, containing perhaps sixty of the *Hajji* we had seen at the border post. They looked even iller than they had done two days previously. Their faces were grey and pallid; their eyes dim and expressionless. When the bus drew to a halt in the middle of the street, many remained rooted in their seats, too exhausted to move. Those that did make it out did so with dragging feet, muttering under their breath and glancing around them, puzzled and bewildered. I picked up my rucksack and rushed, shrieking, out of the cara-vanserai to look for Lou. The bus seemed our one chance and I was determined to leave with it, even if it meant clinging to the roof rack.

I behaved unforgivably. With the ill *Hajji* too weak to argue, I led Lou into an assault on the bus, out-manoeuvring the con-ductor who was guarding the back door. Then, like suffragettes chaining themselves to the railings of Parliament, we seized a corner of the driver's cabin, and refused to budge. As the *Hajji* began to stumble back into the bus, a murmur of protest rose to a furious crescendo. The driver and the conductor screamed 'Posh! posh!' at us: an exclamation normally reserved for intransigent cattle. We did not move. We had absolutely no right to hijack the *Hajji* in this manner, but the idea of spend-ing another day in Tashkurgan had made us desperate. We stood our ground and set about perjuring ourselves. Lou pre-tended she was violently ill, then changed her mind and decided she was pregnant. She tried miming morning sickness, the later stages of pregnancy, labour, childbirth, and caesarian section. I performed an elaborate charade which hinged on my visa expiring unless I was able to get to Kashgar to renew it. I gave quite a passable mime show of my arrest, imprisonment, torture and eventual deportation from China. This rather impressed the *Hajji*. It certainly confused them.

Too exhausted to remove us violently, perhaps a little sympathetic towards the deranged Europeans, the driver eventually gave up screeching at us and started the engine. We had escaped.

Around us the *Hajji* began to nod off. Women in wimples slumped forward, capped heads fell to one side. One old man, returning from Mecca with two parrots, covered their wicker cage with a drape, then rested his head on top. Looking down the length of the bus from the driver's cabin all I could see was a mass of hoods, veils, headscarves and chimney-pot mufflers. Snores began to echo above the whine of the engine. Lou and I settled ourselves on our rucksacks, and discussed all the things we would do when we arrived at Kashgar, now only a seven-hour journey away.

Suddenly the bus lurched to one side. Everyone sprang back to life, and peered out of the window to see what had happened. The street in Tashkurgan had been tarmacked, and was straight and smooth. This impressive piece of engineering came to a sudden end one hundred yards outside the town. At the end of the main street, the road dissolved into a Somme of construction trenches, ditches, mud and craters. The bus, overloaded with three months' luggage for sixty people and a museum of religious souvenirs, groaned from side to side, accompanied by the screams of women and the grinding of metal. Twice the bus seemed to be on the verge of toppling over the embankment. The wheels stuck in ruts. Quarter of a mile later the road gave up completely. The bus driver stopped, got out, looked around and tried to decide where to go. He got back into the cabin, and drove slowly on. After a few minutes we came across a diversion sign. The driver steered left and we bumped off across a stubble field. At the far end we found a track and followed it into an avenue of trees. The trees had never been polled and the branches hung down, obstructing our passage. They snapped before us, twigs brushed into the bus through open windows. The engine started to make alarming crunching noises. The women wailed. One or two jumped out of the back door.

We pressed on until it became impossible to continue. A substantial pond lay across the avenue. On it a small white duck was swimming in contented circles. We were ordered out of the bus and the luggage was unstrapped from the roof. We flexed up against the rear and pushed the bus over a drainage ditch into a ripe field of barley. There, to the amazement of a party of reaping peasants, the driver swung the bus around in a full circle, and drove it down the field, cutting a long swathe through the crop. We regained the road, and there followed about ten minutes of calm during which we saw a camel caravan trotting across the plain. They were not the tobacco-coloured Arabian camels we had seen in Pakistan, but Bactrian dromedaries, with two humps and hairy thighs and ankles, not unlike preened poodles. Then the horrors continued. Halfway up a steep slope the bus paused, hung motionless, then gently slid back down the incline, gaining momentum as it went. It keeled over violently to the right.

The journey thereafter assumed an unreal nightmare quality. I can recall the slow, tedious climb into the Ata Dagh, the breakdowns, the blizzards and the terrible cold. I remember the horrible judderings, and the speed of the bus slowly sinking until we began to crawl along at walking pace. I remember the engine noise which seemed to increase in volume the slower we went. I remember the symphony of creaks and groans and clangs rising to its climax, and the bus drawing to a halt on a high Turkestan plateau. A series of repairs kept us going until, sometime after midnight, we drew into a freezing castellated caravanserai. There we bedded down on the floor in one big dormitory. The next morning, to Louisa's horror, we were given soup to drink with great lumps of greasy yellow yak-fat floating in it.

It took another whole day of travel before we reached the plains. As we pulled into the Kashgar bus station we made a vow never to visit Turkestan again. But within a day of reaching Chini Bagh, the old British consulate, we were already beginning to reconsider our decision.

SEVEN

In the early years of this century Chini Bagh was distinguished by its lavatory. It was a 'Victory' model with a sturdy mahogany seat, the only flushing thunderbox for two thousand miles. As if this were not enough to secure its place in legend, between its arrival in 1913 and the consulate's demise in 1949, it graced such distinguished bottoms as Sir Aurel Stein and Peter Fleming. The 'Victory' was brought by Sir George Macartney, the British consul who was sent to Kashgar in 1890 to keep a watch on the Russians. Over the final years of the nineteenth century the armies of the Tsar had rolled relentlessly across Turkestan adding Bokhara, Khiva and Kokand to the Russian Empire. The government of India suspected that Sinkiang would be the next province to fall. Not only did this put the Russians in an excellent position to move eastwards into western China, it also threatened the safety of the Pamir passes into British India. This was something Britain could never allow. Macartney, then only twenty-four, was packed off to Kashgar to raise the only Union Jack between India and the North Pole.

The Manchu authorities furnished him with a large but primitive house at Chini Bagh (Chinese garden), and there Macartney lived for twenty-eight years, surviving the conspiracies of the Russians, the elusive behaviour of the Chinese *Taotai*, the daily trials of life in Asia and, at first, the extreme loneliness. Apart from a defrocked Dutch priest and a couple of gloomy Swedish missionaries, the Russians were the only other Europeans in Sinkiang, and with them Macartney was forced to maintain cool relations. His humourless Russian adversary, Nikolai Petrovsky, was determined to turn the rivalry of the two empires into a Victorian Cold War, and he

strained relations between the two countries whenever possible. An evening visit by the explorer Younghusband to the
Russian consulate was construed as a deliberate insult. In diplomatic circles the proper time for a call was the morning, and
as a result relations were broken off for some weeks. Later, a
copy of *Punch* sent to the Russian consulate in an exchange of
newspapers was found to contain a caricature of the Tsar kicking the Jews out of Russia. Petrovsky refused to believe that the
Punch had been sent accidently, and between November 1899
and June 1902 he did not address a single word to Macartney.

But Petrovsky was a subtle politician. He nearly succeeded
in persuading his superiors to annex portions of Sinkiang,
either by directly forcing the Chinese to redraw their borders,
or by provoking the Chinese to violence and then occupying
territory to 'protect Russian interests'. His threats were backed
up by the consulate guard of seventy-five ferocious Cossacks, a
force which could at any moment be supplemented by a
whole regiment waiting only a few miles away on the Oxus,
the Russian border. Against this were ranged a degenerate,
opium-sodden Chinese garrison (whom one English traveller
described as being 'good at gardening') and the consulate staff
consisting of Sattur, 'a gnome-like little man, perfectly honest
but with the mind of a boy of twelve', Isa, the dairyman who
liked to sing his cows to sleep, and Daoud the gardener, who
used to have conversations with his plants. After Macartney
married in 1898, the anti-Tsarist forces in Kashgar were supplemented by the consul's formidable wife, Catharine, and
Miss Cresswell, the no less formidable nanny, who used to go
to bed armed with a large carving knife, so as to be 'prepared
for all eventualities'.

Catherine had never left Scotland when her fiancé turned
up unannounced at her house in Dumfriesshire. He told her
that he had only limited leave and that she had one week to get
married and set off for Kashgar. Used to the genteel ways of
rural Galloway, she was unimpressed with the Uigurs she
found around Chini Bagh. 'The natives are essentially docile
and easily managed,' she wrote, 'with no strong characteristics

either good or bad. Nearly all of them have venereal diseases. . . .' The younger Kashgaris also came in for censure. 'The babies and small children go *naked* in warm weather. They become brown like little niggers. . . .' Much more to her taste was competing with the Russian ladies at the tennis club which was formed after Petrovsky retired and relations between the two consulates began to thaw: 'We ladies took it in turns to supply tea twice a week, and we vied with each other as to who could produce the best cakes, ices, or strawberries and cream.' She was very much the Victorian memsahib, but there was a certain heroism in the way she made the best of her lonely posting, making Chini Bagh civilized, keeping it warm and homely, and creating the beautiful garden which so impressed visitors.

She would be heartbroken to see it now. The rooms have been divided up into dormitories, the stables turned into rows of stinking squatter loos, the garden left to run riot. The plaster walls are peeling and only nail holes remain where the British coat of arms used to hang. The Russian consulate, christened 'HOTEL SEMEN: Joint Hotil With Civilation', is now an expensive lodging house for foreign tourists. Chini Bagh is more down-market. It is used as an overnight stop for long-distance truck drivers, mainly Pakistanis. In the evenings they lounge around their rooms or build little fires in the courtyard on which to cook their *dal* and rice. Money changers after rupees and dollars flit from group to group. Drying *charwal chemise* hang from clothes lines.

If Chini Bagh has lost some of its romance since the days of the Great Game, then so has Kashgar as a whole. A gloomy dust haze hangs over the town like a shroud. The old city walls have been pulled down and only fragments remain. Large open streets have been punched through the bazaars, with separate lanes for cars, buses, bicycles and pedestrians. There are no cars yet in Kashgar, there is a five-year waiting list for bicycles, and few of the buses are ever in working order (Sinkiang gets them secondhand after they are too old to ply the streets of Peking), but the Chinese want to give the impression that

Kashgar is looking forward to the next century. For this reason the streets are now lined with charmless totalitarian buildings and in the centre of the principal boulevard stands an outsized statue of Mao, hand raised in benediction towards the empty expanses of People's Park. Muslim Kashgar is under assault from Marxist Peking, and the town still bears the scars of the Great Proletarian Revolution of the late Sixties. The Uigurs, the only people in Asia who did not bother resisting Ghengis Khan, have stood by as Manchu armies of occupation were replaced by Maoist armies of occupation. In the last two decades, they have continued to watch while Red Guards burned down their mosques, banned the Koran, imprisoned their mullahs and closed the schools, bazaars and *medresse*. The Uigurs have many fine qualities, but they are not a gallant race.

They do, however, possess a certain knack of survival. Our first afternoon in Kashgar we explored beyond the modern streets and soon found the remains of the old city. In the back-street bazaars, newly rebuilt after the destruction of the mediaeval town, we stumbled across a world very different from the regimented drabness of the modern communist town. The traditional ways of the Uigurs had gone to ground for a few years, then quietly reasserted themselves when it was safe to do so again. Wandering past low mud houses through dusty lanes, we suddenly came across a wider space. On either side of the road lean-to shacks had been erected, and in the centre a long tarpaulin had been hung over a brick dais. Under this, and in and around the shacks, sat vendors arranged in groups according to produce. First we came to the hat sellers, then the wood turners, ironmongers and knife makers. Beyond lay a range of *cay* stalls, an expanse of carpets partitioned into separate cubicles by canvas slats. On the far side was the fruit and vegetable market. The road was blocked by a gaggle of donkey carts piled high with figs, grapes, apples and apricots. Squawking chickens dangled from handlebars. One escaped from a coup and hopped off over a crowd of carts pursued by the owner. Donkey carts reversed into stalls, collapsing tarpaulins on squatting groups of tea drinkers. Little boys poked sitting dromedaries, who got up and disturbed herds of sheep. The sheep scattered over crowds of cross-legged fruit sellers. Runaway donkeys sent old men flying; little children got their feet stood on; stall-holder mothers were tripped up by nasty boys in flat caps playing hide and seek. There was a ringing of bicycle bells and camel bells and a smell of dust and charcoal and spicy cooking. It was a far cry from the days of the Cultural Revolution when a boy selling peanuts could be arrested as a capitalist. We had seen finer bazaars in the East, but none so unexpected. Coming to it from the wide empty streets of the Chinese town was like discovering some rare animal thought long extinct.

It was the human variety that was the most exciting thing about the bazaar. There were a few diminutive, nervous-looking Han Chinese in fatigues or Mao outfits; nearby sat turbaned Tadjiks and Kazakhs with high foreheads, coarse skin and twisting cavalier moustaches. There were Uzbecks with big ears and pork-pie hats, Uigurs in homespun cotton shirts, bell-shaped coats and knee-length leather boots. There were little boys in dirty trousers who cracked sunflower seeds and swarmed around the side alleys like urchins escaped from a Dickens novel.

It seemed that there was nothing that these people did not have: plough shares or dried ginseng, bamboo tree trunks or small boiled sweets, donkey-cart axles, millstones, white carrots, even crystalline sugar lumps two and a half feet long. Nothing, that is, except perhaps a competent dentist. The entire population of the market could not have had a complete set of teeth between them. Smiling faces revealed cavernous holes punctuated in exceptional cases with a solitary surviving incisor. This situation worried me as I could feel my own false front tooth beginning to wobble, and I did not give much for my chances of finding someone who could stick it in again. The last time it had come loose was in 1984 in Leh, the capital of Ladakh. There I discovered that there was but one dentist. It was the town mechanic and he used the same spanner for both his jobs.

*   *   *

Our room at Chini Bagh was cosy and comfortable. It was rectangular with a low ceiling and large windows. Inside the furniture was arranged symmetrically with two beds and two desks placed against the side walls, and a charcoal-burning stove (with no charcoal) and a steel wash-stand (with no water) in the centre of the room. There was only one problem: Madam Curd. Our first morning Madam Curd appeared at the quite reasonable hour of nine o'clock, knocked politely at the door, and sold us two bowls of thick, creamy yoghurt. We ate them with sesame rolls, and before we went to bed that night we placed the bowls outside the door. The next morning Madam Curd appeared at eight. The third morning she was outside our door just before six. There was a quiet knocking. Then a pause. Then came a louder knocking, and finally an hysterical shaking of the door. I got out of bed, shouted at Madam Curd, and foolishly bought some more yoghurt.

Madam Curd was unusual among Uigur women in that she wore no *chador*, and had the bearing of a person of some power and importance. In build she was small and squat, but she had a magnificent nose and a proud chin which was covered in a shadow of sharp stubble. She spoke with a fearsome, piercing voice and was held in great respect by the other yoghurt-women. Under her direction these women were distributed around the corridors of Chini Bagh peddling their wares. We, however, were her exclusive property. She remained remarkably unmoved by my tirade, and set about explaining herself in a rattle of loud, guttural Turki. Madam Curd appeared to be a subscriber to the theory (often thought to be exclusively British) that to be understood by a foreigner she had merely to speak louder than he. Having tired of explaining she sidestepped into the room and wandered over to Louisa's bed to inspect its contents. Louisa was still asleep and only a few strands of her blond hair could be seen above the quilt. At these Madam Curd tugged with a surprising forcefulness. Louisa emerged from beneath her bed clothes like a snail from its shell. Slightly less than half awake, she stared at Madam Curd with a mixture of fury and bemusement. Madam Curd stared adoringly back. She lifted her hand and began running her fingers through Louisa's locks. She beamed. She had never seen blond hair before.

Madam Curd was not our only morning visitor, though she was invariably our earliest. Hot on her heels, usually around nine, there would come a further invasion, this time of the moneychangers. Historically, Uigurs have always been the usurers of the East, and during the golden age of the T'ang they had a monopoly on moneylending at Ch'ang-an, the great eastern terminus of the Silk Road. The moneychanging of the Uigurs today is a less glamorous affair. Its object is to buy FECs (Foreign Exchange Certificates), the Mickey-Mouse money given to foreigners entering China, and to exchange it for normal Chinese currency. The foreigner ends up with a large quantity of Chinese money while the Uigur gets some FECs with which he can buy luxury Western items on the black market. Because the transaction benefits both parties the moneychangers assume that Europeans are longing to enter into negotiations at any time of the day, and the earlier the better. They charge into hotel rooms without knocking and corner the occupant, scribbling offers on dirty scraps of paper. Whether or not the foreigner is enthusiastic about the invasion (and at nine in the morning he is generally unenthusiastic) the moneychangers tend to regard themselves as honoured guests and assume an open invitation to sit down and sort through the foreigner's rucksack. Sony Walkmen, picture books, brightly coloured pills and digital watches will all be brought out and offered in exchange for flat caps, bowls of yoghurt, Mao suits and pieces of fruit. Other moneychangers take the opportunity to practise their English. One man sat on my bed for an hour and a half reciting a curious litany presumably learned from an eccentric English textbook: 'I have a dog; Mr Brown has an umbrella; I have a dog. . . .'

We had one other visitor, although he rarely appeared before mid-afternoon. Mick was a tall, languid hippy with a spindly body and a baffled expression. He had long locks which were held in place by a headband. He played early Bob

Dylan songs on an old guitar and nursed an enormous lump of hashish the shape of a loaf of Hovis. It lived on a breadboard on the desk in his room, and when he came to visit us he would carve off a sliver and bring it through. He smoked reefers the size of Havana cigars. Occasionally he would speak.

'Kashgar is . . . amazing,' he said one afternoon. We were sitting on the flat roof of the consulate. Below you could see the red headscarves of the women gleaning the fields by the river. Mick had his guitar with him and while he talked he strummed a few chords. Then he put down the guitar and relit an old joint.

'In Rishikesh in the old days we used to smoke a lot to help us reach . . . to help us meditate. Now I just smoke.'

'You don't believe in meditation any more?'

'Hare Krishna and all that crap?'

'It's not crap. Edward was into Hare Krishna after he left Winchester.'

'Who's Edward?'

'My boyfriend.'

'What about fatso here?'

'We're just friends,' said Louisa. 'But you were saying?'

'What was I saying?'

'You were saying about Hare Krishna.'

'Oh yeah,' said Mick. 'Hare Krishna . . . Cosmic Consciousness: bunch of transcendental bullshit, in my opinion.'

One afternoon Mick summoned up the energy to take us on a tour of Kashgar. He said he knew the least spoilt quarters of the town. He had travelled to Asia in the great days of overlanding in the late Sixties, and had lived for a year in an ashram on the Ganges. Then he moved to Kabul with his girl-friend Lynn. She had taught English, he had written poetry ('stream-of-consciousness stuff. Basically about makin' love'). They had got out in '79, before the invasion, and moved to Goa. Goa was amazing too. But they had been thrown out when the Indian Government started refusing residents' permits in 1985, and Mick had been in Chini Bagh ever since.

We followed Mick into the old town below Chini Bagh. He lolloped along leading us deeper into a maze of side alleys. Here the houses had latticed windows, and inside you could see rooms dimly lit by flickering oil lamps. In some streets he took us into tiny mosques hidden behind mud-brick walls. The *mihrab* were whitewashed and the roofs were supported by wooden pillars with stalactite capitals. We came across street acrobats, a dancing bear, some magicians and a mullah in riding boots, jodhpurs and frock coat. We passed barbers who shaved the beards and the heads of their customers, and tribal doctors who examined their patients' palms and prescribed shaman remedies: bats wings and powdered antler. But most intriguing of all were the noodle makers. Never for a moment did I imagine the skill involved in making normal, everyday Chinese noodles. A lump of dough was rolled, squeezed and bounced on a table top until it was soft, oozy and supple. Then the noodle maker rolled it out into a long sausage. He held it up and pulled and twisted it into a plaited pigtail. He brought the two ends together and repeated the process. Slowly the sausage grew in length. It was subjected to further ordeals of rolling, slapping and dismembering until it became thin and thread-like. Then, in a final show of dexterity, the threads were tortured into a cat's cradle and dropped neatly into a cauldron of boiling water. It was a fascinating sight and we watched hypnotized.

I left the others near the town centre and went to sit in the Id Gah mosque. You enter through a great domed portal and immediately the Peace of Islam is upon you. The Id Gah is the largest mosque in China and has room for eight thousand worshippers. It was partially burned down in the Cultural Revolution but has since been renovated; it now looks a little gaudy with its bright yellow-ochre brick. The façade follows the standard Persian model: an arcade of arches flanked by two pepperpot minarets, centring on the great *ivan*. But inside, lying the far side of a grove of lime trees, the architecture breaks away from the orthodox. The main prayer area is not a basilica but an open-fronted pavilion in the manner of the Chihil Sutan in Isfahan. Raised on a platform, a forest of octagonal wooden pillars supports a flat, gabled roof and gives onto a prayer wall lined with niches. The façade projects in the centre which serves to emphasize the tile-covered central mihrab. The arrangement is ingenious and extremely beautiful. When the *muezzin* called for evening prayers and the Uigurs trooped in from the bazaar and lined up in between the trees and the pillars, the effect was like holding a prayer meeting in a pavilioned pleasure garden.

I spent an idle evening in the Id Gah pretending to work. After the prayers a young Uigur came up and watched me writing. He was wearing a faded blue Mao jacket and a green embroidered skullcap. I was about to write some nonsense about old and new in perfect harmony, when the boy began speaking to me in fluent if idiosyncratic English.

'You like Islam?'

'I like many Muslims,' I replied.

'I am a Muslim,' he said. 'An educated Muslim.'

Salindi told me that he was a student at Urumchi University. There Islam was discouraged, as was the Uigur language. All teaching was in Mandarin, and the Uigur students were taught to despise their tongue and their Islamic culture. Many of his friends had dropped their faith and he now found himself in a difficult position. He was over-educated for the taste of most Muslims, but considered old-fashioned and backward by his contemporaries at university. Recently he had applied for permission to go on *Hajji*, and had been refused. No one between the ages of ten and sixty was allowed to leave the country.

'Mecca is so beautiful,' he told me. 'I have seen pictures. The buildings . . . the crowds. . . .'

I told him I would like to see it too, but was also unable to get permission. No non-Muslim was allowed into the Holy City.

'Do you believe?' he asked.

'Yes, I think I do.'

'In Allah?'

'In the Christian God. It probably comes to much the same thing in the end.'

His face darkened. 'No. I do not think so.'

'What do you mean?'

'If the Christian God were as mighty as Allah the West would not be like it is. In Europe you have no morals.'

'How do you know what the West is like?'

He blushed. 'I have seen James Bond films.'

'Here?'

'Yes. We now get many European films in Sinkiang. Also books.'

'What sort of books do you get?'

'I am reading a book about Britain at the moment. Would you like to see it?'

I followed him to the gatehouse where he had left his bag. The book was an English language textbook entitled *A Survey of Great Britain*, written by a certain Zhang Guo Yung and 'examined and approved' by Huang Hong Xu. It turned out to be a remarkable work. Its findings included the following: the five biggest mass organizations in the country are the TUC, the CBI, the NUS, CND and the Society of Anglo-Chinese Understanding. To send a boy to public school costs 'very much – about £90'. The Conservative and Labour parties both represent the landowning and capitalist class and the only difference between them is that 'the Labour Party likes to argue about theories, for example the theory of Socialism, but the Conservatives do not'. As for newspapers: 'The *Guardian* has made progress among intelligent people', while the *News of the World* 'specializes in court cases'. London meanwhile is a city beset by pollution problems. These are due, so it says, to a combination of marsh mists sweeping in from the east and the 'citizen's love of open smoke fires', the combination of which means that the Londoner can seldom see a yard in front of him.

As we sat reading, an old *hoja* sidled up and began asking my friend questions.

'What is he saying?' I asked.

'Forgive this man,' said Salindi. 'He is old and stupid.'

'No, please. What is he saying?'

'He is a very foolish man. He is asking who is the Chairman of England.'

'Tell him our chairman is called Elizabeth.'

Protesting, Salindi told him. The Mullah asked another question.

'What did he say?'

'Sir, do not worry about this man. He is asking uneducated questions.'

'Really, I don't mind. What questions?'

Salindi frowned. 'He wants to know how many sheep, donkeys and camels your chairman owns.'

'Tell him she owns no camels, but has very many horses and a great number of corgi dogs.'

The information was passed on. The old man nodded his head as he listened.

'Sir, this man is now asking about the dog which is called *khor-qi*. He asks whether these *khor-qi* are good to eat.'

'Tell the old man that they are delicious.'

'And your chairman has many flocks of these dogs?'

'Very many.'

'Sir, the mullah says your chairman must be very rich. But he asks one more question. You must forgive him, sir, he does not know better. He wants to know why you dye your hair blond. He says it looks very stupid. He asks why you do not leave it black like it should be. If you do not like it he thinks you should shave it off or wear a hat like other men. Sir, he does not understand. . . .'

The following day I met Salindi outside the Id Gah at one o'clock. He had promised to take me to a matinée. I had never been to an Asian cinema, and was anyway interested to check his claim that English-language films were on show in China. I had always understood that Western films were kept well away from the People's Republic to make sure no one ever got a hint of the life enjoyed on the affluent side of the Bamboo Curtain. This idea had been confirmed by my guidebook to China which maintained that the Chinese were kept going on a cinematic diet of *The Chuang Minority Loves Chairman Mao with a Burning Love* and *The Production Brigade Celebrates the Arrival in the Hills of the Manure Collectors*. But Salindi had been telling the truth. At the Kashgar Odeon (or whatever name it went by) two films were currently being shown. One was advertised by pictures of the familiar 'Happy Peasant' variety, and that film might well have been about manure collectors. But there was no mistaking the second film. It was *Dr No*. We bought two tickets and went inside. The film had just begun.

The auditorium was not large by English standards, but was packed full. The audience consisted entirely of Uigur men and all were in a great state of excitement. It seemed not to matter that very few had seats, and had to sit on a floor glazed with spittle. Going to the cinema was clearly a great treat, and everyone was determined to enjoy themselves whether or not conditions were perfect, indeed whether they could see or hear anything at all. I assume this because the Uigurs can in fact have understood almost nothing of what was going on. The film had been dubbed out of its original English, not into Turki but into French, which cannot have aided comprehension greatly. And, although there were subtitles, this also did not greatly help. The Uigur subtitles were placed at the bottom of the frame, beneath those in Tibetan and Chinese, and because of a technical error in the projecting box, all of these had disappeared below the screen and now rested on the backs of the heads of the people in the front two rows. This same error also deprived Sean Connery and Joseph Wiseman of their heads, which were projected beyond the screen and could just be seen, along with everything else from the top of the frame, wildly distorted at the front of the hall.

Despite all these irritations, the Uigurs were tolerant. There was an excited murmur every time a character bent down and his face could be fleetingly glimpsed on the screen, and the Muslim audience behaved with remarkable restraint during the sex scenes. Even Ursula Andress coming out of the sea, enough to craze the most worldly-wise Western audience, failed to move the Uigurs to any really dramatic behaviour, although this may have been because none of the audience had ever seen the sea (Kashgar is further from it than any other town in the world) and so were distracted from the more inflammatory aspects of the sequence. It may also have had something to do with the fact that the more inflammatory parts of Ursula Andress's body had missed the top of the screen and could only be seen indistinctly (if hugely enlarged) on the front wall.

There was, in fact, only one scene in the film which really impressed the Uigurs. This was when James Bond wakes up to find a large and very hairy tarantula crawling up his crotch and making for his torso. There cannot be many tarantulas in Kashgar, but the audience still got the gist of what was happening. They went berserk. As the spider crawled upwards the background murmur in the cinema got louder and louder. At the moment Bond tossed the beast off his chest and onto the floor, crushing it with his shoe, the cinema exploded. The Uigurs rose from their seats and bawled 'Allah-i-Akbar' (God is all powerful). A very old man next to me took off his shoe and started thumping the floor with it. Hats were thrown in the air. Urchins made wolf whistles. It was like the winning goal in the Cup Final. After that, even the twenty megaton nuclear explosion in the SPECTRE headquarters came as bit of an anti-climax.

Coming out of the cinema, I noticed for the first time a winter nip in the air. The Kashgar nights had been cold ever since we arrived, but now the air was beginning to blow chill during the days as well. It was, after all, mid-September and summer had gone.

It was time to be thinking about moving on. We had been in Kashgar ten days. The Cambridge term was due to start in three weeks. I was supposed to be changing faculties and before I returned to university was expected to have spent at least a month in earnest study of Anglo-Saxon Gospel Books. It all seemed very far away and very unimportant, but nonetheless left me with a nagging feeling of guilt. Reminded of England by the chilly evening, I stopped by at the Kashgar Public Security Headquarters (the police station) on my way back to Chini Bagh.

It had become clear that it was going to be difficult to follow the next stage of Polo's route. The Venetian took the southernmost of the two Silk Roads leading eastwards from Kashgar, that which skirted the northern flank of the Kunlun mountains, following the line of oasis towns between the hills and the Taklimakan desert. The northern route via Urumchi and Turfan is open to foreigners, but Polo's journey crossed much more sensitive country: land disputed with India, and now used by the Chinese for the testing of their nuclear weapons (although we did not know this at the time). Permits to the area are almost impossible to obtain. Nevertheless it seemed worth having a go. Against the odds we had got out of Israel, into Iran and over the Karakoram Highway, and I saw no reason not to try fate a fourth time.

My interview with the Chief of Police was surprising in every way except for its ultimate failure. The chief was a small, elfish Han Chinaman, who spoke good English, said he admired the British Constitution and offered me tea to prove it. We crippled each other with courtesies. I said how much I admired the triumphant achievements of the People's Republic, and he returned by complimenting in generous terms the achievements of Winston Churchill, who he seemed to believe was still our Prime Minister. I remarked how I was enjoying seeing Kashgar, and he replied by apologizing for the stubborn, ignorant natives of the Sinkiang Autonomous Region. He promised that by the time I next visited Kashgar the place would at long last have been modernized: the last of the old bazaars would have been swept away, cars and bicycles would be everywhere and camels and donkeys would be banished for ever. I applauded the scheme with enthusiasm. How nice

Kashgar would look with a bit more concrete and the odd flyover. Slowly I moved the conversation round to the possibility of a permit. I told him about Marco Polo. What a fine symbol he was of East–West cooperation! I showed him the Cambridge letters and echoed how the journey would bring China and Great Britain into ever closer fraternal relations. He nodded sagely. I hinted darkly that I might have a word with Winston when I got back, and we would see what we could do about a word of commendation to Peking.

The police chief evidently did not believe a word I said. He rose from his seat, shook my hand and wished me luck. Sadly, he said, unless I had relations along the road it was beyond his jurisdiction to grant a permit, but he knew that the Chinese International Travel Service would be delighted to help. He showed me the location of the CITS office on the map then showed me out. I caught the CITS just before closing time. The entire staff, which exists solely for aiding foreign tourists, boasted not one English speaker. I battled on in pidgin Turki. The CITS was unable to grant me a permit unless I first had a letter of introduction from the Chief of the Public Security Corps. I returned to the police station. I explained what I wanted. The officer at reception apologized. He was very sorry, but the police chief had just been taken ill and would be unable to see me. Had I thought of going to Urumchi and trying the police chief there?

I returned to Chini Bagh, defeated. It was clearly going to be impossible to get along the southern Silk Road legally.

It was a bad night. I was first woken by a loud clattering noise outside the window, and looking at my watch I saw that it was four a.m.

Crash-bang-crash-clatter-crash! Still three-quarters asleep I pulled on my *charwal chemise* and went out into the corridor. Mick was already halfway to the door.

'Did it wake you too?' I asked.

'Nah. I haven't gone to bed yet.'

'Haven't gone to bed? It's four o'clock in the morning.'

'Yeh.'

'What were you up to?'

He flashed a glazed grin. 'Smokin' the pipe of peace.'

His pupils were the size of soup plates.

We padded outside and searched for the cause of the noise. Round the back of the consulate, immediately under my window, we found two pigs enthusiastically jumping up and down on top of an old rubbish bin.

'Some whacko's tabbed those goddamn pigs,' said Mick.

'What?'

'That, fatso, is bacon on acid.'

We chased the pigs away then I went back to bed. Four o'clock in the morning was no time for freak jokes. Nor was six o'clock. Less than two hours after the pigs finally desisted from their snufflings, Madam Curd appeared on her morning visit. She hammered relentlessly on the door for five minutes, then began to break the thing down. Too tired to make even a token protest, I opened up and bought all the yoghurt she could sell me. It seemed a small price for being left in peace.

Back in bed I found to my surprise that despite being shattered and semi-comatose I was still incapable of getting to sleep. I tossed and turned, counted sheep, counted pigs, listed vicious ways of incapacitating Madam Curd – but all to no avail. I gave up and went off to have a shower. But here lay only further frustration. The hotel was owned and run by an organ of the Central Government, and so (like everything else official) it worked on Peking Time. This ran two hours behind Sinkiang time, and was quite ill-suited to the region. According to Peking Time, dawn is at half past nine in the morning, and sunset takes place sometime towards midnight. In this manner the hands of the Central Committee, which manipulate everything in China, turn even the shower knobs of Chini Bagh. I arrived at the bath house to find it closed. In Peking it was still only five a.m. The showers were not due to open for another three hours.

Returning to the room, I saw that Louisa was still asleep. The sun had risen outside, but the curtains were drawn and the room was filled with a dim yellow half-light. Some of Louisa's covers had slipped off and I could just make out the long, lovely curve of her back and her left breast, pressed gently against the sheets. I sat on my bed and took it all in while I got back into my *charwal chemise*. It was only then that I noticed what had happened to her. What I had at first taken for shadows were in fact terrible weals and blotches on her skin. Great red bruises and smaller pink swellings covered all the exposed parts of her body. Something terrible had happened to her overnight.

When she awoke soon afterwards she was feeling dizzy and ill. What I had taken for the ravagings of vicious bed bugs was beginning to look more serious. Lou lay in bed all morning, getting paler and paler and feeling less and less well. She was not hungry and there seemed to be little I could do other than read to her. By lunchtime this had only succeeded in giving her a headache.

When Mick got up early in the afternoon he too took a look at Lou. He diagnosed an allergy and prescribed plenty of sleep and a diet of hashish and curd. This had no immediate beneficial effect and so at teatime I finally set about looking for a doctor. Armed with a Chinese phrasebook I made inquiries at the reception. In China, so it seemed, doctors never came to see patients, however ill they were. The halt, lame, crippled and infirm were all expected to get to the doctor. In Kashgar, this meant either crawling to the shaman in the bazaar and getting the prescribed fix of bat's wing, or else somehow arranging a lift to the hospital, on the far side of the town. We opted for the hospital.

The problem was getting there. I wandered the streets for an hour before I found a *tonga*. The first three made a point of not understanding what I wanted. The fourth refused to take me. The fifth tried to run me down. Finally, a sweet-natured ten-year-old agreed to take me for only three times the normal fare. It was a memorable moment. Then the Chini Bagh *chowkidar* refused to let the *tonga* come inside the consulate's gates. He justified his action by pointing at the horse's back end and loudly repeated a word I assumed to be the Turki for dung. I tried to help Louisa to the *tonga*, but she was too weak now to walk more than a few steps. The *tonga* would have to be carried to Louisa.

The sweet-natured ten-year-old did not like this plan, and spat at my shoes when I suggested it. He relented only when I doubled the agreed fare. He helped me unstrap the harness, then squatted moodily on the ground while I pulled the carriage down the half-mile drive to the main consulate building (to the delight of the consulate sweepers who jeered, shouted insults and threw things at me as I passed). The Pak truck drivers looked on impassively from their cooking fires.

We eventually got Lou to the *tonga*, the *tonga* to the horse, and the horse to the hospital. There followed an hour the likes of which I hope never to have to go through again. The hospital was a filthy place and smelt of urine and incontinent Uigurs. It reminded me of archive photographs of field hospitals on the western front in 1916. Men lay groaning on camp beds. Muffled shrieks echoed down the corridors. As I carried Louisa in, two *tonga*-driving ambulance men carried a corpse out. Then Louisa ran out of strength. She sat slumped forward on a chair while I tried to explain the problem to a Uigur doctor. He took very little interest, partly I think because he spoke no English and partly also because ten Uigur women were trying to explain their problems to him at the same time. In the middle of my explanation he simply turned heel and walked off. It was over an hour before we were finally ushered into a surgery. Here a Chinese doctor ordered Lou to bare her arm. He then disappeared behind a curtain and emerged carrying an enormous syringe. It was an antihistamine dose about ten inches long by two inches wide. Ordering a Uigur nurse to hold Louisa still, he jabbed the needle into her bared upper arm. He did this with such violence that Louisa sobbed with pain. Then, rather than giving the injection in one go, he delivered the dose in short bursts over a period of five minutes, during which time the needle remained firmly stuck in Louisa's flesh.

She was beginning to have difficulty breathing: frightened, exhausted and in considerable pain, she became hysterical. She started screaming, and was sick all over the doctor, a bucket and the floor. The injection over, she collapsed onto a bed on the far side of the surgery, where she fell into a deep sleep. When she awoke three hours later, her swellings were down. By the time I got her back to Chini Bagh all the blotches and weals had completely disappeared, but she was still very weak and it was clear that she would not be able to move from her bed for several days.

For three days Lou languished in bed. She felt dizzy, weak and nauseous, and was unable to eat. I stayed by her bedside, or at any rate within Chini Bagh, nursing her, talking to the Pak drivers and searching for the 'Victory' loo. The quest for the latter was becoming something of a crusade for me, and I became adept at lying in wait for sweepers entering locked parts of the consulate, then rushing past them and making frantic searches before I was thrown out. By the time Lou recovered I had searched nearly every inch of the building. The 'Victory' was nowhere to be seen; perhaps it was destroyed in the Cultural Revolution. My only discovery was a hidden storeroom smelling of dustsheet and attic. It was full of solid-looking Victorian furniture: a couple of massive and very tatty chintz armchairs, an old stove, and a few enormous carved bookshelves, all of which must originally have been brought to Chini Bagh by mule-train. Most melancholy of all was the discovery, in one corner, of a pile of old, scratched 78s: some Beethoven, a little jazz, and four or five Chopin waltzes. These must have been the records described by Peter Fleming in *News from Tartary*. 'We led a country house existence,' he wrote of his time in Chini Bagh. 'One night we slept on the floor, drank tea in mugs . . . twenty-four hours later we were sitting in comfortable armchairs, with long drinks and illustrated papers and a gramophone playing. . . .'

It is difficult to know whether any of the furniture I saw

would have been recognized by Lady Macartney. When she arrived the consulate was a mud-built bungalow, and all the furniture homemade and very primitive. It was built of 'white, unpainted wood as there was neither paint nor varnish to be got', and included one chair, the handiwork of the defrocked Dutchman, 'so high,' reported Lady Macartney, 'that I had almost to climb up to the seat. The back was quite straight and reached far above my head, and the seat was no more than six inches wide. There was no possibility of having a rest on it – all one's time was taken up with keeping oneself balanced.' Nevertheless, by the time the Macartneys returned to England in 1918, a new consulate had been built (according to a design of Mr Hogberg, one of the dour Swedes), and it had been filled with furniture brought from Europe. I rather fancied that Lady Macartney would have sat in one of the heavy chintz chairs. They conformed to what I imagined would have been her taste.

If I was unlucky in my search for the 'Victory', I had more success in checking Polo's description of Kashgar. He seems to have liked it as much as he disliked the Kashgaris: 'The inhabitants live by trade and handicrafts,' he wrote, 'and have beautiful gardens and vineyards and fine estates. They grow a great deal of cotton beside flax and hemp. From this country many merchants go forth about the world on trading journeys. The natives are a wretched set of people, and include many Nestorian Christians, who have churches of their own. The people of the country speak a peculiar language.'

Nothing remains of mediaeval Kashgar. The mosques and the fortifications are all nineteenth century, although the decayed mud brick gives the impression of greater antiquity. Situated in territory disputed by four empires, the town has been sacked too many times for anything genuinely ancient to survive. Yet much of Polo's description still rings true. The hammering and hawking in the bazaar indicates the importance of trade and industry probably little developed from Polo's day, and the beautiful gardens and vineyards still survive. They line the roads, vine trellising and maize heads visible behind the whitewashed walls. The growing of hemp also still goes on apace (as Mick never tired of pointing out) but cotton cultivation seems to have died out. Certainly the Uigurs still wear simple cotton clothes, but they must import it for, as far as I could see, they do not seem to grow it themselves. This may, of course, have been because I arrived outside the cotton season, but there is another possibility. In Kashgaria there is a considerable amount of sheep farming; is it possible that Polo mistook the carts full of teased wool (they still trundle past) for convoys of picked cotton? Teased wool and cotton look almost identical. As for growing flax, it may well still go on, but as neither I, Lou, or Mick knew what flax looked like, we were unable to establish whether it is still cultivated.

The most exciting discovery we made was that, according to Salindi, there are still Nestorian Christians in Kashgar. Nestorius was a fifth-century Syrian bishop who had fine eyes, flowing red hair and controversial views on the nature of Jesus's manhood. Accused of over-emphasizing the humanity of Christ to the point of denying the divinity, he was hounded out of the Church at the Council of Ephesus in 431. He was sent into exile in the Libyan desert, while his supporters fled east to Persia, Khorassan and beyond. There they lost contact with other Christian sects, thus preserving many of the ideas and practices of the early Church forgotten elsewhere. At the same time they took on many of the mores of the Eastern peoples they found around them: in Persia they abandoned clerical celibacy and authorized repeated marriages; later, under the influence of Islam, they came to hold Friday as a holy day and used to perform ablutions on entering church. Theirs became a remote and exotic sect. Kashgar was one of the centres of the faith, and from the twelfth century was the seat of a patriarch.

But it was among the Mongols that the Church became really influential. Nestorian missionaries penetrated the vastness of the Mongolian steppe just a century before the Mongols swept out to conquer Asia, so that when they did so they took Nestorianism with them. Ghengis Khan was brought up by a Nestorian guardian, and many of the Imperial Mongol family received baptism. It was probably Uigur Nestorians from Sinkiang who taught the Mongols to write, and Nestorians held many of the most important posts at the Mongol court. There appeared to be a real possibility Kubla Khan would convert and that Mongol Asia might become a Christian Empire. In 1253 Friar William of Rubruck was sent to the Mongol capital of Karakoram to investigate. He returned with news both good and bad. Certainly the Khan favoured Christians and attended their services, but the conduct of those services and the intellectual capabilities of the Nestorians left a little to be desired:

> The Nestorian priests are ignorant and debauched . . . they say their prayers and have their sacred books in Syrian, a language that they do not understand. They are userers, drunkards and some live with the Tartars and have like them several wives. The bishop rarely visits their country, perhaps only once in fifty years. At that time all the male children are ordained priests, even those that are still in the cradle. Then they marry, which is completely contrary to all the teachings of the Fathers, and they are bigamists because after the death of their first wife they take a second. They are also all simoniacs, not administering any sacrament without pay. . . .

Particularly horrifying was the service Rubruk saw performed in front of the wife of the Great Khan:

> On the octave of Epiphany, all the Nestorian priests assembled in their chapel before dawn, sung matins solemnly, donned their vestments and prepared the censer and incense. And as they were waiting in the church, the first wife, called Cotota Caten, entered the chapel with several ladies and her oldest son Baltu, fol- lowed by several of his brothers. They prostrated them- selves, touching the ground with their foreheads. . . .

Then the priests brought us mead to drink, made of rice and of red wine, like the wine of La Rochelle. The Queen, taking a full cup, knelt and asked for our blessing, and all the priests sang in a loud voice while she emptied her cup. When she drank once more, we had to sing, for it was our turn. Everyone was a little drunk; meat of a sheep was brought, which was quickly devoured; after that fish. . . . So the day passed until evening. Then the Queen, tottering with drunkenness, mounted her chariot in the midst of the singing and howling of the priests, and went her way. . . .

After the thirteenth century, not perhaps surprisingly, Nestorianism went into decline. By the end of the nineteenth century it was thought to have died out in the Far East, and only known to survive in any strength in eastern Turkey. The massacres of 1917 put an end to that. In the Armenian Genocide, the Turks failed to distinguish between the Armenians and the Nestorians and within a few nights both peoples were massacred, often burned alive within their churches. Today, the only known survivors are those few who managed to escape through Kurdistan to Iraq. Salindi's news that there remained a few families of the sect still practising in Kashgar was thus a genuinely important discovery. Moreover, they would be fascinating to meet. One of their liturgies, the Mass of the Holy Apostles, dates from before 431 and is certainly the most ancient of those now in use. Isolated from the rest of Christianity since the fifth century, the Kashgar Nestorians might preserve untold numbers of ancient rites and practices. They have certainly never been studied.

Salindi promised to take me to meet the Nestorians although it was his last day in Kashgar before he returned to Urumchi. We arranged to meet at four o'clock outside the Id Gah mosque, on the the day following our trip to the cinema. Tragically, at that time I was rushing Lou to the hospital and so missed the appointment. As soon as Lou was well enough for me to leave her, I went back to the mosque to search for

Salindi. But he had gone, and I never saw him again. No other Uigur I talked to knew anything of the sect. I had missed my chance to talk to the only Nestorians I am ever likely to meet.

On Friday night there was a frost in Kashgar. Madam Curd, perhaps woken by the cold, appeared outside our door that morning at five-thirty. She screeched for half an hour before I rose to let her in. It seemed an appropriate moment to put a stop to her visits. Using a number of props, I made it clear to Madam Curd that if she ever again disturbed us before ten o'clock she would be received, at the very least, with a bucket of extremely cold water.

Saturday saw the departure of a number of the Pak truck drivers. Winter was pulling in fast, and the Pakistanis were worried about the closing of the Karakoram passes. Even Mick was getting ready to pack up. He had spent one freezing winter alone in Kashgar and did not wish to spend another. He had received a letter from Lynn, who was in Sri Lanka. She had rented a beach hut near Colombo and Mick had decided to join her there.

We, however, had not moved. Nor did there seem any immediate prospect of our doing so. Lou was now sitting up, but was still too weak to leave her bed, and the difficulties of getting away from Kashgar down the southern Silk Road remained intractable. A visit to the bus station confirmed that it was impossible for a foreigner to buy a bus ticket to Khotan without a permit, nor was it easy to find an English-speaking Uigur to buy one for us. The bus station was in complete chaos. Some buses were leaving empty (an unheard-of event in Asia) while others were packed full and surrounded by mobs of angry, fist-waving Uigurs. I circled among the crowds, jostled and shouted at, unable to find anyone who spoke English. Only the moneychangers showed any interest in me. They followed me around shouting 'Change moneys? Change dollar?'; attempts to get them to go away only increased their enthusiasm. They were soon noticed by the bus station security guards.

I and my suspicious-looking entourage were pursued around the bus station, in and out of bus queues, through ticket halls and waiting rooms until we eventually lost them in the mêlée outside.

My perseverance was eventually rewarded. In a dark booth behind the bus station, I found a degenerate-looking Uigur smoking a hashish pipe. He spoke enough English to understand what I wanted, and in due course stumbled off to the ticket office with a bundle of my money. To my surprise he came back again, but he had not got a ticket: the travel office, so he said, only reserved seats one day in advance. Hoping that we might be able to leave on Monday morning, I agreed to meet him at five o'clock the following day to try again. I roamed off towards Chini Bagh.

In the bazaar, fur hats and woolly jumpers were being hung out on the shop fronts, and the ironmongers were pulling stoves out from the storerooms. The air was cold, and some of the puddles on the ground were iced over. People seemed less willing to linger in the cafés. Everyone was hurrying home. I sat in a tea house, warming my fingers around a bowl of green tea, talking to an old russet-skinned Uigur. He said that snow had fallen the day before in Urumchi, and people were expecting a freeze. He then explained the chaos at the bus station: winter, he said, had officially begun that day, and the clocks had been changed that morning. One bazaar rumour had it that Peking time had gone back an hour; another had spread that Sinkiang time had gone forward: both rumours gained only partial credence. As a result Kashgar had ended up operating on four separate times, and the transport system had completely broken down. Back at Chini Bagh things were little better. The reception closed at sunset and the showers never opened. That night Louisa and I went to bed dirty.

The following morning Madam Curd knocked timidly at our door at seven-thirty (Sinkiang winter time). We did not use her bucket of water: it could have been six-thirty, seven-thirty, eight-thirty or nine-thirty as far as she was concerned, and we decided to be lenient.

Woken by Madam Curd's ministrations, I went out to buy some bread. I found the town totally transformed. Streams of villagers were pouring in from all over Kashgaria with great caravans of donkey carts piled high with hay, wood, or sacks of grain. Some held families of Uigurs eight or nine strong; others led horses, goats or bulls. Strings of camels ambled along the footpaths, wary both of the donkey carts and the tarmac. Sheep trotted past, fat tails flapping. Chickens squawked from wicker boxes, urchins tottered under outsized flat caps. We had forgotten the central event of the Kashgar week: the Kashgar Sunday Market. I ran back to the hotel and rose Louisa from her death bed. Together we hired a *tonga*, and joined the hordes as they poured in one solid stream towards the market.

Our cart jolted down the hill along winding willow avenues. As we neared the market the crowds thickened and the dust rose. We crawled along at walking pace. We smiled at a family in the next cart. Some of them smiled back. Everyone seemed to be enjoying themselves, if in a slightly stolid, farmerly way. Then we turned a corner. In front of us was a vast field of swarming humanity cloaked in an enormous haze of risen dust.

In its details the market resembled the weekday bazaar, but the total effect was very different. It was a fair and a carnival, a masque and a festival, crowds and noise, smells and treasures, a mirage through a dusk of dust. We wandered until our legs buckled beneath us, then we sat cross-legged in the tea tent of the silk merchants. We sipped *cay* from great porcelain bowls, and nibbled *tsepale*, a Tibetan delicacy of dough and fried yak's meat. The *tsepale* were tinct with hot spices. It was our last day in Kashgar and we were exhausted and happy.

Afterwards a shaven-headed *tonga* driver took us to the tomb of Akbar Hoja. There we lay in a garden of shrubs and trees surrounded by poplar avenues and vineyards still heavy with fruit. It was a cool, quiet, peaceful place and we stayed there all afternoon, wandering through the forest of brightly coloured pillars, looking up at the roof murals of paddle steamers and snow-capped mountains. They were a little incongruous and naive, but rather lovely.

That evening I got the tickets to Khotan. We washed our clothes, wrote a last clutch of letters, and went to bed early. We had a long journey ahead of us.

The security forces of the People's Republic work in strange ways. At six o'clock the bus station security guards hauled us off the morning bus to Khotan. They took us into their office and shouted at us. Although the lecture was in Chinese and we lost the finer points of the speech, we still got the general gist: if we made another attempt to enter a forbidden zone we would be fined and deported back to Pakistan. Then, only half an hour later, having decided to try hitching, we got our first lift from a convoy of army trucks. The last truck in the convoy, a little behind the others, drew to a halt and a khaki-clad China-man peered through the window. At first we thought the man was going to arrest us, but instead he smiled and opened the door to the driver's cabin. Happily unaware that he was aiding and abetting a crime he beckoned us in. He said he was going to Yecheng, halfway to Khotan. We jumped in. The convoy was waved through the police checkpoint at the edge of the town. It was thus as the guests of the People's Liberation Army that we left open Kashgaria and headed off into forbidden territory.

The road rapidly assumed the character that it was to main-tain along its length. The Kashgar oasis extends well beyond the limits of the town itself, and at the end of the avenues of poplar and the whitewashed garden walls, we came to a belt of large state farms. Within half an hour the fields of maize were giving way to fields of wilting sunflowers, and these in turn gave way to scrub. We passed a PLA road team with sweat-wet backs, a last cluster of houses, a water tank, and then the white desert beyond. There were no dunes. The desert was flat, harsh and depressing. Ahead the lines of the tarmac road converged in the distance. There was not one tree, one bush, not one solitary clump of pampa grass to break the horizon. We had entered the Taklimakan.

The Uigurs regard the desert as an evil place. In Turki its name means 'go in and you won't come out'. In the bazaars there are strange tales of the demons and half-men who live within its borders. These tales have a long pedigree, and are recorded by many of the travellers who have passed through the desert. The first European to make the journey was the hugely corpulent Friar John of Pian de Carpini. His account of the local legends perhaps reads a little uncritical to the modern eye:

> The inhabitants of this desert are reported to be wild men, who cannot speak at all and are destitute of joints in their legs. If they fall they cannot arise alone by themselves. But they are prudent and make felts of camel's hair, with which they clothe themselves, and which they hold against the wind. If at any time the Tartars, pursuing them, chance to wound them with their arrows, they put herbs into their wounds, and fly strongly before them.

Polo's account is also full of strange legends.

> There is a marvellous thing related of this desert, which is that when travellers are on the move by night, and one of them chances to lag behind or to fall asleep or the like, when he tries to gain his company again he will hear spirits talking, and suppose them to be his comrades. Sometimes the spirits will call him by name; and thus shall a traveller ofttimes be led astray so that he never finds his party. Many have perished in this way. Sometimes stray travellers will hear the tramp and hum of a great cavalcade of people away from the real line of the road, and taking this to be part of their own company they will follow the sound; and when day breaks they find that they are in an ill plight. Even in daytime one hears these spirits talking. And

sometimes you shall hear the sound of a variety of
musical instruments, and still more commonly the
sound of drums. . . .

At first sight, Polo's tale looks just as fanciful as that of Pian de
Carpini. But while the Friar's account is obviously ridiculous,
the story Polo tells is a common one, first recorded in the
seventh century and still current in Kashgar in 1916 when
Ella and Sir Percy Sykes heard it at first hand from a Hindu
trader. The Hindu had been in the Taklimakan after dark
when a sudden light revealed a broad road along which
marched an army, dressed, so he thought, in Turkish uniforms.
Then the army vanished only to give place to droves of cattle
and sheep. The account is almost identical to that of the great
Buddhist traveller Hsuan Tsang, who saw, one thousand three
hundred years before the trader, 'a body of ghostly troops
amounting to several hundreds covering the sandy plain – and
the soldiers were clad in fur and felt. And now the appearance
of horses and camels and the fluttering of standards and
lances. . . .'

The only soldiers we saw were those of the People's Liberation Army, and they were far from ghost-like. At eleven
o'clock the leading truck slowed down, and the convoy pulled
to a halt in the middle of the desert. Soldiers spilled out to uri-
nate and stretch their legs. We were just about to do likewise
when our driver signalled for us to stay where we were, and to
keep our heads down. The truck in front of us had also taken
on a hitchhiker, a Uigur boy a few years younger than ourselves. There had been no room for him in the driver's cabin so
he had sat outside on a tarpaulin at the rear of the truck. There
he was spotted by the officer in charge of the convoy. The officer first reprimanded the driver, then ordered the boy to come
down. Nervously he did so. Towering above the boy, the officer
shouted insults at him. The Uigur lowered his head, but did
not reply. Then the officer gave the boy a vicious shove. He
stumbled backwards, and fell heavily on his backside. The
officer rounded on him. He kicked him in the ribs and the

arms, and directed one blow at the boy's head. The Uigur squirmed in the dust and cried out when struck but made no attempt to defend himself. The other soldiers stood by, laughing. Eventually the officer kicked the boy off the road, and returned to his truck. The convoy moved off. The boy was left lying by the roadside.

By early afternoon we had passed through another police checkpoint, and entered the oasis at Yarkand. Its boundaries were marked by a straight line of poplars: one minute we were in open desert, the next amid fertile farmland cross-cut with irrigation channels and mud-brick walls. Expanses of paddy were interspersed with vineyards, vegetable gardens and orchards. The relief of escaping from the desert was almost physical, yet was mixed with the fear of being spotted by the police and sent back. In the middle of the principal street of Yarkand a lorry carrying melons had crashed into a tractor, overturning the lorry and scattering the melons. The scene of the accident was swarming with Public Security guards, and our truck drew up in the middle of them. The tractor driver, a Uigur, was in deep argument with the lorry driver who was a Han Chinaman. No one was picking up the melons. Encouraged by our driver, who had now realized that he was carrying an illegal cargo, we got back down below the dashboard. There we crouched uncomfortably for half an hour, able to see nothing except the gear stick and the crotch of our driver. The collision was cleared up and we moved on. We determined to buy a basic disguise as soon as possible, and in the meantime took in as much of Yarkand as we dared. Polo says that the inhabitants are plagued by goitre ('a large proportion of them have swollen legs, and great crops at the throat') and the same complaint was noticed by Sven Hedin, one of the handful of Europeans to get down this road in the nineteenth century. There were certainly one or two unusually portly burghers around, but they were swollen around the waist rather than the legs, and of the disease we could see no trace. Goitre is an iodine deficiency, resulting from bad drinking water, so the water supply must have been improved at some point this century.

But the inhabitants of Yarkand still look remarkable: the men are furiously moustached and sport high Cossack busbies. These have white cotton tops and perch on their heads as precarious as the plates of an acrobat's balancing act.

The Yarkand oasis is enormous; it continues without a break to Yecheng, forty kilometres away. We were dropped on the edge of the town by our driver, who shook our hands then drove quickly away, understandably nervous of being caught helping us. We set off through back lanes and across garden plots, trying to avoid the main streets of the town. Even so we attracted a considerable following. The people of Yecheng had never seen Europeans before, and they seemed determined to make the most of the opportunity. Peasants dropped their hoes; workmen left their lathes. Schoolchildren coming back from their lessons turned around and joined the growing throng who dogged our footsteps. The sensation of being a Pied Piper might have been quite enjoyable in Hamelin; now it was not only irritating but dangerous. Conceivably we might just slip past the Public Security guards if we were on our own, but it was difficult to see how anyone could avoid noticing a baying crowd of at least sixty people. It was not even particularly flattering. As we had discovered in Kashgar, Uigurs regard Europeans as enormously ugly. Pakistanis think us the very image of perfection (fashionable Pakistani women wear suncream designed not to darken their skin, but to lighten it to a fairer, more European shade), but the Uigurs do not share these preferences. In Kashgar, Louisa had received none of the generous propositions she got the other side of the Karakorams. To the Uigurs we resemble ogres in English fairy-tale books: we are too big, our noses are long and flared, our lips flabby, our features misshapen and unattractive. Louisa's breasts came in for close, incredulous scrutiny from the Uigurs: how could such inflated watermelons exist? To the people of Yecheng we were no more than wondrous circus freaks to be poked and stared at. But for all this our entertainment value was enormous; attempts to shake off the escort were doomed to failure. We hurried; our followers sped up too. We stopped at a road junction, hoping that the Yechengis would lose interest and return home. They did not. On the main road we tried to flag down a truck. It took one look at our escort and accelerated off.

It was three hours before we got another lift. The conveyance was a cattle truck, filled not with heifers, but with thirty loud and argumentative Uigurs. They were crammed into a ridiculously small space with about one and a half square foot for every occupant. It was hot, dark, stuffy and nauseously smelly. One old man was sick; another could be heard sobbing in a corner. Our drivers were three financially acute Uigur farmers. They had set up the truck as a private taxi racket in competition with the irregular and unreliable government bus services; if the fare they charged us was at all representative, they must have been doing very nicely from the business. The journey was extremely unpleasant and was aggravated by a momentary panic when Louisa thought her money belt had been stolen. It had not, but it was only when we stopped at a *han* for the night that I discovered that my side pocket had been ransacked and my razor blades, malaria pills, insect repellent, sun cream and athlete's foot powder were all gone. It was a terrible waste: the Chinese cannot grow beards, do not suffer from malaria or sunburn, and were unlikely to guess what to do with the athlete's foot powder or the Jungle Juice insect repellent. My only consolation was the thought that the wretches might try to eat them.

The next morning we continued our journey on top of a pile of coal.

We arose before dawn and tried to find a truck to take us on from Khotan to Keriya, the next oasis. Of ten trucks in the *han* courtyard, four were broken down and five were returning to Kashgar. That left only one to choose from. Its driving cabin was full and we had to sit on an enormous mound of coal slag in the back. We climbed up, at once regretting the decision to wear our brand new white *kurta* tops from Lahore. But such concerns were soon dwarfed by much greater worries. Accompanied by loud judderings and crunching of gears, the lorry crawled out of the *han* and made its way up the middle of the main street of Khotan. Lou and I, exposed to the world on top of our coal tip, kept our heads down to try and avoid unwanted police attention. We need not have bothered. The truck trundled up the principal thoroughfare, turned left and headed straight for the police station. We parked directly outside the main entrance. The driver waved at us and went in to fetch a permit. We scrabbled around in the coal trying to dig ourselves into foxholes, covering our heads with jerseys in an effort to pass off as sleeping peasants, well aware that our clothes and rucksacks must have screamed out to every passing Public Security officer. Yet no policeman emerged from the Public Security Bureau and after a few minutes the driver returned proudly bearing the new permit in his hand. He got back into the cab and turned the ignition. The truck coughed, coughed again and died. We held our breath while the driver tried a third time. Nothing happened. Into our foxholes we dived, pulling our jerseys back over our heads. For twenty minutes the driver and his friend hammered away at the engine, until eventually it spluttered grudgingly back to life. At half its previous speed the truck crawled out of the police station and headed at walking pace into the main street. We were overtaken by a man on a donkey. Then, suddenly, we were in the desert. On all sides the shale flats stretched off into infinity. It was difficult to believe that anything could move slower, yet we again managed to cut our speed by half when, soon after Khotan, the tarmac road gave out and was replaced by a gravel track, pockmarked with boulder-sized potholes. It took a great effort of imagination to believe that we were travelling along the fabled Silk Route, one of the most famous highways in the world. In Scotland I have travelled along many more imposing footpaths.

The day wore on and the truck's speed sunk lower and lower. We headed deeper into the desolation. A desert wind rose, covering us with sand and coal dust. At noon we had travelled for five hours and put no more than twenty miles behind us. Then, early in the afternoon, we came across a farmstead lying alone in the middle of the desert. It was a strange place. Surrounded by sand, with no water and no cultivation, it was difficult to see how the Uigurs who lived there could survive. There was nothing for them to eat except a few ill-looking chickens (how did the chickens survive?) and although they must earn some money feeding truck drivers, only a handful of trucks could pass by in an entire year. So I mused as the patron strangled and plucked one of the unhappy chickens. He burned it over a fire then hacked it to pieces with a carving knife. We ate it in silence. Then we drove on. Lou lay on her back amid the coal dust, listening to her Sony Walkman. I laboured through *The Mayor of Casterbridge*. Only one event of the afternoon impressed itself in my mind. This was when I soaked myself performing the difficult task of balancing on the back flap of the truck and urinating into the slipstream.

Hours later, bored, caked in coal dust, smelling of urine, we pulled into the oasis of Keriya. The sun was setting. We had been driving, literally, from dawn until dusk, and in that time we had covered thirty-five miles.

But Keriya proved full of surprises.

The lorry dropped us off in a side street and we scuttled off to find the *han* before the Public Security guards found us. In the caravanserai compound we were confronted with a most unexpected sight. There, facing us, were not the usual burned-out beaten-up haulage trucks, but a row of gleaming, new Toyota Land Cruisers. More unexpected still was the boy we found cleaning them. He was dressed in a Japanese tracksuit and welcomed us in good English, which he spoke with a slight American accent. The boy, we discovered, was from Hong Kong, as were the Land Cruisers. They belonged to a party of German geomorphologists who were cooperating with the Chinese in a geological survey of the Tarim basin. The party consisted of twenty academics from Germany and

China; the expedition had taken a decade to plan and was the first to be given permission to enter the area since the proclamation of the People's Republic in 1949. Slightly annoyed at having been beaten down the road, but looking forward to meeting the geomorphologists, we took a room and set about cleaning ourselves up before joining the Germans for supper.

Half an hour later, sweet-smelling, and wearing a marginally fresher set of clothes than those in which we had arrived, we crossed the compound to the *han* refectory. The air was full of smoke and the buzz of conversation. Fifty men and one or two fat German women were sitting at five large, round tables. In the middle of the tables were great heaps of food, the likes of which we had not seen since leaving the Begum's table in Lahore. There were plates of meat covered in delicious sauces, kebabs, mountains of noodles, exotic Chinese vegetables, small batter envelopes filled with fascinating spicy confections, water chestnuts, great drifts of pilau rice. The seating had been arranged so that the Germans were alternated with orientals, and the latter were busy trying to teach the Germans to use chopsticks in a civilized manner. Their efforts met with only limited success and the conversation was punctuated with louds guffaws of hearty Teutonic laughter.

Having broken in on this feast unexpected and uninvited, we thought it best to keep a low profile. We quietly took our seats in a corner and waited to be served. No one came to take our orders, nor did any of the Germans invite us to join them. After ten minutes, slightly embarrassed at not having done it sooner, I got up and went over to the senior German. I introduced myself, and held out my hand for him to shake. The German professor was struggling with a hundred-year-old egg as I approached, and he looked up, outraged that I should butt in at such a rare moment of pleasure. His moustache bristled. Leaving my hand unshaken, he looked me up and down, frowned and said: 'Who are you and what are you doing here?' Before I had time to answer, the professor turned to his left and consulted with a small Mao-jacketed Uigur. The conversation hushed. I stood beside the professor, hand still outstretched, grinning inanely. After what seemed like half an hour, but what could not in fact have been longer than thirty seconds, the professor turned around and addressed me again.

'The District Governor,' (he motioned to the Uigur), 'says that he did not expect two extra foreigners at his banquet. Go back to your seat. You will be served.'

I went back to my seat. Lou looked at me and shook her head. A waiter brought us some leftovers. The game was up. Attempting to outwit the police, we had stumbled across a gathering of the entire local Party officialdom. We picked at our supper in gloomy silence. The following morning we would be sent back to Kashgar and maybe deported to Pakistan. It was the end of the expedition.

Meanwhile the noise level rose. Unworried by the intrusion of the two renegades, the Party cadres drank and laughed freely. The Germans downed the remaining bottles of Chinese pilsen, wiped their plates, burped, then began singing. The cadres countered by playing a noisy drinking game. It was a kind of human snap. Two cadres faced each other, and on the count of three (*yi, er, san!*) slammed their fists on the table, extending as they did so a certain number of fingers. The rules were simple. If both parties extended the same number of fingers, both had to drink a large glass of *mao tai*, the fierce rice wine which the Chinese love and which Westerners find difficult to distinguish from methylated spirits.

Soon everyone was very drunk. The Germans rolled from side to side, cried, laughed, bawled out guttural drinking songs and slapped the Chinese on the back. The governor stood up and started to make a speech. After a few sentences everyone began clapping and the governor gave up. He had anyway forgotten what he was going to say. He sat down, waited for everyone to shut up, then stood up again. This time he proposed a toast. The professor followed suit. Minor party officials proposed further toasts and were followed by minor academics. More bottles of *mao tai* were brought and quickly emptied. A kind waiter brought a half-glass to each of us.

The evening wore on. Germans began to slump forward

onto the table tops. The songs got slower and increasingly emotional. The cadres stumbled off to bed. The governor got up, held himself steady and then, to our surprise, tottered over to our table, propped up by his two interpreters. He clasped us both to his chest and wished us good night. We were welcome in Keriya, he said. He was the friend of all enlightened foreigners. He poured us both glasses of *mao tai*, then politely inquired how we had got here. We explained our story to him, and told him that we had come to Keriya by coal waggon. He expressed horror at the danger and discomfort we had exposed ourselves to, and offered to arrange bus tickets to Charchan for us. Tomorrow, he said, we were to be his guests at a dancing display. Then, the following morning, we could catch our bus. So saying, he poured three last glasses of *mao tai*, drank our health and staggered off to bed.

We assumed that the governor's pleasantries had been the drunken ravings of a man unstudied by too much rice wine. We were proved wrong, however, when two bus tickets to Charchan were delivered to our door at ten o'clock the next day. The bus was not scheduled to leave until five a.m. the following morning but with the governor as out protector we considered ourselves safe from the attentions of the Public Security guards, and celebrated our new-found freedom by breakfasting out of doors. Then we went back to bed.

Late that afternoon we ventured out of the compound to explore. It did not take us long to appreciate that we had been stranded in one of the most beautiful places that either of us had ever seen. We roamed along mud-walled alleyways, past a set of perfect mediaeval street scenes: blacksmith's hammering, children playing in broken donkey carts, old ladies in smocks sitting beside the road, nuts and dried apricots laid out in front of them. Men bent under the weight of shoulder poles staggered home carrying water from irrigation runnels; a boy squatted on his hams drawing in the dust with a bent stick.

Aksakal, the white-beards, set out in groups of three to take the evening air. They were dressed in flowing robes of khaki serge, tied loosely at the waist. On their heads they wore mountainous white turbans. Some had Caucasian features. When they greeted other *aksakal* coming in the opposite direction they would clasp each other's hands, shake firmly, then stroke their beards with their right hands and conclude the ritual by touching themselves on the back of the neck.

Most of the houses we passed were of mud brick, but a few had walls built from bundles of pampas grass tied together to form thatched fences. The fences were broken with rickety wickets. They reminded me of English cottage gardens. Over the walls we could see Uigurs sitting under the shade of vine trellising, sipping *cay* from clay bowls. Others tended their sunflowers and climbing roses. There were poplar trees and apricot trees, mulberries and ash. There were sparrows in the branches and the leaves rustled in the breeze. After two days of desert it seemed nothing short of paradise.

At one place in the main street a crowd had gathered in a ring. We pushed forward and found an acrobat in the middle. His daughter was his assistant and together they performed a series of age-old circus tricks: fire-breathing, balancing acts, and sword-eating. The girl concluded the show with a display of simple cartwheels. The crowd clapped enthusiastically then tried to make off before the acrobat passed the hat around. Not knowing the proper tactics we hung around and ended up paying for all of the Uigurs.

In another part of the oasis we visited the new mosque, as yet still unroofed. While Lou sketched the mullah, the *muezzin* drove away the inevitable urchin escort with a six-foot-long knob kerry. Built of wood by the villagers themselves, the mosque was simple and lovely – an open-air wooden pavilion, giving onto a wooden basilica. It was similar to the Id Gah mosque but spared the clumsy *ivan* and dome of the Kashgar model. It was cheering to know that the traditional crafts still survive here; in other parts of Islam the concrete mosques erected by 'progressive' governments rival the worst modernist horrors in Europe. The Iranians are the worst offenders, followed closely by the Jordanians and the Turks.

Hence, by the back door of the mosque, into open countryside reminiscent of an eighteenth-century Dutch painting: long, sinuous lines of poplars set in a flat, green, fecund landscape. The ground was soft and springy and there were hens and white ducks picking around the irrigation channels. Sitting on the banks of a brook a Uigur peasant came up to us. He was wearing a bell-shaped skullcap edged in sable and he asked us if we were from Hindustan. Taking the remark as a compliment to her healthy suntan, Lou replied that we were.

We returned to our rooms to learn that we had had two visitors in our absence. The first was the governor who had called in person to deliver tickets to his dancing display. The second was an officer from the Public Security Bureau who wanted to see our permits. Hoping that our first visitor would protect us from the second, we adjourned to supper where we found the Germans slightly more friendly since our adoption by the governor. The German professor was in a great state of excitement. The reason for this was explained to us by a young expert in glaciation from Hamburg. Apparently the governor, after delivering our tickets, had gone straight to the professor and asked him whether he would be so good as to sleep with his (i.e. the governor's) new and very attractive young wife. This offer had been made two years previously when the professor had first visited Keriya to prepare the ground for the current expedition. Then he had refused saying that he was too old for such pleasures. It seems the governor had misunderstood him and thought that the professor meant the proffered wife was too old. Far from being put out by this observation, the governor had instantly divorced his wife and married his current belle, a renowned Uigur beauty from Khotan. When the professor had refused a second time the governor was mortified: 'I want some noble, enlightened blood in my family,' he had begged. 'Are you sure, Professor, that your loins are too tired?'

The strange thing is that a similar offer may have been made

Mullah praying on the banks of the Indus, Thakot.

Camel driver, Kashgar Sunday market.

Hajji pilgrims walking to Kashgar after the breakdown of their bus.

Coal truck on the Southern Silk Road between Khotan and Keriya. While Louisa sleeps, a Uighur battles with her Sony Walkman.

Looking smug afterwards, Neville's Court, Trinity College, Cambridge.

to Marco Polo when he came here. It is the origin of one of his few saucy anecdotes. 'The people of Pein [Keriya] have a custom,' he writes, 'which I must relate. If the husband of any woman goes away upon a journey and remains away for more than twenty days, as soon as that term is passed the woman may marry another man, and the husband may also marry whoever he pleases.'

Sir Henry Yule, in his footnote to this passage, writes rather disapprovingly that this 'may refer to the custom of temporary marriages which seem to prevail in most towns of Central Asia which are the halting places of caravans, and the morals of which are much on a par with those of our own seaport towns, and from analagous causes. Kashgar is also noted in the East for its *chaukan*, young women with whom the traveller may readily form an alliance for the duration of his stay, be it long or short.'

As there seemed to be no *chaukan* available at supper, Louisa and I were forced to sit next to the young expert in glaciation. He was an appalling bore.

German: My father is in semi-conductors. I too vood have gone into semi-conductors, had I not discovered moraines.

Louisa: How interesting! What is a moraine?

German: Tzere are three principal kinds of moraine. Tze first is called a lateral moraine, tze second a medial moraine. Some people are interested in lateral and medial moraines. I am not. *I* am interested in *terminal moraines*!

Louisa: Gosh.

German: Terminal moraines are tze deposit left when tze rock fragments in a glacier are left stranded by tze melting ice pack. For tzis to happen it is very important zhat ze glacier is neither retreating nor advancing. It must be stationary! Stationary I say!

WD: Some more tea?

German: However if tze ice advances *over* a terminal

moraine, tze sediments become contorted and folded. (*Much gesticulation.*) Zis produces structures resembling tectonic deformation. Such a feature is known as a push moraine. Push moraines are BEAUTIFUL! BEAUTIFUL!

(*Rambles on at great length and tedium.*)

We were saved from more of this by an envoy of the governor who came in and announced that all our company was requested by the Keriya Communist Party at the Keriya People's Hall. It was, on this occasion at least, an invitation we could not refuse.

The governor was being characteristically modest when he called the performance that he laid on for us a dancing display. It was Keriya's answer to the Royal Variety Show, an extravaganza of local Uigur farming talent, comprising singing, dancing, strumming on balalaikas, a little light operetta, and some curious slapstick comedy sketches. It was rounded off by a little Uigur pantomime whose meaning remained obscure. The show was an interesting reflection of Sinkiang's position as a cultural crossroads: the gestures of the dance seemed to be drawn from India, the twanging balalaika from Russia, the costumes and facial features from China. But as entertaining as the performance itself was the audience of excited Uigurs who, led by a row of mentally handicapped children at the rear of the hall, expressed their enjoyment in a chorus of hoots, whistles and inarticulate (if appreciative) gargling noises. The governor seemed to be enjoying the show more than anyone and himself put on a splendid performance: he showered us with sweets, melons, nuts and drinks, asked us at the end of every act whether we were enjoying ourselves, and enthusiastically offered his wife around the junior German academics. After nearly three hours of this, the cast appeared for a last bow, the audience exploded into tumultuous applause, and the handicapped children began weeping. We filed out led by the governor, who invited us all back to the *han* dining hall for a quick glass of *mao tai*. We excused ourselves saying we were tired, and crossed the compound to our room.

The door was open and the light was on. Two men were inside bending over my rucksack. I rushed in, then stopped. The men were not burglars as I had first assumed. They were Chinese Public Security guards.

There followed a very unenjoyable three hours at the Keriya Public Security Bureau. We played ignorant foreigners. We played outraged Englishmen. We played harmless idiots. We threatened and cajoled, flashed our letters, smiled and flirted. We outlined the nasty things that would happen to them all when our friend the District Governor came to hear about our arrest. We listed the honours that would be heaped on the officers for helping our expedition. I went and fetched an interpreter and we went through the whole rigmarole again, this time in Chinese. Despite now being mutually comprehensible, we made no visible progress. They repeated their position over and over again. We had illegally entered a forbidden area. We had no permit. We must be fined and sent back to Kashgar. But gradually, as our claims to influence grew, a seed of doubt lodged itself in their minds. Perhaps the imminent royal visit would be called off. Perhaps Britain really would break diplomatic relations. Sometime after midnight we wrung our first concession. Before they deported us they would telegraph their superiors in Urumchi. By one we got them to agree to a second concession. They would let us go to bed, and wait until the next morning before telegraphing or pursuing their inquiries any further. Everyone was tired. Everything could be sorted out amicably the following morning.

We went back to the *han*, packed our bags and went to sleep for four hours. At five we were up and creeping past the Public Security Bureau like naughty children off to raid a larder. Using the tickets the governor had bought us, we got aboard the dawn bus. The checkpoint the far side of Keriya was unmanned. Feeling very uncourageous and more than a little worried as to the consequences of our escape, we juddered off out of the oasis and back into the cold wastes of the Taklimakan.

I dreamt that I was swimming across a sea of golden syrup. The air overhead was a pleasing shade of orange and the syrup was warm and pleasantly sticky. At first I swam happily, but I slowly became aware that I was sinking, or rather being sucked down. Surprised and rather alarmed, it dawned on me that I had managed to swim into a whirlpool. I made a mental note: watch out for whirlpools the next time you go swimming in seas of golden syrup. Sadly there was little chance of doing anything constructive to save the situation. I was shooting downwards in a perfect swirling spiral, dizzy and sickly fast. Suddenly the swirling stopped and I realized that although I was still covered in golden syrup, I was now sitting trussed up in a dentist's chair. Everything was as a dentist's surgery should be, except that the dentist, whose back was turned to me, was dressed in a strangely familiar black cowl. The dentist turned around and came towards me clutching a huge pair of pliers. She said: 'Now William, this won't hurt,' and as the pliers plunged into the recesses of my mouth I suddenly realized that the dentist was Laura.

I woke up screaming. Feeling the front of my mouth with my tongue, I realized that the loose front tooth which had been worrying me since Kashgar was now very wobbly indeed.

'Are you all right?' asked Lou.

'What do you mean?'

'You've been whimpering for the last five minutes.'

'I'm sorry,' I said. 'I just saw Laura.'

'Laura?'

'Yes. She was coming at me with a pair of pliers.'

Lou, bemused, shook her head, and returned to *The White Hotel*. Around us our fellow passengers were beginning to wake up. It was very cold and the Uigurs had come fully equipped with sheepskins and massive fur pelts which gave the bus a rather neolithic look. Some of the Uigurs nibbled seeds, others cut slices of watermelon with savage-looking knives. All smoked fat cigarettes emitting a smell suspiciously like hashish. The geography textbooks have us believe that hemp is cultivated in China exclusively for its rope-making qualities. This is nonsense. As our journey demonstrated, the Uigurs are far from blind to the ability of hashish to make a long, boring bus journey pass in a pleasant state of euphoric semi-dormancy. It is to the Sinkiang People's Autobus Company what McEwen's Export is to British Rail.

The disadvantages of travelling with a busload of stoned Uigurs only became apparent later. An hour after sunrise the early winter winds began to blow and by noon they had turned into quite respectable sandstorms. The windows were shut and everyone waited to see what would happen. Polo's *The Travels* contains descriptions of many of the horrors of the desert, but does not mention sandstorms. This is surprising as the *buran* of the Taklimakan are some of the most ferocious of any desert in the world. Of the descriptions of *buran* left by those who experienced them, none is as evocative as the much-quoted passage in von Le Coq's *Buried Treasures of Chinese Turkestan*:

> Quite suddenly the sky grows dark . . . a moment later the storm bursts with appalling violence. Enormous masses of sand, mixed with pebbles, are forcibly lifted up, whirled around and dashed down on man and beast; the darkness increases and strange clashing noises mingle with the roar and howl of the storm. The whole happening is like hell let loose. . . .

Nothing quite as bad as von Le Coq's *buran* hit us, but as the wind increased in strength the sand from the dunes began to drift onto the road. At first this simply slowed us down, but gradually it began to make the going almost impossible. The bus finally drew to a halt in front of a huge drift thirty miles outside Keriya. The driver covered his mouth with a rag and disappeared outside with a shovel. A handful of the more *compos mentis* Uigurs and I went out to help him; the rest stayed in the bus puffing at their reefers. We shovelled away at the sand and placed wooden sleepers under the wheels to give the tyres some purchase. It worked. After an hour of hard labour the bus moved on, but drew to a halt only five miles further up the road. Again we all got out and shovelled.

The rest of that day was spent edging forward in this manner. At six the sun set over the distant Kunlun mountains, darkening the vast emptiness of the desert. Through the rattling of the bus came the quiet murmur of the Muslims saying their evening prayers. It was nearly midnight when we arrived at Niya.

The caravanserai was filthy, cold and had no food, but neither, thankfully, did it have any Public Security guards. We slept like children, but only until five o'clock. To keep ahead of the police we knew we had to be off before dawn. We also thought it wiser to change our transport. If the Keriya police had telegraphed forward to Charchan, the Public Security there would be expecting us on the bus. We guessed that we stood more chance of getting through travelling by truck. So, feeling ill and exhausted, we tramped around the different caravanserai dormitories looking for a driver who was leaving immediately, heading in the right direction and prepared to take us with him. Only one filled all these criteria: as at Khotan, we set off into the desert on top of a pile of coal. To mark the occasion we wore for the first time the 'disguises' we had bought in Keriya. Mine consisted of a Mao suit topped by a green Uigur skullcap; Louisa wore a printed dress and a white veil. From front-on, in broad daylight, neither disguise fooled anyone. Indeed on several occasions they caused hysterical peals of laughter from Uigurs who otherwise might never have noticed us. Nevertheless we thought that the 'disguises' did look vaguely convincing from the back. If ever we came to a checkpoint, we planned to fall forward on our faces and pretend to be asleep. Only the most officious guard would be rude enough to wake a sleeping couple, or so, at any rate, we hoped.

The next two days were exhausting. The constant worry of being detected, occasional pangs of hunger and thirst, the physical effort of digging ourselves out of sand dunes, the daytime heat and the extreme night-time cold, all these different strains began to take their toll. Particularly unpleasant was the aggressive old man with whom we shared our coal slag. Our relationship got off to a bad start on the first day when, during a mid-morning *cay* stop, I blew my nose in his presence. For this unforgivable *faux pas* I earned myself a violent torrent of abuse. It appears that my crime was twofold: firstly blowing my nose while he was drinking, secondly using a handkerchief. Apparently polite Uigur etiquette demands that one walks away from any imbibing company, raises one's left hand to the ridge of one's nose and blows heartily through the nostrils, aiming to discharge the deposit onto the ground. Any overhang should then be wiped away, and the hand then cleaned on the shirt front. This was certainly how the old man approached the problem. It was on this same *cay* stop that my false front tooth finally fell out. This had a disproportionately lowering effect on my morale. It was now four days since my razor blades had been stolen and the combination of an unshaven yet unbearded face, a weatherworn visage and a gap-toothed smile was clearly an unpleasant one. It was several days before I next saw a mirror and was able to take in the full horror of it myself, but its effects on those around me was immediately obvious. It was about this time that little Uigur children began running away from me, screaming and shrieking for their parents.

That night we reached Charchan. Outside the caravanserai we ate the best kebabs in the world, then slunk quickly off to bed before our 'disguises' caused a riot. Long into the night we could hear the shrieks of laughter outside. Neither of us could sleep. A day exposed to the full glare of the desert sun had given us both bad sunburn, while the night chill was unbearable. We lay awake in our coal-grimed clothes, at once burning and shivering, a combination that was as unpleasant as it was unusual. We were up and waiting for the truck driver when he appeared at four-thirty the following morning.

The strain was now really beginning to show. We had been on the move for nearly a week and in that time had only one full night's sleep. Louisa was silent and irritable; I had sunk into a state of exhausted, toothless gloom. We had diarrhoea. Our clothes were torn and we were both filthy: neither of us had washed since Keriya. I was a terrible sight; poor Lou looked a little better but felt much worse. The colour had gone from her cheeks and she had ceased to take trouble with her appearance; for the first time she was beginning to look a little dishevelled. The next morning, after another sleepless night in another filthy caravanserai, she finally reached the end of her endurance. The coal truck left Waxari before dawn. Shortly afterwards she said: 'I think that I am going to be sick,' then was, several times. We arrived at the oasis of Charchalik about nine in the morning. There she announced that she was quite simply incapable of going on.

'If I spend one more minute on this truck,' she said quietly but very firmly, 'I will die.'

We took a bedroom from the club-footed caravanserai keeper. There we ordered a basin of hot water, then washed, dried and lay on our beds wondering how long it would be before the police came to hear of our arrival. They heard very quickly. At quarter past ten there was a knock on the door. Lou was asleep so I got up to open it. Outside stood two Public Security guards.

We were fined and made to sign a confession but we were not sent back. We had got far enough to make it more effort than it was worth. Instead, the next day, we were bundled into a police Jeep and deported northwards out of the security zone to the town of Korla near Turfan. There, still under arrest, we were made to buy tickets to Peking and seen onto the train.

We had got as far as the border of the desert of Lop, what we learned later was the Chinese nuclear testing ground. It was this discovery that gave our final day in Charchalik a special poignancy.

After the police discovered us in the morning, they locked us up in our hotel room, perhaps for lack of anywhere better to put us. That evening they let us out to eat supper. Lou did not feel like eating, so I was taken on my own to a shabby restaurant owned by a deaf mute. As he was possibly the only other person for five hundred miles who was unable to speak or understand either Chinese or Uigur I felt a certain bond between us and lingered in his café, toying with a bowl of chop suey, while the Public Security guard waited by the door. It was only after half an hour that I began to notice how many other cripples there were in the restaurant. It seemed that there was not a single healthy person in the town: some had terrible contorted limbs and strange disfiguring marks on their skin. A few were completely bald; others were thin and wasted. There can only be one explanation for this gathering in one small town. It must have been something to do with radiation from the testing ground. No wonder the police were so quick to deport us: we appeared to have stumbled across an oasis populated by mutants.

EIGHT

USSR

OUTER MONGOLIA

XANADU ☆ Duolon

Korla

INNER MONGOLIA

Jiayuguan

PEKING

LANZHOU

XI'AN

CHINA

0   200   400   600
        kilometres

We arrived in Peking six days later and several pounds fatter.

Much has been written on the supposed discomfort of Chinese trains. They are meant to be overcrowded, noisy and filthy, their occupants displaying all the worst Chinese vices: boorishness, arrogance and insensitivity. But after the lorries that had taken us across the Taklimakan, we found our Hard Seat (Third Class) carriage on the local freight train pure luxury. It seemed scarcely possible that travel could be so smooth, fast or noiseless. The simplest things gave unimaginable delight. After a fortnight of empty desert the serried ranks of healthy Chinamen seemed something verging on the miraculous. One billion people! And a few of them neither Uigurs or mutants. We stared with numbed incredulity at the fleet of blue-jacketed, pigtailed girls who marched up and down the train, efficiently cleaning the floors, swilling out the loos, and playing patriotic ditties on the in-train tannoy. Through the window, the Taklimakan, as Godforsaken from the north as it had been from the south and the east, looked now as distant and harmless as a picture on a television screen. Nothing out there could pursue us, arrest us, or fine us any longer. We were safe, happy and very nearly comfortable.

At Daheyong it got better still. Here we changed trains and promoted ourselves to a Soft Sleeper (First Class) compartment. There I peeled off my old, stained travelling clothes, and set about relishing the onset of middle age. I vowed never again to travel on a heap of coal slag, never again to stay in a hotel that smelt like a morgue, never again to use a squatter which belched up its contents over the user. I had done all that. If something needed to be proved it was proved. From now it would be a holiday cottage by the seaside, a rocking chair and some new, relaxing hobby, perhaps knitting or crochet.

The Soft Sleeper was a good start to this projected lifestyle. It was the sort of thing we had been dreaming about on top of our coal slag. Each compartment consisted of four beds, two bunks on either side, with a cavernous central space in between. This space was half filled by a wooden table covered by a tablecloth. On top of this floated a porcelain tea set, a pot plant and a reading lamp. Beneath our feet the floor was carpeted in thick Burgundy pile, the bed furnished with a silken quilt. The compartment was as soft as the cell of a lunatic.

We shared it with a most agreeable character. Mr Flying Chicken was a gentleman of Singaporean origin who was remarkable chiefly for his kingly girth and his efforts to maintain it by constant feeding. Mr Flying Chicken was, appropriately enough, a seismologist. He was just returning to Peking after several months working on the earthquake problems of Urumchi. His company clearly valued the services of Mr Chicken for they had supplied him with all that was needed to keep him in good spirits for the duration of the journey, namely one very large hamper. This he tucked into with great enthusiasm. Before our eyes, in a matter of minutes, he consumed batteries of boiled eggs, bean curds barely unwrapped from their boxes, half-salamis imported at great cost from Italy, great lumps of dried pickled fish. These he washed down with cans of Chinese beer and inter-course slices of pineapple pie. But it was the poultry that was most dear to him. From a separate compartment in the hamper Mr Chicken produced a whole, cold boiling fowl. He lifted it aloft with the same reverence as a Catholic priest might lift the host at the elevation. He looked at Louisa and me with hungry eyes.

'Fly Chikky,' he murmured.

After we had made friends with Mr Flying Chicken the journey turned into something of a dorm feast. He shared his poultry with us and in return we offered him a bag of melons we had bought in Turfan. As the afternoon went by we slowly ate our way through Mr Chicken's hamper, until, sometime towards sunset, we reached the bottom. Mr Chicken surveyed the empty hamper with great sadness.

'No chikky, no agg, no pie-pie,' he said.

He picked at the pile of bones on the floor of the compartment, and looked around for something else to consume. There was nothing, and, as a glance at his watch revealed, it was more than two hours until the dining car opened. A look of infinite melancholy clouded his face. For a moment I thought he was going to cry. Then, suddenly, his face brightened.

'Tray slow down,' he said.

We listened. He was right. There was no doubt about it. The train was pulling into a station. Mr Chicken rose and made to leave the compartment. As he did so he turned and flashed a smile in our direction.

'I go gi' foo. I go gi' fly chikky.'

He returned laden with groceries. It was like the miracle of the loaves and fishes. Where there had been one pie there were now two. Where there had been ten eggs there were now twenty. Mr Chicken's new hoard also contained many delicacies that had not previously graced his hamper. There were sponge cakes and apricots, bags of apples, piles of prawn crackers, great sacks of nuts. But most of all there were chickens. From cradled arms he unloaded a great pile of poultry and stacked up the carcasses on his bed.

'One chicky, two chikky, three chikky, four. . . .'

Outside, we had left the desert and were passing a textbook vision of China I had known since childhood: chequer-board paddy fields, wide-brimmed straw hats, swarms of harvesting peasants. We were now passing through the Gansu Corridor and the train chugged along between two parallel ranges of mountains. The chequer-boards were interrupted by wooden farmhouses and gravel farm tracks. As we pushed on up the corridor, the paddy slowly began to give way to narrow fields of russet-brown soil, newly harvested of grain. The blue-jacketed peasants tending the paddy-shoots were replaced by other groups of villagers standing in circles around yellow piles of harvested wheat. They were winnowing the chaff from the grain, throwing spadefuls in the air and letting the chaff drift away in the breeze. Some of the men were leaving the group, bent double under great bundles of straw. Others were digging the fields, either by hand or with the aid of a horse plough. On the fallow strips, horses and sheep were grazing, watched by shepherds. One squatted some distance away from his flock chewing on a straw.

That evening our compartment was invaded by a Chinese engineer and his wife on their way to a conference. They ignored Mr Chicken and ourselves and lay in the same bunk groaning into the small hours. We listened like outraged spinsters. But the engineer went on to commit a far more terrible crime. After we had all drifted off to sleep he furtively arose and turned on the Tannoy. The ability to turn the Tannoy off is perhaps the single most enjoyable luxury of travelling Soft Sleeper. As with the telescreens in *Nineteen Eighty-Four*, silence and privacy are privileges jealously guarded by senior Party members and high officials. Our engineer was neither of these, and must have been unnerved by the silence. He certainly seemed relieved by the five a.m. news broadcast. We were less sure as to its merits. We swore at the engineer and turned it off again. Lou and I tried to get back to sleep; our Singaporean friend sought solace in a chicken sandwich. But the disruptions continued. Soon after the news had finished, our compartment became the venue for a morning gathering of all the engineers on the train.

The engineer and his paramour left us at Xi'an. Henceforth the only intrusion in our compartment was a succession of drunk Party cadres looking for the lavatory. The Soft Sleeper carriage was full of Chinese bourgeoisie, a class that officially does not exist. As I wandered up the carriage, open doors revealed competent-looking men in Western clothes: Fair Isle jerseys, stripy cotton shirts and tweed jackets. An old soldier and a provincial Party official alone wore Mao jackets. They looked as old-fashioned and out of place as a stockbroker in a bowler hat might do in Britain; they had an air of living up to a vanished stereotype. The younger Party officials had haircuts that were as distinctive as their clothes: they were smart and carefully styled. It distinguished them from the peasants just as clearly as the Manchu's *queue* (pigtails) distinguished the native Chinese from the northern invaders in late Imperial times.

Some of the cadres read, smoked or played chess. Others sat in groups toasting each other, chuckling and slapping each other's backs. A particularly noisy drinking bout was going on in the next compartment. From behind the partition could be heard the sound of toasting, the clinking of glasses and, a little later, the noise of retching. I lay on my bunk reading the Chinese section of *The Travels*, disgusted to note that Polo thought rice wine (*mao tai*, the filthy meths-tasting drink so beloved of Communist Party officials) to be the 'finest wine in the world'. This alone confirmed the worst I had come to expect of the Venetian.

Late that morning we crossed over the Yellow River and by early afternoon had passed into rolling hill country. Around the river the soil had been so carefully tended it looked as if it had been combed: every available inch was used, right up to the drop of the river gully. But in the hills there was a more relaxed attitude to the land. There was more meadowland, more room between the steeply pitched tile roofs of the farmsteads and the first browns of the arable soil. By evening the train had begun to gather speed and was heading out of the hills into flat plains. The hills receded and the sun sank behind the hills and the colour drained slowly from the landscape. The train lights came on, and we thundered into the gloom.

The setting of the sun was a signal for the sleeping-car attendants, who rose like vampires from their compartment. They set about the carriage, mops and dusters in hand, working themselves into a frenzy of hygiene. Windows were cleaned, floors swept and sideboards dusted. The beds were stripped of their sheets and we were forbidden to sit on the upper bunks. To get out of the attendant's way we took Mr Flying Chicken to supper with us in the dining car. We got there with difficulty.

In the Hard Seat carriage a fierce dispute was in progress. Some Uigurs were kneeling in the aisle saying their evening prayers while a pair of attendants were trying to clean up around them. There was a lot of shouting and it was difficult to make out exactly what was going on. But it was clear that the Uigurs were not winning. They were being gradually swept back into their seats and the floor was being brushed, washed, soaped and disinfected. Islam was on the retreat. During supper, just as Mr Chicken was about to embark on his second course, the train pulled to a halt in a station and the attendants leapt outside and began feverishly swilling down the outside of the carriages. The train was due to arrive in Peking in less than an hour and the attendants wanted to spend as little time as possible cleaning up after we arrived. After supper we returned to our carriage to find that Mr Chicken's cake, nuts and melons had all been thrown away. He was still trying to retrieve them from the attendants when, at ten-thirty, the train pulled into Peking Central.

That night a ferry of buses took the frightened provincials to a dimly lit hotel in the west of the city, the East Acton of Peking.

All the diplomats, most of the correspondents and even a few of the tourists complain that Peking is a dull town, all flyovers and glass hotels. Arriving from New York or Tokyo it might appear so. Coming to it from the Taklimakan, however, it appeared dauntingly sophisticated. True, it did not quite conform to my Fu Manchu ideal of a Chinese city. There were no paper-lantern prostitutes or opium-den gangsters, no gambling Triad smugglers, no American agents in Burberrys, no exploding firecrackers. Nevertheless it seemed a huge and exciting place; we went to bed like schoolboys on the last night of term.

At first light we ate a hurried breakfast, then hired bicycles and set off into the slipstream. At the traffic lights we would pause, waiting with one black car and ten thousand other bicycles. When the lights changed we would shoot off down wide avenues, past crocodiles of schoolchildren, past groups of tourists photographing each other, past cranes and building sites and department stores. Outside, hordes of Chinamen would squint through the plate glass, watching the ranks of black and white televisions displayed in the shop fronts. Everything seemed so big – the crowds, the buildings, the articulated buses, the roads. . . .

There were many things that we liked about Peking: the grinning dentists caressing their pliers outside the surgeries, the delicate boys in the barber shops, the old women hobbling past on unbound feet, the lines of plane trees and the silver poplars, the bird cages hanging from the street lamps. But best of all we loved the chocolate eclairs. Mr Flying Chicken would have been proud of us. At a small corner table at the back of Minim's a low-budget appendage to Yves St Laurent's new Peking Maxim's, we spent one of the happiest afternoons of the whole journey. We drank small porcelain cups of espresso coffee and ate our way through the café's entire patisserie shelf: fourteen chocolate eclairs in three hours. When the café closed, we stumbled out into the cold night air, bloated, ill and guilty. We had spent more money in three hours than we had in the previous three weeks.

We had sometimes talked as if Peking were our journey's end. Now we wished that it were. We were tired. We had little money left. Our curiosity and appetite for novelty was long satisfied. We longed for home, for comfort and for stability. Most of all we desperately wanted to stop moving. If there was one thing we had learned on the journey it was that we were not nomads. But we could not stop, at least not yet. In the inside pocket of my torn, soiled old waistcoat I still had the phial of oil from the Holy Sepulchre. Had Marco Polo arrived in China one month later, he would have delivered his phial to Kubla Khan in his new capital at Khan Balik, now in Peking, under the site of the old Forbidden City. But as it was, Polo arrived in May, and during that month Kubla Khan was away north of the Great Wall at his summer palace, Shang-tu, or, as it was called by Coleridge, Xanadu.

Xanadu was Kubla Khan's favourite residence. In the capital he pined for the steppe and to remind him of his home he planted a patch of Mongolian grass in the palace gardens. In the hot months he made straight for the summer palace 'my vast and noble capital. . . . My splendidly adorned. . . .' Xanadu was built on the first plateau of the steppe, the nearest piece of real grassland to Peking. The Chinese traveller Wang Yun visited the city soon after its foundation and wrote that it was encircled on four sides by mountains and surrounded by luxuriant and beautiful countryside; to the north lay pine forests famous for their falcons, nearer at hand were pastures teeming with herds of goats and sheep. But it is Polo who gives the finest surviving description of the palace itself; it is perhaps the most beautiful piece of descriptive prose in the whole of *The Travels*:

There is at this place a very fine marble palace, the rooms of which are all gilt and painted with figures of men and beasts and birds, and with a variety of trees and flowers, all executed with such exquisite art that you regard them with delight and astonishment. . . .

Round this palace a wall is built, enclosing a compass of 16 miles, and inside the park there are fountains and rivers and brooks, and beautiful meadows, with all kinds of wild animals, excluding those which are of a ferocious nature. . . . There are more than two hundred gerfalcons alone. The Khan himself goes every week to see his birds . . . and sometimes he rides through the park with a leopard behind him on his horse's croup; and then if he sees any animal that takes his fancy, he slips his leopard at it. . . .

Moreover at a spot in the park where there is a charming wood, he has another palace built of cane, of which I must give you a description. It is gilt all over and most elaborately finished inside. . . . On each column is a dragon whose head supports the architrave, and the claws are stretched out right and left. The construction of the palace is so devised that it can be taken down and put up with great celerity; and it can all be taken to pieces and removed withersoever the Emperor may command. When erected, it is braced by more than two hundred cords of silk. . . .

The ruins of the palace were accidently rediscovered in 1872 by the physician at the British legation in Peking, Dr S. W. Bushell; he happened to pass the city while on a botanical expedition north of the Great Wall. The landscape he saw sounded fairly similar to that described by Marco Polo. But the scene at Xanadu itself was very different.

> . . . a wide rolling prairie, covered with long grass and fragrant shrubs, the haunts of numerous herds of antelope. The only building in the neighbourhood is a small Lama monastery, the abode of several wretched priests. The city has been deserted for centuries. The site is overgrown by rank weeds and grass, the abode of foxes and owls, which prey on the numerous prairie rats and partridges. . . . The ground in the interior is strewn with blocks of marble and other remains of large temples and palaces, the outlines of the foundations of some of which can still be traced; while broken lions, dragons and the remains of other carved monuments lie about in every direction, half hidden by the thick and tangled overgrowth. Scarcely one stone remains above another, and a more complete state of ruin and desolation could hardly be imagined.

Before he left, Bushell discovered a broken memorial tablet. On it was inscribed a form of ancient Chinese character, surrounded by a border of dragons, boldly carved in deep relief. Later, when the inscription was translated it was discovered that the tablet had been raised by Kubla Khan in memory of a Buddhist chief priest. The inscription left no doubt about the identity of the ruin on which the botanist had stumbled. It was indeed the Xanadu of which Coleridge had written, a name known to every schoolchild. But this did not lead Bushell to trumpet his discovery. He quietly wrote it up inside the scholarly botanical report that he submitted to the Royal Geographical Society in 1874. Fellow scholars carefully noted his findings (Yule refers to Bushell's expedition in his footnotes to *The Travels*), but the world at large remained ignorant of the doctor's work. Although the ruins lay only one hundred miles north of Peking, no other expedition was mounted to investigate the remains of Kubla Khan's summer capital. Despite its mythical fame, Xanadu itself seems to have remained a scholarly lacunae. If we were to reach the city, we would be the first Europeans to see the ruins for over a century.

It was not far to go, but the same circumstance which had for centuries left the ruins in obscurity hindered us from reaching them. Inner Mongolia is a sensitive border region facing China's old enemy, the Soviet Union. The area is closed to foreigners. If we were to have any hope of reaching Xanadu, the journey would involve us getting back into our ridiculous disguises and undergoing the same exhausting routine we had followed on the southern Silk Route. It was a terrible prospect. But having come this far, we had to try and finish the journey.

The following two days were full of confusion. It was now the first week of October and the Cambridge term was due to begin in four days. If we were to try and get to Xanadu it would mean arriving late for the beginning of term; not in itself any great loss, but a bit undiplomatic with finals drawing in. With this in mind, Lou and I agreed that before we left for Mongolia we had better arrange the flight home and organize a transfer of funds from London to pay for it. It sounded simple. In fact it took forty-eight hours of negotiating with bankers, pleading with bored airline officials and telephone calls across the world – ages sitting in hot waiting rooms – before we had two seats booked for the following Thursday and the necessary funds on their way. We had a very tight schedule. We calculated that it would take two days of nonstop travelling to get to Duolon, the nearest town to the ruins, and two further days to return. Our charter flight, the only one we could afford for a fortnight, left in six days. This left only one day spare in which to get to the ruins from Duolon, a distance of about twenty-five miles. We had no accurate directions and our only guide, Bushell's article, was over a century out of date. For all we knew the ruins might be miles from any road. Whether or not we succeeded in finding Xanadu in that one day left to us, we would have to return to Peking or else miss our flight.

To minimize complications we booked a seat on the train north and a hotel room at the end of the line in Chengde. By Friday evening we were ready to set off on the last leg of the journey. We packed what we needed for four days' travelling into one rucksack and placed the spare in the hotel's safe room. The following morning we got up at five-thirty and caught the train to Chengde, the old Jehol, site of the summer palace of the Manchu dynasty.

The train was nearly empty. On the seat opposite us, two Chinese students were sitting tenuously holding each other's hands. Neither spoke. The girl, who was taller than the boy, wore a frilly blouse and an embroidered jersey. She looked out of the window. The boy chain-smoked.

The transition from town to country took place very gradually. As we neared the suburbs the gardens backing onto the railway line grew in size. Blocks of flats and lines of warehouses gave way to allotments. The buildings were spaced further apart; gradually we came to farmsteads and high pitched roofs and thatched outhouses. There were maize fields and vines. In some of the strips peasants were ploughing with teams of blinkered ponies or pairs of long-horned cattle; at the edge of one strip you could see clusters of hives and a bee keeper shrouded in netting. Then, slowly, we began to rise. The hills had jagged peaks, cleft like a dragon's back. It got colder and the Chinese girl shivered and pulled a jacket out of her bag. In the valleys the arable fields turned to hill pasture. The villages had water mills. The hills grew higher and a purple haze hung over the water meadows. We crossed the Great Wall and passed into Manchuria.

The railway follows the route of the old Imperial road. It was the route taken by Lord Macartney, the first English ambassador to the Chinese court, when he came to negotiate a commercial treaty with the Chinese Emperor, Ch'ien-lung, in 1783. He travelled in a neat English post-chaise drawn by four Tartar horses. Behind him followed a cart full of presents for the Emperor; these included two full-length Joshua Reynolds portraits of King George III. Macartney, an ancestor of the consul at Kashgar, thought the scenery 'uncommon picturesque' but the views he enjoyed were to be the only reward he was to get for his labours. The Chinese, as he discovered, had no interest in trade. In his letter of reply to George III, the Emperor wrote that he acknowledged the receipt of the 'local products' presented as 'tribute articles' but regretted that the Celestial Empire had not 'the slightest need' of England's manufactures. A court letter went further. 'The English are ignorant barbarians,' it read, 'totally uninformed as to the proper ceremonies. It is not worth treating them with too much courtesy.' The Chinese had no interest in the English; they knew little about them and had no desire to enlarge on that knowledge. According to the *Huang Ch'ing chih-kung t'u*, an illustrated Imperial handbook to 'the tribute nations', England belonged to Holland. 'The men mostly drink wine,' it maintained, 'and the unmarried women lace up their hips in their desire to be slim. They keep snuff in metallic wire boxes and carry these boxes about with them.' Another authority, the *Hai-lu*, written by a Chinese sailor who had visited Europe, filled out this somewhat sketchy picture. Holland, England's overlord, was in fact a region in north-west France and its people were 'all the same as in Portugal'.

Ch'ien-lung may not have been interested in the English, but he was very interested in his gardens at Chengde. Here, at the back of his summer palace, he created a huge willow-pattern world of lakes and pagodas. It was an impossible rural idyll – a kind of Chinese Petit Trianon, but there was no doubt as to its beauty. Macartney thought it exquisite and wrote that if he had not known that Capability Brown had never visited China, he would have sworn that he had drawn his happiest ideas from the Imperial gardens at Jehol. What was unclear was what state of preservation they would be in. When Peter Fleming visited Chengde (the old Jehol) in the 1930s the temples were already in a bad state of decay and I had heard in Peking that the Cultural Revolution had accelerated the destruction.

We arrived late in the afternoon; the town straddled a ridge below a rim of lavender-coloured mountains. When Fleming came here, Chengde was a garrison town for the occupying Japanese and was full of short soldiers in gaiters performing mock assaults on pagodas; he thought it like 'staying in Windsor in 1919 supposing the Germans had won the war'. There was also a curious complement of American missionaries, including Mr Panter ('very tall, very doleful . . . the voice of Doom'), Mrs Panter (who played the harmonium) and young Mr Titherton ('on probation, a kind of apprentice missionary'). But the town we saw had a very different character. There were neither missionaries nor soldiers to be seen and Chengde now had the unmistakable air of a summer resort out of season.

Our visit got off to a good start. We found a taxi driver who spoke English and was prepared to help buy us a ticket to Duolon. He did not even ask for a commission. At the hotel, however, things were a little more difficult.

'My name is Dalrymple,' I told the receptionist. 'We have a reservation.'

'It has been cancelled,' replied the girl.

'Not by me it hasn't.'

'It has been cancelled,' the girl repeated.

'Who by?'

The receptionist consulted a register.

'It was cancelled yesterday by Yu San.'

'Who is Yu San?'

'I don't know,' said the girl. 'She is your friend not mine.'

No convincing explanation for this incident ever emerged; I knew no one called Yu San. But there was certainly no problem with the hotel being booked up. It was cold and damp and empty. The season had turned and we were the only guests. It was a strange, grey place with wide stairs and long, echoing half-lit corridors, but I rather liked it. It reminded me of a Highland fishing lodge where I had once been stranded on a cold night in late November.

I left Lou there, and went to explore the summer palace before it closed. At the entrance the postcard sellers were packing up their stands, but I persuaded the custodian to let me in and I slipped off behind the palace to the lakes beyond. The gardens were as beautiful as they were unexpected. I marvelled at the care with which the park had been laid out: the winding paths and the deserted potpourri pavilions; the weeping willows, the walnuts and the corianders reflected in the lake; the lilies and lotus flowers floating beneath the flying eaves of the temples – and all shrouded in mist and smelling of wet earth and falling leaves. The dying light of autumn. As I wandered along the lake shore, I suddenly realized how long I had been travelling. Summer was gone. There is no autumn in the desert; when travelling through the great expanses of sand, one's sense of passing time and changing season becomes numbed. It was only now, when I found myself suddenly propelled halfway to winter, that I realized for how long I had been on the move. Jerusalem and Acre seemed many weeks distant; I could barely remember a time when the day did not begin by packing a rucksack and paying a hotel bill. Now the imminent prospect of reaching my destination seemed slightly alarming. To stop moving was going to be very odd. A whole segment of life was going to end. A whole new series of responsibilities loomed: getting home, getting back to Cambridge, finals. . . .

Wandering around Chengde that afternoon one thing did become clear. At long last I understood the Chinese arrogance that fostered the dismissive attitude to Lord Macartney and the first English to visit China in the eighteenth century; an attitude which still lingered, despite the decline of the Middle Kingdom, into this century. The gardens in Chengde were the one place I saw that had retained some glimpse of the fragile elegance and dignity of Imperial China. They made any European garden I had ever seen seem stiff and crude and formal; here you could easily understand the Chinese thinking Westerners barbarians: of course they had no interest in England's manufactures! But if the beauty of Chengde made some things clear, it made other things more difficult to understand. In the Cultural Revolution the monks who were still clinging on in the Lama temples when Peter Fleming visited were all lined up and shot; many of the temples were demolished, the others were left to fall apart. Over China as a whole one million people were killed and thirty million persecuted. What I did not understand was how the nation which, for five thousand years had produced the most delicate and elegant art the world ever saw, could suddenly turn face and became viciously, violently iconoclastic. Paul Scott was puzzled by a similar paradox in India: how could the Indians, the most courteous and gentle people on earth, suddenly turn to frenzies of orgiastic violence? Scott's answer was that the Indian really was emotionally predisposed against violence; hence his hysteria when he surrendered to it. 'He goes beyond all ordinary bounds, like someone mad, because he is going against his own faith as well.' By analogy, I thought, perhaps the Cultural Revolution was as brutal as it was simply because it went so deeply against everything Chinese culture stood for. The fragile ideal represented by Chengde was a testament to that.

The light was fading. I turned heel and headed back along the damp paths towards the hotel. The following morning we rose early, pulled on our 'disguises' and caught the dawn bus to Duolon.

The journey into Inner Mongolia proved surprisingly easy. We got onto the bus without problems and found the border checkpoint unmanned.

It was a lovely chill Sunday morning. The water meadows were edged by windbreaks of silver birch and the peasants had left sunflower heads on the thatched roofs of their huts to dry in the autumn sun. The trees had turned gold and auburn and the light picked out the colours and reflected them onto the water in the flooded fields. In the streets there were Mongol dogs with curling, upturned tails and gaggles of Canada geese. It was cold and there was a high wind.

We rose up from the Manchurian valleys onto the tableland of the Mongolian steppe. It grew colder and the light faded. The hills flattened out and there was thunder in the distance. By lunch we had reached Banjieta; the others got out and bought some food but we were afraid of the police and stayed where we were. It began to rain and the bus leaked.

Waiting in the bus, Lou looked at the map and compared it with the diagrams attached to Bushell's article. According to the modern map there was a small hamlet called Zheng Lan Qi about thirty mies west of Duolon. There was no sign of it on Bushell's sketch, but if the modern map was accurately plotted, she calculated that it should be much nearer Xanadu than Duolon. More importantly, the map showed that Zheng Lan Qi was built on a river, unnamed on the modern map, but apparently the same as that marked 'Shang tu R' on Bushell's sketch. The river Shang-tu was Coleridge's Alph; it was the river that once watered Xanadu. She had found our guide. All we had to do was to get to Zheng Lan Qi that night; the following morning we could follow the river upstream, until, sooner or later, it brought us to the court of Kubla Khan.

Our decision was confirmed when, that evening, we saw Duolon. When Bushell visited it, the town was bustling, dirty and prosperous thanks to its monopoly on the manufacture of 'idols, bells and other ecclesiastical paraphernalia of Buddhism'. Now it was still dirty, but was very far from either prosperous or bustling. The town had suffered from the decline of Buddhism. A pair of stocky Mongol horses chaffed at their bits beneath the pagoda of a ruined temple; a pockmarked Mongol tried to sell us horrible-looking toffee apples (a Mongol speciality). The people looked tired and weather-beaten; the place had that same sense of chill desolation that I have only ever experienced before in Glencoe or some of the clearance villages in the Highlands. It was damp, dreich and brooding. We skirted the town and caught a lift from a truck across the steppe to Zheng Lan Qi.

We arrived just as darkness was falling. Zheng Lan Qi was small and new. It was made up of a handful of grey shacks of pre-stressed concrete and corrugated iron; the caravanserai was the one stone building. Like Duolon, the town was damp, cold and exposed. It sat incongruously in the middle of the steppe and the wind whistled straight through it. If our calculations were right we were now less than five miles from Xanadu, but anything less like Coleridge's vision – of gardens bright with sinuous rills, forests ancient as the hills and sunny spots of greenery – was hard to imagine.

The Mongols were ugly and inquisitive. They had narrow, high-set eyes and tight, dark skin. When we sat in the caravan-serai kitchen that night, forty of them gathered to watch us eat. It was difficult to see where they all came from; there were barely ten houses in the town. Lou suggested that they were all cousins and had interbred: that, certainly, would explain both their unusual stupidity and how so many of them managed to live in so few houses. We wolfed down our supper of mutton soup and mutton omelette then fled to our rooms, terrified of attracting more attention.

The next morning the alarm went off, as usual, at five-thirty. Thousands of miles away in East Anglia the Cambridge term was about to begin. Everyone would be rushing off to Heffer's to buy their textbooks, Lever-Arch files and file paper. We should have been there too; instead we were in the middle of Mongolia and had twelve hours to find Xanadu. Looking outside we could see that it was about to rain; ahead of us was the prospect of a long, cold, wet walk. But we were in good spirits; while we got dressed, I remember Lou describing a dream she had just had – some tale about eating scrambled egg with Edward in a cave beneath Easter Island. She had just set about interpreting this story for me when there was a knock at the door. Without waiting for us to answer, two Mongol Public Security guards burst in.

To begin with, everything moved too quickly for the full implication of what was happening to hit us. The policemen shouted at us in Mongol and gestured that they wanted to see our passports. It was only when we handed them over, and the policemen took them away and locked us in our room that we realized what this meant. The idea of travelling twelve thousand miles, only to be detained and deported five miles from our destination was too much to bear. I sank onto my bed. When planning the expedition, I had never for a moment imagined that we would get this far. But having arrived in Zheng Lan Qi, I had ceased to think anything could stop us finally completing the mission. Now there was nothing to be done. I lay on my bed; Lou lay on hers. Neither of us spoke. We waited.

The security guards returned half an hour later. This time they brought with them two teachers – a husband and wife – to act as interpreters. Neither spoke English with any great facility; both were terrified of the security guards. We tried to explain what we were doing. We were following Marco Polo. We wanted to get to Shang tu. We had come twelve thousand miles to see it. We had to get there today. The teachers passed this on. The security guards were uninterested. Have you a permit? they asked. No. Have you a special endorsement on your passports? No. The interview was brought to a swift conclusion: 'These men say you must go Peking. You no allow here.' We protested, but it had no effect. The teachers simply repeated what they had said before. 'Vey soy. Vey soy. You must go Peking. You no 'low here.' With that the guards and the teachers left us; the door was locked shut. There was nothing we could do. I sank back onto the bed. I felt like bursting into tears.

We waited for three hours. Outside it was as dark as evening; a storm was brewing and the air was heavy. The door was unlocked late in the morning. This time the teachers were accompanied by a middle-aged man in a black Mao jacket, presumably some sort of Party cadre. He spoke halting English and asked us to explain what we wanted. We did so, this time with the aid of the maps and plans in *The Travels*. Lou drew her finger along the dots, dashes and crosses of the Grand Master Map drawing to a halt just before Shang tu. 'The court of Kubla Khan,' she said. The cadre nodded: 'Hoobilay Han, Hoobilay Han.' This was more encouraging, but our spirits began to flag again when nothing happened for a further three hours. It would be dark shortly. Time was running out.

It was after four o'clock when the security guards and the teachers returned. There was no sign of the man in the black Mao suit and the security guards were just as brusque as before. 'You have money?' they asked through the teachers. Lou opened her wallet and counted out all that remained of her money, ninety yuan, about eighteen pounds. The guards took all of it, counted it again and smiled at each other. It was unclear whether we had just paid a fine, an inflated taxi fare or a bribe. The teachers did not make it any clearer. 'Jeep, jeep,' they said. We were ordered to pack our rucksack and were marched outside. A police Jeep was waiting; the cadre was inside. The security guards motioned for us to get into the back seat.

We set off: an incongruous party of two Cambridge under-graduates, two security officers and one Mongol Communist Party official. The teachers waved us goodbye. In the distance we could hear the sound of thunder; it began to pour. One of the guards turned on the tape player and drowned out the sound of the storm with some wailing Mongol music. At the main road we turned right, back towards Duolon. It was still unclear where we were being taken.

We drove for two miles along the road, before I became con-vinced that we were being sent back to Peking.

'They're deporting us,' I said to Louisa. 'They're bloody well deporting us.'

One of the security guards turned around, smiled, and for the first time indicated that he knew some English.

'Mongol music: good, good,' he said.

'Fuck,' I said, quietly and to no one in particular. 'Fuck. Fuck. Fuck.'

Then the Jeep swung left off the road and jolted off across the heathland. We passed two mounted Mongols leading a third pony; they were making slow progress in the pelting rain. We splashed past them, spraying liquid mud in the air. The storm was now raging fiercely like some scene from a Gothic novel, and the steppe was illuminated by flashes of lightning. We were heading north across a plain bounded on either side by a range of hills. On either horizon, Louisa noticed that the mountain peaks were topped by cairns. The cadre saw her pointing it out to me and scribbled something on a sheet of paper. He handed it to her. He had written the numeral 108. According to Bushell the Mongols called the ruins of Xanadu *Chao Naiman Sume Khotan*; in English it means 'The City of 108 Temples'. It was only then that we knew for sure that we were finally on the threshold of our destination.

We came down over a range of shallow hills and suddenly in front of us we saw a vast rampart stretching across the plain. We crossed the river Alph and headed towards it; gradually the shape resolved itself. It was one side of a square earthen bank, twenty-five feet high, enclosing an area of about four square miles. As we drew alongside we saw that originally it had been a double wall with a ditch in the middle. They were built out of rubble and mud and shaped steeply on the inside, with a lower angle facing out. The second wall was now very denuded. At the top of the taller bank stood a Mongol shepherd covered in animal skins; around him were a few wet and bedraggled sheep.

We drove into the ruined city and headed for the inner enclosure, the Jeep slipping in the mud. Our vision of Xanadu was nearer the heath scene in *Lear* than the exotic pleasure garden described by Polo. There was no sign of the marble palace, the gilt rooms or the lovely murals 'that you regard with delight and astonishment'. Nor was there anything left of the 'perfect arch twenty feet high, twelve feet wide' which in

Bushell's day still stood over the South Gate of the Inner City. Instead, through the pelting rain we saw the shattered foundations of pavilions and temples, with column bases, capitals, roof tiles and pottery fragments littering the ground. The enclosure was crisscrossed with earthworks, ditches and craters. In the centre, raised on an earth platform, were the remains of the main palace. All that still stood to any height was the back wall, a mud-brick structure with timber lacing. It was centred on a deep fireplace in which some sheep had taken shelter. The jeep pulled to a halt below the throne dais.

Only one artefact remained still intact. In front of the dais stood a three-foot-tall statue cut in flat relief, portraying a figure holding a cup. It was pockmarked and had a narrow beard and a malevolent expression. There was nothing remotely Chinese about it. It was a dark and brooding image, more like a pagan Celtic fertility statue from a northern hill fort than anything you might expect to find in the court of the Khan.

The worst of the storm had passed and we all got out. The Mongols leant on the roof of the Jeep, lit cigarettes and began chattering. Louisa and I were more reverent. We had travelled twelve thousand miles to get to this spot. We stood at the base of the ramp leading up to the throne dais. Here seven hundred and eleven years before, Marco Polo had also stood at the end of his outward journey.

> When the Two Brothers and Mark arrived at that great city, they went to the Imperial Palace, and there they found the Sovereign attended by a great company of Barons. So they bent the knee before him, and paid their respects to him, with all possible reverence, prostrating themselves on the ground. Then the Lord bade them stand up, and treated them with great honour, showing great pleasure at their coming, and asked many questions as to their welfare, and how they had sped. They replied that they had in verity sped well, seeing that they found the Khan well and safe. Then they presented the credentials and the letters which

they had received from the Pope, which pleased him right well; and after that they produced the Oil from the Sepulchre, and at that also he was very glad for he set great store thereby. . . .

I took out the phial of oil from my waistcoat pocket and, with Lou two steps behind, we very slowly climbed up the ramp. At the top I knelt before the place where the throne of the Khan used to stand. I unscrewed the phial then tipped the oil onto the ground. For a second it floated on the surface, then it slowly began to sink into the earth, leaving only a glistening patch on the mud where it had fallen. Then, in the drizzle, halfway across the world from Cambridge, Louisa and I recited in unison the poem that had immortalized the palace in whose wreckage we stood:

> *In Xanadu did Kubla Khan*
> *A stately pleasure-dome decree:*
> *Where Alph, the sacred river, ran*
> *Through caverns measureless to man*
>   *Down to a sunless sea.*
> *So twice five miles of fertile ground*
> *With walls and towers were girdled round:*
> *And there were gardens bright with sinuous rills,*
> *Where blossom'd many an incense-bearing tree;*
> *And here were forests ancient as the hills,*
> *Enfolding sunny spots of greenery.*

Below, beside the Jeep, the Mongols stood shaking their heads. As we walked back towards them the Party cadre revolved his index finger in his temple. He grunted something in Mongol. Then he translated it for us:

'Bonkers,' he said. 'English people, very, very bonkers.'

'Personally,' said Louisa as we got back into the Jeep, 'I think that he could well have a point.'

EPILOGUE

When Sir Richard Burton left Mecca having spent a year there in disguise, despite having just accomplished one of the greatest-ever feats of exploration he found himself overcome with depression.

> The exaltation of having penetrated and escaped the Holy City without damage was followed by languor and disappointment. I had time upon my mule for musing upon how melancholy a thing is success. Whilst failure inspirits a man, attainment reads the sad prosy lesson that all our glories 'are in shadows not substantial things. . . .'

I had never understood Burton's feelings until I left Xanadu. Within the hour, the euphoria of having reached our goal and delivered the oil began to wear off. As the Jeep neared Duolon I began to fuss about what we had failed to achieve. The security guards had forbidden us to take photographs, and I worried that nobody would believe our tale, just as they had refused to believe Marco Polo himself. In fact my anxieties were needless: pieces of roof tile we had managed to smuggle out of the site were later dated by the Fitzwilliam Museum as thirteenth-century Mongol, thus somewhat buttressing our claims. But that lay in the future. As soon as the security guards left us at the caravanserai in Duolon, I immediately began planning to return to Xanadu the following morning to take photographs and make further notes.

It was not to be. At dawn the next day the security guards reappeared and escorted us onto the bus to Zhangjiakou, the provincial capital. There a second group of security guards were waiting for us. They picked us up off the bus and escorted us to the train station. They kept guard over us in the waiting room until the train to Peking arrived; when it did, we were consigned to the care of the train's guard.

As we headed back to the capital, I experienced a strange sensation of vacuum. After weeks of worry, the goal had been achieved. Facing me, in the empty first-class carriage, Lou was now fast asleep. Yet I could not relax. Time hung heavy. I tried to read. I looked out of the window. I ate some of the snacks we had bought at Zhangjiakou. I fidgeted. Then from my waist-coat pocket I took out the blue logbook with its pages of illeg-ible notes. I thought back to the beginning of the summer and that first morning in Jerusalem, rising before the sun for the first time and setting out to fetch the oil from the Holy Sepulchre.

I got out a sharp pencil, opened a blank page and began to scribble.

Glossary

Aksakal	'White beards', imperial Chinese village official.
Birasi	Beer shop.
Buran	A ferocious Turkestani sandstorm.
Caballarii	A cavalryman from the Byzantine free peasant militia.
Caravanserai	Merchants' lodging house. Same as a *han, khan* or *rabat*.
Cay	Tea.
Chador	Woman's veil. Can involve anything from a headscarf or a sack to something verging on a tent.
Chai-khana	Tea or coffee house in Iran. Much in favour since the bars were closed down.
Charpoy	Rope-strung bedstead on which the population of India and Pakistan pass much of their time.
Charwal	Baggy pyjama bottoms. Bottom half of a *charwal chemise*.
Charwal chemise	Pyjama suit; the unofficial national dress of Pakistan.
Chattri	Mogul helmet-shaped dome.
Chaukan	Turkestani whore.
Chorba	Thin Turkish soup.
Chowkidar	Watchman, guard or groundsman in India or Pakistan.
Coolie	Porter.
Dal	Pulses.
Demlik	Turkish samovar with attached teapot.
Derzi	Tailor.
Dhobi	Indian or Pakistani laundryman.
Divan	An oriental sofa.

Dolmus	Turkish minibus.
Fida'i	Initiated member of the sect of the Assassins.
Funduq	Merchants' inn or warehouse.
Gunbad	Tomb tower.
Hajj	Muslim Mecca pilgrimage.
Hajji	Pilgrim who goes thereon.
Hammam	Turkish baths.
Han	Merchants' lodging house. Same as a *caravanserai, khan* or *rabat*.
Hoja	An old man.
Hookhah	Water-pipe. Same as a *nargile* or hubble bubble.
Ivan	Open-fronted hall.
Jihad	Islamic holy war.
Kausia	Macedonian helmet, as used by the soldiers of Alexander the Great.
Kebabji	Kebab shop or restaurant.
Keffiyeh	Arab headscarf. Particularly associated with Palestinians.
Khan	Merchants' lodging house. Same as a *caravanserai, han* or *rabat*.
Kibitka	Nomad's tent.
Kibbutznik	Someone who works on a Kibbutz settlement in Israel.
Kilim	Turkish rug.
Kufic	Arabic calligraphy used for monumental purposes.
Kumbet	Turkish tomb tower. Same as a *gunbad*.
Kurta	Long-tailed man's shirt. Top half of a *charwal chemise*.
Lathi	Wooden truncheon.
Magi	Zoroastrian class of priests.
Mali	Indian or Pakistani gardener.
Medresse	Islamic college.
Mescat	Small kiosk-mosque usually raised on legs. Common in Seljuk caravanserai.
Mihrab	Prayer niche indicating direction of Mecca.

Muezzin	Prayer leader. In old days used to wail from minarets five times a day. An endangered species since the advent of the cassette recorder.
Muhajir	Indian Muslim refugee in Pakistan since 1948.
Mujahedin	Muslim freedom fighter, especially in Afghanistan.
Mullah	Muslim priest or holy man.
Muqarna	Stalactite-style decoration over mosque or *medresse* doorway.
Nargile	Water-pipe. Same as a *hookhah* or hubble bubble.
Passagium	The 'months of the passage' or trading season during the time of the Crusader Kingdom.
Patou	An all-purpose Afghan blanket.
Queue	Chinese pigtail.
Rabat	Merchants' lodging house. Same as a *caravanserai, han* or *khan*.
Sadhu	Hindu holy man.
Shin	Gujar animist ceremony.
Shuravi	The Soviets (in Dari).
Taotai	Imperial Chinese district governor.
Terzi	Tailor.
Theme	Byzantine province.
Tonga	Horse trap.
Tsepale	Tibetan delicacy of dough and fried yak's meat.
Yurt	Mongol tent.
Yuruk	Turcoman nomad.
Zenana	Women's part of the house; the harem.

Bibliography of Principal Sources

Chapter One, pp. 1–26

Meron Benvenisti, *The Crusaders in the Holy Land* (Jerusalem, 1970)

T. S. R. Boase, *Kingdoms and Strongholds of the Crusaders* (New York, Bobbs Merrill, 1971)

K. A. C. Creswell, *Early Muslim Architecture* (2 vols., Oxford, Oxford University Press, 1932 and 1940)

Richard Ettinghausen and Oleg Grabar, *The Art and Architecture of Islam 650–1250* (London, Pelican, 1987)

Ibn Jubayr, (trans. and ed. William Wright) *The Travels of Ibn Jubayr* (London, Luzac & Co., 1907)

George Michell, *Architecture of the Islamic World: its History and Social Meaning* (London, Thames & Hudson, 1978)

Paul Pelliot, *Notes on Marco Polo* (3 vols., Paris, 1959–73)

Joshua Prawer, *Crusader Institutions* (collected papers) Essay on The Italian Communes (Oxford, Oxford University Press, 1980)

Joshua Prawer, *The Latin Kingdom of Jerusalem* (London, Weidenfeld & Nicolson, 1972)

Joshua Prawer, *The World of the Crusaders* (London, Weidenfeld & Nicolson, 1972)

Sir Steven Runciman, *A History of the Crusades. Volume III: The Kingdom of Acre* (Cambridge, Cambridge University Press, 1954)

S. Fatima Sadeque, *Baibars I of Egypt* (Oxford, Oxford University Press, 1957)

Sir Henry Yule (trans. and ed.), *The Book of Ser Marco Polo* 3rd edn. (2 vols., London, John Murray, 1929)

Chapter Two, pp. 27–58

T. S. R. Boase, *Castles and Churches of the Crusader Kingdom* (Oxford, Oxford University Press, 1967)

Robert Fedden, *Syria* (London, Robert Hale, 1946)

Francesco Gabrieli, *Arab Historians of the Crusades* (London, Routledge & Kegan Paul, 1969)

Philip K. Hitti, *Usamah Ibn Munquid: Memoirs of an Arab Syrian Gentleman* (New York, Columbia University Press, 1929)

M. G. S. Hodgson, *The Order of Assassins* (The Hague, Mouton and Co., 1955)

Bernard Lewis, *The Assassins: A Radical Sect in Islam* (London, Weidenfeld & Nicolson, 1967)

W. Muller-Weiner, *Castles of the Crusaders* (London, Thames & Hudson, 1966)

Chapter Three, pp. 59–114

T. S. R. Boase, *The Cilician Kingdom of Armenia* (Edinburgh, Scottish Academic Press, 1978)

Claude Cahen, *Pre-Ottoman Turkey* (London, Sidgwick & Jackson, 1968)

N. J. Dawood (trans.), *The Koran* (London, Penguin, 1956)

A. Evans (ed.), *Francesco Pegolotti: La Pratica della Mercatura* (Cambridge, Mass., Harvard University Press, 1936)

Benjamin Z. Kedar, *Merchants in Crisis* (Yale, Yale University Press, 1977)

Manuel Komroff, *Contemporaries of Marco Polo* (New York, Boni & Liveright, 1928)

Leonard Olschi, *Marco Polo's Asia* (Berkeley, California University Press, 1960)

T. A. Sinclair, *Eastern Turkey: an Architectural and Archaeological Survey* (3 vols., London, Pindar Press, 1987)

Tamara Talbot-Rice, *The Seljuks* (London, Thames & Hudson, 1961)

Chapter Four, pp. 115–46

Ibn Battuta, *Travels in Africa and Asia* (London, Routledge & Kegan Paul, 1929)

J. A. Boyle (ed.), *Cambridge History of Iran*, vol. 5, *Seljuks and Mongols* (Cambridge, Cambridge University Press, 1968)

J. A. Boyle, *The Mongol World Empire 1206–1370* (collected papers) (London, Allen & Unwin, 1977)

J. A. Boyle (trans.), *Rashid al-Din, The Successors to Ghengiz Khan* (New York, Columbia University Press, 1971)

Edward G. Browne, *Literary History of Persia* (4 vols., Cambridge, Cambridge University Press, 1928)

Robert Byron, *The Road to Oxiana* (London, Macmillan, 1937)

Basil Gray, *World History of Rashid ad-Din* (London, Phaidon, 1979)

David Morgan, *The Mongols* (Oxford, Basil Blackwell, 1986)

Leonard Olschi, *The Wise Men of the East in Oriental Tradition* (in William Poper (ed.): *Semitic and Oriental Studies*)

Amir Taheri, *The Spirit of Allah: Khomeini and the Islamic Revolution* (London, Hutchinson, 1985)

David Talbot-Rice, *The Illustrations of the World History of Rashid ad-Din* (Edinburgh, Edinburgh University Press, 1976)

Arthur Upham Pope, *Introducing Persian Architecture* (Teheran, Soroush Press, 1969)

Arthur Upham Pope and Phyllis Ackerman (eds.), *A Survey of Persian Art* (6 vols., Oxford, Oxford University Press, 1939)

Chapter Six, pp. 177–223

Babur (Annette Beveridge trans.), *The Baburnama* (Memoirs) (2 vols., Oxford, Oxford University Press, 1921)

William Foster (ed.), *Early Travellers in India 1583–1619* (Oxford, Oxford University Press, 1921)

Bamber Gascoigne, *The Great Moghuls* (London, Jonathan Cape, 1971)

Robin Lane Fox, *Alexander the Great* (London, Allen Lane, 1973)

John Keay, *India Discovered* (London, Collins, 1988)

David Kopf, *British Orientalism and the Bengal Renaissance* (Berkeley, University of California Press, 1969)

Sir Aurel Stein, *On Alexander's Track to the Indus* (London, Macmillan, 1929)

M. E. Strachan, *The Life and Adventures of Tom Coryat* (Oxford, Oxford University Press, 1962)

Chapter Seven, pp. 225–75

V. V. Barthold, *Turkestan Down to the Mongol Invasion*, 4th edn. (London, Luzac & Co., 1968)

Louis Boulnois, *The Silk Road* (London, Allen & Unwin, 1966)

E. A. W. Budge, *The Monks of Kublai Khan, Emperor of China* (London, Religious Tracts Society, 1928)

Peter Fleming, *News From Tartary* (London, Jonathan Cape, 1936)

Peter Hopkirk, *Foreign Devils on the Silk Route* (Oxford, Oxford University Press, 1980)

Lady Macartney, *An English Lady in Chinese Turkestan* (London, Ernest Benn, 1931)

M. Rossabi, *China Mong Equals*, essay by T. A. Allsen, *The Yuan Dynasty and the Uighurs of Turfan in the Thirteenth Century* (Berkeley, University of California Press, 1983)

W. Samolin, *East Turkestan Down to the Twelfth Century* (The Hague, Mouton & Co., 1964)

Diana Shipton, *The Antique Land* (London, Hodder & Stoughton, 1950)

C. P. Skrine and Pamela Nightingale, *Macartney at Kashgar* (Oxford, Oxford University Press, 1973)

Sir Aurel Stein, *Ruins of Desert Cathay*, (2 vols., London, Macmillan, 1912)

Sir Aurel Stein, *Sand Buried Cities of Khotan* (London, Fisher Unwin, 1903)

Ella and Sir Percy Sykes, *Through the Deserts and Oases of Central Asia* (London, Macmillan, 1920)

Peter Yung, *Xingiang* (Oxford, Oxford University Press, 1987)

Chapter Eight, pp. 277–302

Sir Richard Burton, *Personal Narrative of a Pilgrimage to El-Medina and Meccah* (3 vols., London, John Murray, 1855–6)

Peter Fleming, *One's Company* (London, Jonathan Cape, 1934)

Christopher Hibbert, *The Dragon Wakes* (London, Longman, 1970)

Witold Rodzinski, *A History of China*, (2 vols., Oxford, Pergamon Press, 1979)

Witold Rodzinski, *The Walled Kingdom* (London, Flamingo, 1984)

Index

Abaqa Khan, 121
Abbotabad, 190
Abd al-Malik, caliph,
  built Dome of the
  Rock in 687, 16
Acre, 7, 18 ff.
Acts of Saint Blaise, 87
Afghans, nine, on truck
  journey, 212
Ain Jalud, 65
Akbar Hoja, tomb of,
  Kashgar, 253
al-Garb valley, 34, 37
al-Muqaddasi,
  chronicler, 144
Aleppo, 49, 50, 52–3, 65
Alexander the Great,
  202, 205 ff.; *Alexander
  the Great*, Robin Lane
  Fox, 211
Ali, son-in-law of
  prophet Mohammed,
  129
Ali-Akbar Hashemi-
  Rafsanjani, Speaker of
  the Iranian
  parliament, 118
Alp Arslan, ('The
  Conquering Lion'), 85
Amassya, school at, 67, 87
Anarkali bazaar, Lahore,
  182
Antioch, capture of 1268,
  7
A Survey of Great Britain,
  Zhang Guo Yung, 237
Aornus, 202, 206
Aras Nehri, tributary of
  the Euphrates, 111
Armenian Genocide, the,
  1917, 250
Arrian, chronicler, 211
Ashoka, Maurya emperor,
  195; script, 196
Assassins, the, 34, 36;

Persian mullah quoted
  on, 34–6
Ata Dagh, the, 223
Attaturk, 80, 118
Aubrey, John, 74
author's great aunt, 169 f.
Ayas, Asia Minor, 9, 58,
  62 f.
Ayatollah Khamanei,
  159
Ayatollah Khomeini,
  113, 159
Ayatollah Sadeq
  Khalkali, Judge of the
  Revolution, 118
Azerbaijan Museum,
  Tabriz, 124

Ba'albek, 31
Babur, first Mogul, great
  grandfather of
  Jehangir, 199
Baburnama, quoted on
  Ferghana, 199
Babvlon, Hanging
  Gardens of, 111
Badiet esh-Sham, Great
  Syrian Desert, 34, 49
Baffa, valley of, 199
Baibars I, Mameluke
  sultan, 7, 37, 65, 67
Baluchistan, 152
Banjieta, 294
Battagram, valley of, 199
Bayazit mosque,
  Istanbul, 101
Beijing, 243, 296
'biggest liar in the world',
  the, *see* Pattle
Bohemond, prince of
  Antioch, 8
Bombay Fornicators, 169
Book of the Stick, 44
Bosch, Hieronymous, 31
Botham, Ian, 161

Brahmi, Gupta and
  Ashoka scripts, 196
British School of
  Archaeology,
  Jerusalem, 14
Brocardus, priest, quoted
  on the Assassins, 35
Brother Fabian at Holy
  Sepulchre, 3–4, 14
Brunelleschi, 130
*Buried Treasures of Chinese
  Turkestan*, von Le Coq,
  271
Burton, Sir Richard, 134;
  quoted on melancholy
  134; 301
Bushell, Dr S. W., quoted
  on Shang-tu palace,
  287; 294, 298
Byron, Lord, 47; quoted,
  63
Byron, Robert, 4, 125,130

Cala Ataperistan, 'Castle
  of Fire Worshippers',
  136
Catania cathedral, 103
Cape of Storms, Acre, 25
Ch'ang-an,
  moneychanging
  centre, 233
*Chao Naiman Sume
  Khotan*, The City of 108
  Temples, 298
Charchan, 264, 273
Charchalik oasis, 274
Chateaubriand, quoted,
  96
Chaucer, 46
Chengde (old Jehol),
  289–91
Ch'ien-lung, Chinese
  emperor, 290
Chihil Sutan, Isfahan,
  236

THE LAST MUGHAL
The Fall of a Dynasty: Delhi, 1857

In this evocative study of the fall of the Mughal Empire and the beginning of the Raj, award-winning historian William Dalrymple uses previously undiscovered sources to investigate a pivotal moment in history. The last Mughal emperor, Zafar, came to the throne when the political power of the Mughals was already in steep decline. Nonetheless, Zafar—a mystic, poet, and calligrapher of great accomplishment—created a court of unparalleled brilliance, and gave rise to perhaps the greatest literary renaissance in modern Indian history. All the while, the British were progressively taking over the emperor's power. When, in May 1857, Zafar was declared the leader of an uprising against the British, he was powerless to resist though he strongly suspected that the action was doomed. Four months later, the British took Delhi, the capital, with catastrophic results. With an unsurpassed understanding of British and Indian history, Dalrymple crafts a provocative, revelatory account of one of the bloodiest upheavals in history.

History/India

NINE LIVES
In Search of the Sacred in Modern India

In portraits of people we might otherwise never know William Dalrymple distills his twenty-five years of travel in India to explore the challenges faced by practitioners of traditional forms of faith in contemporary India. For two months a year, a man in Kerala divides his time between jobs as a prison warden, a well-builder, and his calling as an incarnate deity. A temple prostitute watches her two daughters die from AIDS after entering a trade she regards as a sacred calling. A Jain nun recalls the pain of watching her closest friend ritually starve herself to death. Together, these tales reveal the resilience of individuals in the face of the relentless onslaught of modernity, the enduring legacy of tradition, and the hope and honor that can be found even in the most unlikely places.

Religion

FORTHCOMING IN FALL 2012

THE AGE OF KALI

In this fascinating book, Dalrymple turns his distinctive blend of expansive insight and remarkable compassion toward the Indian subcontinent. In compelling and diverse portraits of a range of figures who are shaping the region—from a Hindi rap megastar to the Tamil Tigers, from Benazir Bhutto to the drug lords of the North West Frontier—he depicts an area struggling to reconcile the forces of modernity and tradition. The result is a compelling and exciting travelogue, and a unique portrait of a diverse and rapidly changing place.

Travel

FROM THE HOLY MOUNTAIN

A rich, story-filled travelogue chronicling Dalrymple's journey across the entire Byzantine world, retracing the footsteps of two monks who made the same trip in the spring of A.D. 587. When John Moschos and his pupil Sophronius the Sophist traveled from the shores of the Bosphorus to the sand dunes of Egypt, they stayed in caves, monasteries, and remote hermitages, collecting the wisdom of the stylites and the desert fathers before their fragile world finally shattered under the great eruption of Islam. Using Moschos's writings as his guide, Dalrymple recreates that epic journey, and his account of his travels is an elegy to the slowly dying civilization of Eastern Christianity and the people that have kept its flame alive.

Travel

VINTAGE DEPARTURES
Available wherever books are sold.
www.randomhouse.com

ALSO AVAILABLE FROM
VINTAGE BOOKS AND ANCHOR BOOKS

WILD COAST

Travels on South America's Untamed Edge
by John Gimlette

Guyana, Suriname, and French Guiana are perhaps some of the last untamed places in South America. The landscape is as weird and beautiful as it is wild, with hundreds of vast rivers, entire cities built on stilts, and some of the darkest, densest forest in the world. Along with the region's often-bloody history, Gimlette introduces us to some unnerving creatures—from alligators to head-crushing jaguars—and the extraordinary cast of characters who have made the Guianas their home: among them, tribesmen, terrorists, spacemen, Hmong refugees, long-lost Scotsmen, and the descendants of rebels and runaway slaves.

Travel/South America

IN AN ANTIQUE LAND

History in the Guise of a Traveler's Tale
by Amitav Ghosh

Once upon a time an Indian writer named Amitav Ghosh set out to find an Indian slave, name unknown, who some seven hundred years before had traveled to the Middle East. The journey took him to a small village in Egypt, where medieval customs coexist with twentieth-century desires and discontents. But even as Ghosh sought to re-create the life of his Indian predecessor, he found himself immersed in those of his modern Egyptian neighbors. Combining shrewd observations with painstaking historical research, Ghosh serves up skeptics and holy men, merchants and sorcerers. Some of these figures are real, some only imagined, but all emerge as vividly as the characters in a great novel. *In an Antique Land* is an inspired work that transcends genres as deftly as it does eras, weaving an entrancing and intoxicating spell.

History/Travel

VIDEO NIGHT IN KATHMANDU
by Pico Iyer

Mohawk haircuts in Bali. Yuppies in Hong Kong. In Bombay, not one but *five* Rambo rip-offs, complete with music and dancing. And in the People's Republic of China, a restaurant that serves dishes called "Yes, Sir, Cheese My Baby," "A Legitimate Beef," and "Ike and Tuna Turner." These are some of the images—comical, poignant, and unsettling—that Pico Iyer brings back from the Far East in this brilliant book of travel reportage. A writer for Time, Iyer approaches his subject with a camera-sharp eye, a style that suggests a cross between Paul Theroux and Hunter S. Thompson, and a willingness to go beyond the obvious conclusions about the hybrid cultures of East and West.

Adventure/Travel

THE SKEPTICAL ROMANCER
Selected Travel Writing
by W. Somerset Maugham
edited by Pico Iyer

One of the seminal writers of the twentieth century, W. Somerset Maugham was also a fearless and constant traveler who chronicled his adventures with a rare mix of wit and excitement. In *The Skeptical Romancer*, acclaimed travel writer Pico Iyer selects vignettes of Maugham's wise and vivid prose that track his transformation from a boyish traveler to a worldly man of letters, looking back on India, China, Russia, and America. Beginning with an early book on Spain and culminating in excerpts from one of his last books, this collection introduces us to Maugham at his most surprising, charming, and prophetic. In piece after piece, one can see the spirit that continues to cast an unrivaled influence over successors from Graham Greene to Paul Theroux, from Jan Morris to V. S. Naipaul.

Travel/Literature

IRON AND SILK
by Mark Salzman

Mark Salzman captures post-cultural revolution China through his adventures as a young American English teacher in China and his *shifu-tudi* (master-student) relationship with China's foremost martial arts teacher.

Memoir

FROM HEAVEN LAKE
by Vikram Seth

After two years as a postgraduate student at Nanjing University in China, Vikram Seth hitch-hiked back to his home in New Delhi, via Tibet. *From Heaven Lake* is the story of his remarkable journey and his encounters with nomadic Muslims, Chinese officials, Buddhists and others.

Memoir

VINTAGE AND ANCHOR BOOKS
Available wherever books are sold.
www.randomhouse.com

Printed in the United States
by Baker & Taylor Publisher Services